followerfirst

Rethinking Leading in the Church

Second Edition

RUSTY RICKETSON

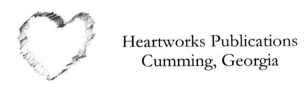

Heartworks Publications
Cumming, Georgia

© 2009, 2014, by Rusty Ricketson

Heartworks Publications
2300 Bethelview Road Suite 110-248
Cumming, Georgia 30040

www.heartworkspublications.com

Printed in the United States of America

Library of Congress Cataloging-in-Publication Data

Ricketson, Rusty
    Followerfirst: Rethinking Leading in the Church /
    Rusty Ricketson - 2nd ed.
    Includes bibliographical references and index
    ISBN : 978-0-9825332-8-4
        1. Leadership
        2. Christian leadership
        3. Followership
        4. Church Growth

Unless otherwise indicated, Scripture taken from the New King James Version. Copyright © 1982 by Thomas Nelson, Inc. Used by permission. All rights reserved.

Cover design by Copper Nelms - coppernelms@me.com

Dedication

To all who truly follow the Lord Jesus Christ and influence others to follow Him.

Appreciation

I am grateful to my family, my colleagues and students at Luther Rice University, participants in the Followerfirst Conferences, those willing learners at the churches I have served as Interim Pastor, and my fellow pastors and friends who have influenced and encouraged and added to this second edition. Your input and participation with me in this project have taught me much about following Christ.

Contents

Introduction

I need to let you know that I am a recovering leader. My journey is not unlike countless thousands: graduate from college, work a job, graduate from seminary, serve a ministry, seek further education to try and become the best you can be at what God has called you to do. Somewhere along my journey, however, I stopped questioning what I was reading and began trying to find someone to tell me what would work in the ministry. The pressures of the pastorate and the internal and external demands to grow a church became my own personal pressure cooker. My thoughts changed from questioning whether or not the information I was reading was biblical to whether or not the information would be the magic pill that would solve the current struggle or at least transform me so that I could lead the ministry correctly.

When I finally began to read more critically, question the assumptions made by much of the leadership literature, and then compare these assumptions with the direct teachings of the Bible, I discovered a life-changing truth: **The Bible is a book written under the inspiration of the Holy Spirit by followers, about followers, for followers.** The thrust of the Bible is not about leading or even teaching people how to become leaders. The Bible is about following and becoming the very best follower of Christ a Christian can be. The implication is simple, wherever the Lord may place me within an organization or within a community of people, I am always first and foremost a follower. This single truth advances the development of a new construct within the leader/follower literature, **"followerfirst,"** and changed my entire perspective with regard to who leaders and followers actually are and how they should respond to one another.

7

What is a followerfirst Perspective?

The followerfirst perspective is predicated upon the idea that the Bible is a book written under the inspiration of the Holy Spirit by followers, about followers, for followers with the purpose of informing these followers of the one true God (Deut. 6:4), and how through teaching, reproof, correction, and training in righteousness (2 Tim. 3:16-17) they might follow the will of God. This assumption provides a biblical foundation upon which a follower-focused rather than leader-centered organizational structure may be built. In addition, the followerfirst perspective provides a framework from which the Scriptures may be read with the desire of discovering specific follower instructions and insights rather than seeking to find leadership principles through historical narrative.

Understanding the following characteristics will give greater clarity to the followerfirst perspective and its subsequent explanations and applications within the church context:

Followerfirst is a Way of Thinking about Life

The followerfirst construct is actually a philosophy,[1] not a program. A philosophy is a set of ideas by which a person thinks and lives his or her life. Followerfirst thinking results in looking at the process of leadership from a unique perspective. After teaching the basics of the followerfirst perspective, students always ask the same questions, "How do you *do* it?" My response is, "You don't *do* followerfirst. You *think* followerfirst, and if you think followerfirst, the doing takes care of itself."

Our churches are so used to 'plug and play' programs where we hear a good idea in one church and simply try to 'plug' it into our church that it may be difficult to initially accept a followerfirst construct. This is due to the fact that in order to gain the desired follower-centered organization, one has to change the thinking of those involved. In a world where being the leader has been the primary thought process for so long, changing these ingrained ideas takes time and perseverance.

Followerfirst provides a way for people to think about the biblical organizing and functioning of the church. Changing people's thinking from leader-centered ideas to follower-centered ideas ultimately impacts how people view their role in the church, their worth to the church, and how they behave within the church organization.

In this book leading and following are understood as roles in which people choose to participate. The role of leader is respected as necessary within an organizational structure, and due respect is given to those who hold particular office within the church (1 Thess. 5:12-13; 1 Tim. 5:17; Heb. 13:7, 17; 1 Peter 5:1-5). However, leaders and the role of leader are not presented as the pinnacle of success. Instead of elevating the role of leader over followers, a followerfirst perspective understands the role of leading as performing a role among fellow followers.

Additionally, the role of follower is respected and understood as a necessary activity within the organized church. Following becomes recognized as the primary unifying factor within the organized church as believers who hold leader positions, and those who do not, humble themselves and follow the commands of Christ and the teaching of the Word of God. For the church to fulfill her purpose the followerfirst perspective needs to permeate every function, program, and activity of the church and be embedded within the organizational culture.[2]

Followerfirst is a Functional Understanding

The followerfirst perspective understands the term 'follower' as the primary functional purpose and responsibility of every Christian. Every person is primarily a follower of some person, goal, or ideal. The term 'follower' is used as opposed to the term 'disciple' because according to the biblical record, a person is first willing to follow before he or she becomes a disciple. This progression is explained in detail later. Also, the term 'follower' is used as a functional rather than a devotional construct. In a leader obsessed society it is too easy to dismiss following as some emotional, obvious response to the love of the Savior rather than understanding following as a crucial function within the church. By accepting the followerfirst perspective, every believer in Christ within the organized church embraces being a follower and has a biblical function and responsibility depending on the role that he or she desires and is willing to assume (see 1 Tim. 3:1) under the leadership of the Head of

9

the Church, the Lord Jesus Christ (Eph. 1:22; 4:15; Col. 1:18; 2:10; 2:19) and the empowering of the Holy Spirit (Acts 1:8).

Followerfirst is the Primary Emphasis

Combining 'follower' with 'first' points to the essence of who we are as created beings. In the beginning, God created Adam and Eve providing them intimacy with Himself and giving them caretaker status over all creation (Gen 1 & 2). Human beings were created to have relationship with the Creator and to follow His directives. We are in essence followers by creation. I will have more to say about this in Chapter 2.

The qualifier 'first' is added to the term follower to form a new construct: followerfirst. By creating a new construct, the idea of following is given primary status regarding: (1) the follower's (believer's) relationship to God as a follower of Christ and (2) the follower's (believer's) functional responsibilities as a part of the church.

The primary status of following can also be understood in that, contrary to the idea that good leaders must first be good followers; the followerfirst perspective posits that good leaders ARE good followers. There is never a time when leaders in the church should not perceive themselves as followers. In the same way, there is never a time when a follower 'graduates' from being a follower to being a leader. Regardless of what role a person has, whether leader or follower, being a follower and understanding oneself as a follower is always the primary thought.

In the church context, followers are only required to follow their leaders when the leaders are following the will of God as revealed in the Word of God. As John Stowell asserted in his book, *Following Christ: Experiencing life the way it was meant to be*, "Leading is a temporary assignment; following is a lifelong calling." [3]

Followerfirst Gives Greater Scriptural Clarity

Reading the Bible with a followerfirst perspective provides clearer insight into the original meaning of the biblical text and an unambiguous understanding of how the text may be applied to one's life. In Chapter One we will see how the Scriptures relative to the purpose of Jesus' coming to earth, as well as Jesus' commands and teachings and those of other biblical writers, add support to the adoption of a followerfirst perspective as the functional organizational perspective of the church.

Followerfirst Defined

The followerfirst perspective may be defined as *a system of thought according to which one willingly follows the Lord Jesus Christ with all one's heart, mind, soul, and strength in every circumstance regardless of organizational position while submitting to fellow followers so that all might fulfill their God-given responsibilities.*

It is no coincidence that this definition mirrors what Jesus declares as the first and second greatest commandments (Mark 12:30). Love is replaced with the word 'following' because following the will of the Lord is how Jesus defines loving God: "He who has My commandments and keeps them, he it is who loves Me" (John 14:21). Submitting to fellow believers is seen as the manifestation of loving one's neighbor. This combination of a love for Christ evidenced through obedience and a love for one's neighbor evidenced through humbly submitting to one another provides a unity within the Body of Christ. The Apostle Paul describes this unity in Philippians 2:1-7.

By embracing a followerfirst perspective, every believer in the church becomes responsible to use his or her gifts, talents, and abilities in the power of the Holy Spirit to fulfill the commands of Christ and the teachings of the New Testament in willing submission and cooperation with fellow followers to the glory of God.

No 'Ships' or 'Isms'

As you read you will notice that except for explanation purposes I write more about leading and following than leadership or followership. This is due to my bias against *ships* and *isms* that we often create to try and make sense of various concepts. We talk of leadership and followership and discipleship and evangelism, but these are terms we create to help codify certain teachings into nice manageable constructs.[4]

The Bible, however, does not speak in terms of *ships* and *isms*. The Bible speaks of leaders and leading but not leadership. The Bible speaks of disciples and making disciples but not discipleship. For instance, we take the action verb *lead* with all its life and power and develop the verb into a noun making it a static construct made up of do's and don'ts. I believe the Lord intentionally wrote "make disciples," "do the work of an evangelist," and "follow Me," so that we would avoid codified *ships* and *isms* that have a tendency to produce organizational inertia by classifying normal Christian activity into specialized spiritual categories. Instead, our energies and organizations are side-tracked by recruiting church members to get involved in evangelism, discipleship, or leadership as we have defined these terms and neatly packaged them in 12 week courses for people to complete but not necessarily apply as a lifestyle. As a result, churches are filled with people who have completed a course of study but see no connection of this teaching to daily life. We educate people enough to make them feel guilty for not doing what they have been taught to do rather than teaching them to be who God has created them to be. This disconnect continues to create inertia in the church and is a major cause of her ineffectiveness.

LEADERSHIP

When I use the term leadership, please understand I am referring to a *process* between leaders and followers and not to individuals or positions. In this book leadership is not solely vested in the titular leader as a person or in a leader's position within the organization.

Leadership is a *process* between a person in the role of leader and one or more persons in the role of follower that is:
(a) *intentional,*
(b) *interdependent,*
(c) *reciprocal,*
(d) *dynamic,* and
(e) *relational*
in order to achieve a common goal.

This definition becomes clearer as we discuss the various parts of the definition.

Process

Defining leadership as a process differs from considering leadership as being merely a list of traits that a person possesses. Process implies that anyone can lead as long as he or she is prepared with the skills and styles needed to relate to others. Thus, leaders are made, not born. This is not to say that some people are born with certain gifts, personalities, and characteristics that may assist them in leading others. But the process view understands that giftedness alone does not make a leader.

As a process, leadership is not a static group of people. We are sometimes prone to addressing the decision makers in an organization as "the leadership." However, such a designation leaves out the important role that followers play in the decision making process and leaves the impression that the leaders are the only ones responsible for the organization.

Role

Leadership involves people with specific roles. Both leaders and followers have roles with specific responsibilities that are essential in the decision making process. Each is accountable for fulfilling his or her responsibilities.

Intentional

Intention is understood as a persons' willingness to engage with another. It is a conscious and deliberate action. Both leader and follower have to be intentional. The leader intentionally introduces an idea and the follower intentionally responds. This leaves no room for disrespecting others by ignoring them or their ideas or responses.

Interdependent

Interdependence is the awareness that accomplishing the mission of the organization is not possible without others. Leadership does not exist without the presence of people. Persons may certainly do a great deal of work within the organization by themselves. However, accomplishing work is not leadership.

Leadership requires that I acknowledge my dependence on you and your dependence on me. Such a requirement helps to keep egos in check.

Reciprocal

Far from the idea of "you scratch my back and I'll scratch yours," in the negative sense, reciprocity in leadership is the awareness that actions usually result in reactions. This awareness informs my communications, behaviors, and overall manner when dealing with others. When involved in a leadership role, it allows me to understand that my actions are important whether I am leading or following.

Dynamic

This aspect of the definition is unique to Christians in that believers are blessed with the presence of the Holy Spirit. When engaged with others in making a decision, we do not have to rely solely on our own perceptions or abilities. We can defer to the influencing of the Holy Spirit. We can avoid trying to manipulate others to our way of thinking, resting instead on the Holy Spirit moving in the hearts and minds of others.

Relational

The most important word in the English language is relationships. Being involved in leadership can be both fulfilling and exhilarating while at the same time frustrating and difficult. This is all due to the fact that within organizations we are dealing with human beings. Enough said.

Achieve a Common Goal

Achieving a common goal begins with an understanding that both leaders and followers have a principled set of values by which they live. Through consistent communication, leaders and followers identify a set of common values that are shared within the organization. These common values not only form the foundation for setting the common goals of the organization, they also serve as guidelines on the behaviors that leaders and followers will employ while seeking to achieve the common goal.

Without leaders and followers resonating with these *strong statements* characteristics, true biblical leadership never occurs, community within the church is never established, and the organization flounders. The church has leaders, but leadership occurs when the Body of Christ, composed of those who hold leader positions and those who hold follower positions, is submissive to and follows the will of God while simultaneously submitting to each member's defined responsibility in the power of the Holy Spirit.

I believe embracing a followerfirst perspective within the church will result in leaders and followers cooperating with each other in their God-given responsibilities and provide a way of 'doing church' that frees both leaders and followers to fulfill their own purpose for living and accomplish the purpose of the church without the usual power plays and petty arguments over turf.

What followerfirst is Not

The most common misunderstandings I've received from the first edition of *followerfirst* has been that it is just repackaged 'consensus leadership' or 'principled leadership' or 'team leadership." These comments evidence a key misunderstanding of what the followerfirst perspective is all about.

The application of followerfirst is most definitely not consensus leadership. Followerfirst gives tremendous respect to leaders and seeks to develop leaders within the Body of Christ. There are leaders. There must be leaders. And one of the fundamental roles of leaders is the responsibility to make a decision. The followerfirst perspective does not discount any of those responsibilities. Instead, followerfirst embraces and challenges the followers within the organization to rally to the leaders, assume responsibility, and seek to make these leaders successful in their decision making.

Followerfirst is certainly based upon core values and principles within the individual person and, as such, can be seen as a companion to the concepts of principled leadership. What differentiates followerfirst from principled leadership is that principled leadership begins with people acting on principle by thinking of themselves as leaders. Followerfirst begins with people thinking of themselves as followers and acting on principle (core values). Changing how people think of themselves from leaders to followers within an organizational context has significant ramifications on how people function within organizations.

The similarity to team leadership stems from the interactions that take place within the dynamics of team development.[4] However, as in the previous misunderstandings, the basic difference between team leadership and a followerfirst perspective is the beginning point of whether a person enters into a team with the desire to be a leader or whether they understand their primary purpose is to follow regardless of any leader designation they may have within the team structure. The followerfirst perspective actually has the potential of allowing for less "storming" in the team development process. As a result, the team may be able to build stronger relationships sooner and become a more effective unit.

It's Time to Rethink Leading in the Church

I realize my thoughts may appear quixotic, idealistic, unrealistic, and impracticable to some. Being a follower, after all, is not a position to which anyone is taught to aspire, especially in American culture. No parent is standing on the sidelines encouraging their child with the words, "Now get in there and be a real follower!"

I was told I needed to become a leader because, in the estimation of others, I had leader qualities. Society, authors, academia, and my own intuition agreed that being a leader was better than being a follower. Many books and leadership teachers stated with confidence that, "Everything rises or falls on leadership." Their implied meaning was, "If you want to really do something with your life you need to become a leader." They might as well have said, "Followers don't accomplish anything." "Followers don't change the world." "Followers don't influence anyone." "Followers are only necessary because without them leaders would have no one to lead."

We have all heard it time and again; being the leader is where the power and the influence are. In much of the leadership literature the prevailing thought regarding followers is: Try to avoid being a follower at all cost.

I challenge you to rethink what being a biblical leader entails. Are these axioms in the leadership literature actually true? Or have they simply been repeated so many times for so many years that we have assigned to them truth status without thoroughly examining their truth claims. As one of my teachers once shared with me, "We might have to unlearn some things before we can actually learn the truth."

I submit to you that the truth lies in being a follower. The beginning point for any Christian leader in any organization, and especially the church, is to understand that because we are followers of Jesus Christ, within our organizations we are always to perceive ourselves as followers first.

God's Unique Church

The church is the most unique organization on earth. It was called into being by God for the purpose of making disciples (Matt. 28:9) who would follow His commands, glorify Him in the process, and enjoy Him forever. To borrow an analogy from the computer world, God created the church with an entirely different organizational operating system. Instead of being based upon systems of power and control, as is the case in most organizations, the church operates with systems based upon role and responsibility (submission and obedience) empowered by the Holy Spirit.

Such an understanding of the organizational nature of the church only serves to reveal the destruction and confusion that occurs within churches if leader-centered power and control philosophies are taught and utilized. Like oil added to water, the two never mix unless the container is shaken. Even then, if left alone, the two products eventually separate themselves from one another. Could such an admixture of leader versus follower be a cause for the growing number of churches in conflict today? Have we become so leader-focused that we have actually failed to recognize that the church operates with a followerfirst perspective? I will have more to say about this later.

I hope within the pages of this book you find an argument that will cause you to reconsider how leadership material is taught and implemented within your church. I also hope you will gain a new appreciation and respect for what it means to be a follower. Far from being people who have no incentive, do not think for themselves, and only follow the crowd, believers with a followerfirst perspective think and act as competent individuals while submitting to the leading of Jesus Christ.

I am indebted to the numerous students, colleagues, church members, and friends who read the first edition of this book and have given their insights, clarifications, and ideas to this second edition. The followerfirst perspective has been 'road tested' by scholars, pastors, and ministers in many different contexts, and their discoveries provide even stronger validation that the church needs to rethink the process of leading and following.

Chapter One studies the life of our Leader, Jesus Christ, and how through His purpose, commands, and teachings He declares Himself to be the perfect follower. Chapter Two challenges the prevailing bias against followers evident in much of the current leadership literature and presents a different perspective on what being a follower entails. Chapter Three investigates the need for followerfirst thinking, especially in light of several unintended consequences that have occurred from leader-centered teaching. Chapter Four challenges the reader to develop his or her own follower identity. Chapter Five examines the idea of follower influence as it relates to power and control within the church. Chapter Six is a new chapter that outlines the crucial element of the Power of Submission. Chapter Seven is another new chapter that investigates the constructs of authority and power and how they are applied within the church. Chapter Eight introduces the construct of the Following-Leader as a model for Christians to embrace within their organizations. Chapter Nine shares how a followerfirst organizational culture can be embedded within the operation of a church. Chapter Ten is another new chapter that explores the need to equip both leaders and followers in the church. Chapter Eleven seeks to identify followerfirst behaviors and introduces a measuring instrument, the Followerfirst Profile, with which to determine follower behaviors within the church. Finally, Chapter Twelve closes the book by looking at the positive impact on the spread of the Gospel and the unified functioning within the local church that will result as churches embrace the responsibilities of a followerfirst perspective and being willing to live according to the Followerfirst Covenant.

A new feature of this second edition is the RETHINK section at the close of each chapter. In the RETHINK section you will find practical applications of the followerfirst perspective as well as more questions for you to consider regarding your own church and how to implement a followerfirst perspective.

Join the Conversation

I understand the scope of such an undertaking is massive and there is no possible way I can address all the various aspects of following and leading within this volume. This book continues to be a work in progress. However, perhaps this work can serve as a catalyst to promote a conversation that needs to be had among those who write and practice leading and following within the church and organizations that have a Christian basis.

I realize my academic friends will be dissatisfied with some of my limited academic investigations. I also realize that my theological friends will question some of my assertions even though I believe I have stayed true to the text and context of Scripture. To all of you, I apologize in advance and only ask that you join the conversation so that we all might discover the truth.

You will notice I refer to the church as an organization rather than an organism, a term some Christians use to describe the nature of the church. I do not disagree with the idea of the church being understood as a living entity because of the life of Christ within the individual members who make up the church. However, I refer to the church as an organization because, from an organizational perspective, that is what the church is.

From my perspective, before the current concentration on leaders and leadership teaching, what the church thought was a crisis of leadership was actually a crisis of following. Now, however, after decades of teaching pastors how to be leaders we have compounded the problem. We still have not taught the followers of Christ how to follow within a church organization, and we now have a generation of leaders who think and act with little to no regard for being followers first. If the church is to make a change, it must begin with a biblical organizational understanding of following.

Now that you know my heart, I invite you to a new journey, a new way of thinking. I invite you to a new freedom, the freedom that comes from being followerfirst. I invite you to explore the possibility of building a bridge between laity and clergy and instigating greater church participation by teaching others that, even though we may have specific God-given roles within the church, we are all followers first. I urge you to consider the influence that can be had when God's people understand they don't have to be a leader or recognized as a leader to make a difference. As followers of Christ we can influence others while in the positions God gives whether those positions are perceived by society as being leadership positions or not, whether they have titles or not, whether they are paid positions or not. I invite you to see that throughout the Bible, God calls His people to follow. It is through following the commands of God that the people of God show their love for God and grow in their relationship with God (John 14:21). It is through following Christ we become "fishers of men" (Matthew 4:19). It is through following Christ we learn to "deny self, take up [our] cross daily, and follow [Christ]" (Luke 9:23).

Does this followerfirst way of thinking resonate within you? Does concentrating on being a follower sound like something so radically counterintuitive to our current organizational way of thinking that it just might be God's plan to change the world? Could it be that this followerfirst perspective is what the church needs to make a greater impact on our culture? From what I have studied in the Bible, I am thoroughly convinced that this impact will not come through robust, charismatic, larger-than-life leaders, but through faithful followers who, through the "foolishness" of following, influence others. Still, the goal of followers is not to become leaders. The goal of followers is to be the very best followers they can be to the glory of God. And if these followers are placed in positions within companies, churches, or ministries in which they are responsible for others, their primary understanding of their position will not be, "I am the leader." Their understanding will be:

I am a follower of Christ FIRST.

**Others may call me a leader, but my primary understanding of
my place on the planet is to be a follower of Christ,
wherever He may lead.**

**The fulfillment of my life will not come from the praise of those
whom I might lead in this lifetime.**

**My goal and fulfillment in life will come when I hear,
"Well done,"
from the lips of Him whom I have followed.**

Jesus said,
If anyone serves Me, let him follow Me; and where I am, there My
servant will be also. If anyone serves Me, him My Father will honor
(John 12:26).

Part I

Follow the Follower

Chapter 1

Jesus: The Perfect Follower

When I first began the process of writing this book I had several friends read the first few chapters just to give me some feedback regarding the material and if what I was writing made sense. The book chapters were arranged in a different order than they are today. As I heard back from these friends one responded bluntly, "I personally don't care what you think about following, and I don't really care what other writers or theories have to say about following. These will not convince me. But if you can show me that the followerfirst perspective was consistent with the life and teaching of Jesus, THEN I'll be sold." I immediately moved this material to the first chapter.

My friend was right. What others propose regarding leading and/or following fades into insignificance when compared to what Jesus lives and teaches regarding leading and following. What makes the followerfirst perspective a powerful force for change is its consistency with the life and commands and teachings of Jesus Christ and other teachings of Scripture.

In most Christian leadership literature, the Lord Jesus Christ is often presented as the perfect leader. I certainly do not disagree with such an assertion. Jesus was, indeed, perfect in everything He did and said. I accept without question that when Jesus led others, He did so perfectly. However, from all that has been written regarding Jesus as a leader, one might begin to think that Jesus' purpose on the planet was to lead others. I would argue that the biblical evidence does not support such a claim. In fact, a close inspection of the biblical text, without the prevailing leader bias, reveals that Jesus' purpose, commands, and teachings were all centered on being a follower.

Jesus' Purpose

Jesus was the greatest follower who ever lived. When we inspect the life and teachings of Jesus it was His acting as a follower that influenced more people than His actual leading a small band of disciples. Consider Jesus' stated purpose for being on the planet. While proclaiming Himself to be the "bread of life" and that those who believe in Him will not be cast out, Jesus said,

> ...For I have come down from heaven *not to do my own will, but the will of Him who sent me.* This is the will of Him who sent Me, that of all He has given Me I should lose nothing but should raise it up at the last day (John 6:38, 39) [emphasis mine].

What is striking about this verse is Jesus' admission that His purpose was to *follow* the will, of His heavenly Father. From childhood, Jesus knew He "must be about [His] Father's business" (Luke 2:49). That business is beautifully portrayed in Philippians 2:5-11:

> Let this mind be in you which was also in Christ Jesus, who, being in the form of God, did not consider it robbery to be equal with God, but made Himself of no reputation, taking the form of a bondservant, and coming in the likeness of men. And being found in appearance as a man, He humbled Himself and became obedient to the point of death, even the death of the cross. Therefore God also has highly exalted Him and given Him the name which is above every name, that at the name of Jesus every knee should bow, of those in heaven, and of those on earth, and of those under the earth, and that every tongue should confess that Jesus Christ is Lord, to the glory of God the Father.

Although equal with God, Jesus "made Himself of no reputation." This translation does not give the full sense of Jesus emptying

Himself as a direct translation of the Greek word *eknosen* requires.[1] The Amplified Bible translates the phrase "but stripped Himself [of all privileges and rightful dignity]." The NIV translates the verse, "but made himself nothing." All of these different translations seek to do justice to the concept that Jesus, although equal with God the Father, willingly humbled Himself and took the role of an obedient follower.

Jesus spoke of His follower status throughout His earthly ministry:

John 5:30
I can of Myself do nothing. As I hear, I judge; and My judgment is righteous, because I do not seek My own will but the will of the Father who sent Me.

John 7:17-18
If anyone wills to do His will, he shall know concerning the doctrine, whether it is from God or whether I speak on My own authority.

John 12:49-50
For I have not spoken on My own authority; but the Father who sent Me gave Me a command, what I should say and what I should speak.

John 14:10-11
Do you not believe that I am in the Father, and the Father in Me? The words that I speak to you I do not speak on My own authority; but the Father who dwells in Me does the works.

The Lamb of God, who takes away the sin of the world (John 1:29), was simply and faithfully following what He had been directed by the Father to say and do. Jesus did **nothing** on his own authority. He was a follower. He is equal with the Father in His deity, yet, for the purpose of the Godhead, Jesus became the follower. The Father is not **better** than Jesus because Jesus is the follower. God the Father, Son, and Holy Spirit, as three distinct and coexisting Persons, do not operate based upon a concept of which Person is better than the other, because each is perfect deity. Rather, the Father, Son, and Holy Spirit operate based upon an accepted role and responsibility.

An oversimplification of this role and responsibility may be stated thus:

- **The Father's role is to be the authority and to bring about His will for His good pleasure.**

  "...for it is God who works in you both to will and to do for *His* good pleasure" (Philippians 2:13). (See Ephesians 1:5, 9.)

- **The Son's responsibility is to follow the will of the Father.**

  "I have come down from heaven not to do my own will, but the will of Him who sent me" (John 6:38). (See Luke 22:42.)

- **The Holy Spirit's responsibility is to follow the will of the Son.**

  "However, when He, the Spirit of truth, has come, He will guide you into all truth; for He will not speak on His own *authority*, but whatever He hears He will speak; and He will tell you things to come. He will glorify Me, for He will take of what is Mine and declare it to you. All things that the Father has are Mine. Therefore I said that He will take of Mine and declare it to you" (John 16:13-15).

In Colossians 1:18 the Apostle Paul said of Christ, "He is also head of the body, the church; and He is the beginning, the first-born from the dead; so that He Himself might come to have first place in everything." Paul understood Christ's position as the head of the church and reiterates this point in Ephesians 1:22; 4:15; 5:23; Colossians 2:10 and 2:19.[2] Paul continues the thought of Christ's place within the Church by adding that Christ is to have "first place in everything." The King James Version translates 'first place' by using the word, "preeminence." This word carries the idea of being "foremost in time, place, order or importance."[3] Because Christ is the head of the church, all who make up the Church fall under His authority.

The Bible makes it clear that in the Church there is no difference in the worth of persons regarding their ethnicity, gender, or background (Galatians 3:28). The Bible does speak to the matter of certain roles within the Body of Christ holding higher degrees of importance because of their responsibility to teach the Word of God (See 1 Corinthians 12.). I will elaborate on this differentiation in more detail in Chapter 7. Yet, we need to always keep in mind that these presumably more important roles are held by those who follow Christ.

Spiritually, we are all equal in that we are all sinners forgiven by the grace of God. Organizationally in the church we are all equal in that we are all followers. Even though we may be gifted differently, no one has personal meritorious rank or worth over any other person within the body of Christ (1 Corinthians 12:12-31). The only ranking member of the Body of Christ is Christ Jesus. Any differentiation among members within the body comes at the level of the responsibilities to which we are called, gifted, and willing to assume.

We all have roles and responsibilities within the Body of Christ. Some church organizations and denominations may vest organizational authority in a particular person or persons in the church. However, this authority does not supersede that of Christ or the Bible and only extends to the individual(s) as the Scriptures allow. Thus, the beginning point of the effective functioning of the Body is an understanding that, under the leading of the Lord and consistent with His purpose, **we are all followers.**

Jesus thought of Himself as a follower of the will of the Father. Contrary to much of the current biblical leadership literature, Jesus' primary role was not to be the leader of a group of men and train them to become leaders of a future group of believers who would establish His church.[4] Instead, Jesus understood His role to be a follower of the will of God, period (See John 6:38-40). A close inspection of the Scriptures reveals that His followerfirst perspective can explain every activity of Jesus recorded in the Bible. Even when Jesus acted as a leader, His actions were predicated upon a

29

followerfirst perspective. Jesus followed the will of the Father until the day He died. Yet, through His death and subsequent resurrection, Jesus became the Savior of the world, a fact that has influenced countless millions of people. The gospel message proclaims that God had a plan to redeem the world to Himself, and this plan was followed perfectly by His only begotten Son. This followerfirst perspective is also evident in the commands Jesus issued to those who would follow Him.

Jesus' Commands

Jesus as Rabbi

Assuming the role of a rabbi, Jesus chose not to gather His disciples as other rabbis had done up until that time. Historically, rabbis would teach, and those who longed to follow would simply inform the rabbi that they were willing to sit under his teaching. Jesus, however, went a step further. There were those who followed Jesus and sat under His teaching according to the common practice of the time. However, for those whom Jesus wanted closest to Him, these individuals would have to respond to His command, "Follow Me."

Vander Laan suggests that Jesus' use of these commands and His personal choosing of His disciples indicate Jesus' embracing the model of the advanced rabbi.

A few (very few) of the most outstanding *Beth Midrash* students sought permission to study with a famous rabbi often leaving home to travel with him for a lengthy period of time. These students were called *talmidim* (*talmids*) in Hebrew, which is translated *disciple*...As the rabbi lived and taught his understanding of the Scripture his students (*talmidim*) listened and watched and imitated so as to become like him. Eventually they would become teachers passing on a lifestyle to their *talmidim*.[7]

Vander Laan continued by stating that in Jesus' time many students would seek out the rabbi they wished to follow (see Mark 5:19; Luke

30

9:57). However, according to Vander Laan, "Jesus broke with this pattern when he chose his own talmidim."[8] A willingness to follow in close proximity with Jesus in obedience to His command, "Follow Me," was the prerequisite before learning would take place.

When we look at these instances in the New Testament, it almost appears that Jesus is deliberately issuing this command to the most unlikely group of people you would want to be on your leader team. I believe the reason for this is quite simple. Jesus was not looking for leaders. **Jesus was looking for followers.**

The Imperative

"Follow Me" are two of the most powerful words in the New Testament. With these words Jesus interjected Himself into the lives of others, and those who responded in the affirmative had their lives changed forever. The Bible uses two different Greek phrases to capture the idea behind 'follow Me.' Written in the imperative mood, these phrases have the force of command.

1. Come After Me

Perhaps the most well-known "Follow Me" imperative of Jesus is when He called Peter and Andrew.

Matthew 4:19
"Follow Me and I will make you to become fishers of men."

Ex. Fallacy

The Greek words, *deute opisow* (δεῦτε ὀπίσω μου[5]) are translated 'follow Me.' However, the words mean, "come after." The words have the idea of lining up after someone. This word for *come* is spoken to those who labor and are heavy laden (Matthew 11:28-30), to those invited to the marriage supper (Matthew 22:4-5), by the woman at the well to summon others to meet Jesus (John 4:29), and nine other occasions in the New Testament.[5]

Peter and Andrew were ardent followers of John the Baptist. John 1:35-40 recounts that it was Andrew who heard John the

31

Baptist declare Jesus to be "the Lamb of God," spent time with Jesus that evening, and then introduced his brother, Simon, to Jesus, whereupon Jesus changed Simon's name to Peter (John 1:42). It was only later as Jesus walked along the shores of Galilee that He uttered the command "Follow Me."

A unique feature of this particular command is the explanation of what the disciples' purpose will be after following Jesus. They will become "fishers of men." I am of the opinion that Peter and Andrew had little understanding of what being a "fisher of men" really entailed. It is possible that in previous conversations Jesus may have inquired, "I wonder what it would be like to fish for men?" But this is mere speculation. What we do know is that Andrew and "immediately dropped their nets and followed Him." Such is the power of the Lord's, "Follow Me." The subsequent calling of James and John (Matthew 4:21) is indicative of the same response of those whom Jesus called. They immediately left their nets and their father and followed Jesus.

2. Follow Me

As Jesus gathered His other followers, He used the imperative form of the Greek word ἀκολούθεω [6] (follow) coupled with the word μοί (me) on eight different occasions. Philip (John 1:43) was called in this manner as well as Matthew (Matthew 9:9). Peter heard these words of Jesus when, after being restored to Jesus for denying Him three times the Lord said, "Follow Me" (John 21:19). Shortly after this event, Peter heard these words again when the Lord reproved Peter's curiosity concerning the disposition of the Apostle John's life by stating, "If I will that he remain till I come, what is that to you? You follow Me" (John 21:22).

These texts also indicate that a willingness to follow precedes becoming disciples (learners). Such a progression becomes clearer when other texts are considered in which Jesus commanded someone to follow but the person refused. Consider the following two encounters: First, to a well-intentioned disciple Jesus said, ""Follow Me, and let the dead bury their own dead" (Matt. 8:22). Second, to the rich young man Jesus said, "If you want to be perfect, go, sell what you have and give to the poor, and you will have treasure in heaven; and come, follow Me" (Matt. 19:2). In each of these instances Jesus utters the command "Follow Me," but the command is disobeyed; the implication being that these individuals never became Jesus' disciples.

In addition, on two other occasions Jesus uttered this command as a response to those who were not following. First, after rebuking Peter for thinking like Satan and being a stumbling block, Jesus said, "If anyone wishes to come after Me, let him deny himself, and take up his cross, and follow Me" (Matthew 16:24). We will examine this verse in detail in a later chapter. However, the progression is clear that to become a disciple one must first follow. Second, in response to certain Greeks who wanted to have an audience with Jesus, He said,

> The hour has come that the Son of Man should be glorified. Most assuredly, I say to you, unless a grain of wheat falls into the ground and dies, it remains alone; but if it dies, it produces much grain. He who loves his life will lose it, and he who hates his life in this world will keep it for eternal life. If anyone serves Me, let him follow Me; and where I am, there My servant will be also. If anyone serves Me, him My Father will honor (John 12:23-26).

From the calling of The Twelve to confronting the disobedient, Jesus' "Follow Me" is a clear command to relationship, proximity, and becoming His disciple. Such a phenomenon is still true today. The power of these words leaves no room for doubt in the minds of those who hear them.

Insights for Recruiting Followers

Looking in detail at seven encounters in which Jesus commanded someone to "Follow Me" offers us new insights into how we might encourage people to follow Christ.

1. Build Relationships *Smerca?*

John 1:43-49
The following day Jesus wanted to go to Galilee, and He found Philip and said to him, "Follow Me." Now Philip was from Bethsaida, the city of Andrew and Peter. Philip found Nathanael and said to him, "We have found Him of whom Moses in the law, and also the prophets, wrote — Jesus of Nazareth, the son of Joseph." And Nathanael said to him, "Can anything good come out of Nazareth?" Philip said to him, "Come and see." Jesus saw Nathanael coming toward Him, and said of him, "Behold, an Israelite indeed, in whom is no deceit!" Nathanael said to Him, "How do You know me?" Jesus answered and said to him, "Before Philip called you, when you were under the fig tree, I saw you." Nathanael answered and said to Him, "Rabbi, You are the Son of God! You are the King of Israel!"

Jesus commanded Phillip, "Follow Me," and Phillip immediately found Nathanael. Having accepted his position as a follower of Christ, Philip influenced others to become followers as well. Are such actions indicative of those within our churches who claim to follow Christ? What relationships do we have or are we building with our family and friends that naturally lead them to want to know the Savior?

In this instance and others we see the followers of Christ moving and living among their everyday relationships while influencing others toward the Savior by confidently sharing what they have found. Philip's obviously excited proclamation; "we have found Him…" expressed the satisfaction of finding what a searching soul had been longing for. Philip's method of attracting others to Christ was to share Jesus from a "you don't know what you are missing" positive position. Undaunted by Nathanael's cynicism ("Can any good thing come out of Nazareth?"), Philip knew that if Nathanael only met Jesus, Nathanael's life would be changed forever. And this is exactly what happened.

2. *Focus on Christ*

Matthew 8:18-22

And when Jesus saw great multitudes about Him, He gave a command to depart to the other side. Then a certain scribe came and said to Him, "Teacher, I will follow You wherever You go." And Jesus said to him, "Foxes have holes and birds of the air have nests, but the Son of Man has nowhere to lay His head." Then another of His disciples said to Him, "Lord, let me first go and bury my father." But Jesus said to him, "Follow Me, and let the dead bury their own dead."

Although these words appear to be harsh, Jesus uses them to teach a key truth regarding being a follower of Christ. Christ must be preeminent in our lives and in our churches and organizations (Colossians 1:18). Our relationship with and to Him takes precedent over every other relationship. We cannot afford to be distracted by good things at the expense of following Him.

Jesus' approach to those who think they want to follow Him is to tell them the truth. The truth is that following Christ may require tremendous sacrifice of comforts and family. Jesus' response differs greatly from many of the appeals we hear today.

Instead we see Christ appealing to the reality of following with a whole heart. In essence what Jesus is implying is, "You may not have a place to lay your head at night, but you will have ME. Is that enough for you? You may not have a home. You may be disowned by your family (as many believers across the world experience every day). Am I enough for you? Or are you looking for ME plus something else? There is no "something else." When you follow Me, all you are promised is ME. Is that enough for you?"

We need to rethink whether or not Christ is preeminent in our lives, our preaching, teaching, and sharing. Can people tell by our actions that we are followers of Christ? Can others clearly hear in our preaching and teaching that Jesus Christ is the central focus of our message? When we share the Gospel, do we offer Christ as the prize and goal of our faith?

3. *Put Aside Pre-judging (Prejudice)*

Matthew 9:9 (Mark 2:14; Luke 5:27)
As Jesus passed on from there, He saw a man named Matthew sitting at the tax office. And He said to him, "Follow Me." So he arose and followed Him.

In my mind's eye I can almost see the shock on Matthew's face as he is confronted by Jesus and challenged by the words "Follow Me." I can imagine Matthew might have looked around to make certain Jesus was talking to him and then pointed to himself as if to say, "Who me?" For Jesus to have approached a hated tax collector was a total contradiction of societal norms.

Think of the person most despised in the culture. Many tax collectors were unscrupulous because they had the backing of Roman government and they arbitrarily padded what a person had to pay or the taxpayer could go to jail. With this backdrop, Jesus comes along and although the Bible does not mention it, it is highly likely that this was not their first encounter because Jesus regularly traveled through this area. What we do know is that Jesus chose one of the most despised people in society to follow Him. Perhaps one of the lessons we can learn from this encounter is that no one, even the most despised, is disqualified from being a follower of Christ.

We need to rethink whether or not we are unconsciously (or even consciously) choosing to share the Gospel with those whom we think would be good candidates to follow Jesus. Have our biases and prejudices become a barrier to the free proclamation of the Gospel to even the most despised people in our communities?

4. *Look Beyond Outward Appearances*

Matthew 19:16-22
Now behold, one came and said to Him, "Good Teacher, what good thing shall I do that I may have eternal life?" So He said to him, "Why do you call Me good? No one *is* good but One, *that is,* God. But if you want to enter into life, keep the commandments." He said to Him, "Which ones?" Jesus said, "*'You shall not murder,' 'You shall not commit adultery,' 'You shall not*

steal,' 'You shall not bear false witness,' 'Honor your father and your mother,' and, *'You shall love your neighbor as yourself.'"* The young man said to Him, "All these things I have kept from my youth. What do I still lack?" Jesus said to him, "If you want to be perfect, go, sell what you have and give to the poor, and you will have treasure in heaven; and come, follow Me." But when the young man heard that saying, he went away sorrowful, for he had great possessions.

I find it interesting that the one person who appears on the surface to have all the qualifications for leadership is the one person who refused to obey the compassionate command of Jesus. Perhaps we might think twice before we invest too much in outward appearances, achievements, personality, and social position when finding leaders for the church. This man may have made an excellent leader. He obviously had riches and was a successful businessman. In leader-centered churches it is possible that such a person could become a deacon or an elder. **It may be that all too often we have looked for leaders, when what we should be looking for are followers of Christ. This rich young ruler may have been a leader among his peers, but he refused to be a follower of Christ to his own peril.**

We need to rethink how we recruit leaders in the church. Are we looking for followers of Christ or are will willing to compromise this standard simply because a person has a successful business track record? Are we willing to face the wrath of fellow church members if we are unwilling to place a person in a position of responsibility who does not share a strong allegiance to Jesus?

If such a scenario did occur, the responses from those within the church might be, "What do you think you are doing? Don't you know that she is the chairman of the Chamber of Commerce? Don't you know he is the president of the bank?" It is likely that some in the church would rise up and NOT call us blessed at that time.

Granted, it is highly unlikely that we would ever have the occasion to challenge someone to sell all their possessions and then become a follower of Christ, but, as in Jesus' encounter, the point is still the same. Just because a person is affluent and holds position in the community does not mean that they actually follow Christ.

What is troubling is that given the prevailing leader-centric attitude in many churches today, such a person could not only find their way into the church but would automatically be asked to serve in a position of responsibility within the church with little or no questioning of their Christ following. Yet, there is NO necessary correlation between a person's position in the community, their business leadership ability, and their capacity to hold a position of responsibility in the church of the living God. This is not to say that those who have social status and financial means cannot be followers of Jesus (see Nicodemus). In fact, we should seek to share the Gospel with all, the down-and-outers as well as the up-and-outers. All need to follow Jesus.

We need to rethink investing too much in outward appearance, social position, human achievements, or personality. We need to keep the same standard Jesus set when people wanted to get involved: Are you willing to follow Christ?

5. *Humble Yourself*

John 12:23-26
But Jesus answered them, saying, "The hour has come that the Son of Man should be glorified. Most assuredly, I say to you, unless a grain of wheat falls into the ground and dies, it remains alone; but if it dies, it produces much grain. He who loves his life will lose it, and he who hates his life in this world will keep it for eternal life. If anyone serves Me, let him follow Me; and where I am, there My servant will be also. If anyone serves Me, him My Father will honor.

Of all the characterizations of Jesus, the idea of the suffering servant is one that strikes at the heart of His character and behavior. The idea of service is so pronounced in the scriptures that Jesus even said that the one who would be the greatest would be the servant of all (Mark 9:35). Servant Leadership is often touted as a biblical leadership theory. From a biblical perspective the theory does have merit. But let us not forget that according to this verse, if we are to serve Christ we must follow Him. Jesus does not say if anyone follows me let him serve Me. Jesus says if anyone serves me, let him follow Me. We cannot claim to serve Christ if we are not following Him. Additionally, it is important to note that the one who seeks to **serve and follow** the Lord Jesus is the one whom the Father will honor.

We need to rethink our own service before the Lord. What is our primary objective? Teaching the people, making disciples and other responsibilities are important functions in the church. However, such responsibilities are secondary to our primary goal of serving Christ. If we are serving the Lord by making disciples and teaching the people we must always follow His commands in the process or we may not actually be serving Him but our own egos and psychological needs.

As Jesus' servant we need to be certain that our own self-concept is that of the "unprofitable servant" described by Jesus in Luke 17:7-10:

> And which of you, having a servant plowing or tending sheep, will say to him when he has come in from the field, 'Come at once and sit down to eat'? But will he not rather say to him, 'Prepare something for my supper, and gird yourself and serve me till I have eaten and drunk, and afterward you will eat and drink'? Does he thank that servant because he did the things that were commanded him? I think not. So likewise you, when you have done all those things which you are commanded, say, 'We are unprofitable servants. We have done what was our duty to do.

If we are serving Christ, we become His servants. If we are His servants we will be where He is. If Jesus is the suffering servant then will we suffer with Him? When things get too difficult in the church, will we leave to find greener pastures, or will we stay and serve? The truth is, only those who are ministering at the time know their own motivation for leaving a ministry context for another. We need to be certain that the leaving is not because the flames are too hot, or the struggle is too great, but rather that God has another assignment for us with new flames, and new struggles that will not only mold us more into the image of Christ, but will extend the Gospel and the kingdom of God.

If we are servants to the suffering servant will we not share in His suffering? Luering stated, "This fellowship in suffering unites us with the saints of God in all times (James 5:10), and is indeed a fellowship with the Lord Himself (Phil 3:10), who uses this discipline to mold us more and more according to His character.[8]"

The beauty of the text is the promise, "If anyone serves Me, him my Father will honor." Those who follow closely are the ones who are honored with an intimate knowledge of the Savior. They are the ones who experience LIFE in Christ in a way that few get to experience it.

6. *Look to Restore*

John 21:17-19
He said to him the third time, "Simon, son of Jonah, do you love Me?" Peter was grieved because He said to him the third time, "Do you love Me?" And he said to Him, "Lord, You know all things; You know that I love You." Jesus said to him, "Feed My sheep. Most assuredly, I say to you, when you were younger, you girded yourself and walked where you wished; but when you are old, you will stretch out your hands, and another will gird you and carry you where you do not wish." This He spoke, signifying by what death he would glorify God. And when He had spoken this, He said to him, "Follow Me."

There is no more beautiful expression of love and intimacy than that between Peter and the Lord Jesus during this time of restoration. Three times Peter denied the Lord Jesus, and three times Jesus pressed upon Peter his responsibility to feed and tend the followers of Christ. Additionally, Jesus loved Peter enough to let him know by what type of death Peter would glorify God. The path to that God glorifying death was through Jesus' command, "Follow Me."

One of the beauties of Jesus is His willingness to restore to fellowship those who have made wrong choices. The church is filled with people who, like Peter, may have turned their backs on Jesus at some point but are now seeking a restored relationship. Evidencing an atmosphere of forgiveness and restoration will allow these people the opportunity to move away from the "God could never use me" attitude to one of hope and fulfillment.

7. Avoid Comparison

John 21:20-22
Then Peter, turning around, saw the disciple whom Jesus loved following, who also had leaned on His breast at the supper, and said, "Lord, who is the one who betrays You?" Peter, seeing him, said to Jesus, "But Lord, what about this man?" Jesus said to him, "If I will that he remain till I come, what is that to you? You follow Me."

It takes all of perhaps one minute for Peter to take his eyes and thoughts off following the Lord and start concerning himself with what others might do. Jesus' rebuke is clear and to the point. In essence Jesus says to Peter, it does not matter what I have planned for John. If I want him to live forever, then that is My business. YOU follow ME.

How often do we allow the thought of what others might say or what others are doing to affect our obedience to follow Christ? As a pastor, I was often tempted to compare my ministry to that of another. Such comparisons always resulted in my either becoming proud because I was comparing my church with another that was not doing as well or my becoming depressed when comparing my church with another that was growing much faster. Either way, such comparisons were not healthy. All of us within the church would do well to avoid comparisons with others and concentrate on comparing our lives and our churches with that of Christ and His commands.

RETHINK

Perhaps now would be a good time to reflect upon our own responses when we hear the Lord's, "Follow Me." At your next team meeting, have the group answer these questions:

1. Am I willing for the Lord to interrupt my daily life, routines, and comfort zones?
2. Is there any delay between reading the Lord's command from the Bible and my response?
3. Am I asking God to enable me through His Spirit to immediately respond?
4. Have I developed a rationalizing mechanism to defer my obedience to another time (i.e. I don't have enough time right now, I don't have enough education, I don't feel prepared, I'm too young, I'm too old, etc.)
5. Am I secretly avoiding obedience because of an unwillingness to humble myself to others, admit my wrongs, ask forgiveness, and/or take a lesser position?
6. Am I too concerned with what others would think?
7. Am I caught up in comparing my ministry with another's?

Jesus' Teaching

When we listen to the teachings of Jesus from a follower's perspective, we recognize His authority loudly and clearly. At the same time, Jesus' teaching centers not on developing leadership skills and traits but concentrating on a relationship with Him. Leading others results from this relationship of following Christ in all things. This is a basic premise of the followerfirst perspective. It is all about relationship. Our primary relationship is with Christ. It is this relationship that impacts all others. Consider the following examples in the New Testament:

Worthy Followers

> Matthew 10:37-39
> He who loves father or mother more than Me is not worthy of Me. And he who loves son or daughter more than Me is not worthy of Me. And he who does not take his cross and follow after Me is not worthy of Me. He who finds his life will lose it, and he who loses his life for My sake will find it.

It is sometimes difficult for us to believe that Jesus would actually place a worth on following after Him. But within this context there is no denying Jesus' plain teaching that only those who know how to carry out a daily dying to self (we will talk more about this in a later chapter) and placing as the most important aspect of life a relationship with Christ are worthy of being in relationship with Him.

Those who have found life in Christ will find the greatest fulfillment of that life by losing themselves in service to Christ. If our greatest personal desire is to know God through Jesus Christ, we will find each day to be filled with opportunity to experience Him. Through our obedience to His commands, Christ is illumined in our hearts and minds as we experience greater intimacy with Him.

My Sheep Follow

> John 10:25-30
> Jesus answered them, "I told you, and you do not believe. The works that I do in My Father's name, they bear witness of Me. But you do not believe, because you are not of My sheep, as I said to you. My sheep hear My voice, and I know them, and they follow Me. And I give them eternal life, and they shall never perish; neither shall anyone snatch them out of My hand. My Father, who has given them to Me, is greater than all; and no one is able to snatch them out of My Father's hand. I and My Father are one."

The above verses are some of the more endearing passages of all Scripture. Jesus stated that His sheep hear His voice. Jesus also said that He knows these sheep, and these sheep have a specific activity:

they follow Him. These sheep count it their greatest comfort to follow Jesus. Jesus gives them eternal life which Jesus defines as knowing God and Jesus Christ (John 17:3).

You Will Follow

> John 13:36
> Simon Peter said to Him, "Lord, where are You going?" Jesus answered him, "Where I am going you cannot follow Me now, but you shall follow Me afterward.

Prior to His crucifixion, death, and resurrection, Jesus sought to prepare His disciples with these words. The disciples had followed Jesus for years. However, now there would be a separation. They would not be allowed to follow: "...you cannot...." However, the promise is extended that they would be allowed to "...follow Me afterward." The entire idea of relationship after Jesus' death, burial and resurrection is couched in terms of following.

Those Who Will Not Follow

> Luke 6:39-41
> And He spoke a parable to them: "Can the blind lead the blind? Will they not both fall into the ditch? A disciple is not above his teacher, but everyone who is perfectly trained will be like his teacher."

In this instance Jesus is referring to leaders who do not follow. They are incapable of following because they are blind. The Pharisees thought themselves leaders in the community because of their great knowledge and adherence to the Law. Jesus recognizes their position. However, He considered them blind because they could not see Him as the Messiah and could not see the real intent of the commands as being the means of growing in relationship with the Father.

From a follower perspective there is no such thing as blindly following leaders because they happen to hold an organizational or societal position as leaders. Followers follow those whom they know follow the Lord Jesus Christ. A point for all to remember is that if you want to know where your leader is going and how he plans to treat you along the way, find out who or what the leader is following, and you will know both where he is going and how you can expect to be treated. If your leader is following fame and fortune and prestige and money, then you can expect to be treated as a commodity or a stepping-stone in the leader's career. However, if the leader follows the Lord, you can expect to be treated with the respect a follower has for God's human creation. This spirit of mutual respect is an almost universal characteristic of those who hold to a followerfirst perspective.

Conclusion

The Bible is clear that Jesus came to follow, call followers, and follow the will of the Father through His life, teaching, death, and resurrection. In the future, Jesus will follow the will of the Father in His second coming (Mark 13:32). The thread of following the Lord is woven throughout the Old and New Testament Scriptures. As following the will of the Father was the purpose and teaching of the Lord Jesus Christ, so ministers and leaders within the church need to begin with a followerfirst perspective as we follow the "head of the church" (Ephesians 5:23).

By concentrating on being a faithful follower, ministers will be able to seek their "well done" from the Lord Jesus rather than from their peers, or denominations, or self. This new freedom will provide a greater motivation to learn to lead from a follower perspective and trust in the enabling and leading of the Holy Spirit more than the often mechanistic practices prescribed by some. Followerfirst thinking will allow ministry leaders the opportunity to reassess how much the follower with responsibilities (minister, elder, deacon, church member) in the church really is dependent on the Lord. It will help all see more clearly how God glorifies Himself through the "foolish things of the world" (1 Corinthians 1:27).

Conversing with Christian ministers and leaders throughout the United States, I find that many are searching for a way of thinking about leading that allows them to lead without succumbing to a type of CEO business model often presented by much of the Christian leadership literature. My personal observations are that ministers and

Christian leaders want to know how to lead others effectively while thinking of themselves as leaders in a way that is consistent with the overall humility of the life of Christ, biblical teachings of humble service before God, and loving their neighbor. The followerfirst perspective fulfills this desire.

Think of Jesus' disciples. Who were they? There was never assembled a more eclectic bunch of losers in the history of mankind. The Bible is silent with regard to why Jesus called these men to "Follow Me." Any conjecture regarding Jesus seeing leadership potential in these men is simply that: conjecture. One truth we do know is these men were Jesus' first followers. The Apostle Paul captured the essence of all true leaders and followers in the church when he said:

> **For you see your calling, brethren,**
> **that not many wise according to the flesh,**
> **not many mighty, not many noble,**
> **are called.**
>
> **But God has chosen the foolish things of the world**
> **to put to shame the wise, and**
> **God has chosen the weak things of the world**
> **to put to shame the things which are mighty;**
> **and the base things of the world**
> **and things which are despised,**
> **God has chosen,**
> **and things which are not,**
> **to bring to nothing the things that are,**
> **that no flesh should glory in His presence.**
>
> **But of him you are in Christ Jesus,**
> **who became for us wisdom from God - and righteousness and**
> **sanctification and redemption -**
> **that, as it is written,**
> **He who glories, let him glory in the Lord.**
> **(1 Corinthians 1:26-31)**

The followerfirst perspective is compatible with much of the current teaching on becoming a leader and leading others. It is also compatible with many leadership styles that are often suggested for Christian leaders to employ. The difference is that the followerfirst perspective does not emphasize what followers and leaders **do** as much as how leaders and followers **think of themselves** within an organization. If you are an organizational leader or follower, I want to challenge the way you think about who you are in the Body of Christ.

When I share with leaders how the followerfirst perspective leads to becoming a Following-Leader, it is as if a large weight is lifted from these leaders as they resonate with the scriptural congruence of the followerfirst perspective. I had one vice president of a large company share with me that he had been looking for a way to express his identity in Christ while working on the job and that the followerfirst perspective gives him greater courage to lead others as he follows Christ on the job. First-time and veteran pastors also tell me that the followerfirst perspective gives them a new understanding and freedom to serve the church. This is the courage and freedom I hope all followers of Christ will find.

RETHINK

When you are recruiting people for positions of service in the church, don't recruit leaders. Recruit followers. You might say it like this:

> I've got good news for you:
> If you think you are foolish,
> if you are ignorant,
> if you are weak,
> if you are despised,
> if you are base,
> if you think you need to learn,
> if you think the world doesn't think much of you…
> Then you are the people I'm looking for
> because this is who I am.

These are the credentials for following Christ. Not titles or the letters after a name, not who you might be related to, not any intellectual capacities, not a position in the community, but who we really are; the ones whom the world's system of thought would think foolish, unworthy, simple, unsophisticated. God chooses in order to confound those who think themselves wise.

As a leader consider this. If God has chosen the foolish things of the world to confound the wise, does it not stand to reason that he would choose the most foolish to lead the foolish?

Some will say you are a fool if you think an organization can operate with people like this. Are we prepared to conduct His church organization to the glory of God in a way that is substantively different from what the "wise" of this world would recommend?

Chapter 2

Followers:
The Overlooked Treasure

I asked several of my colleagues during a roundtable discussion to try and ascertain which type of leadership theory might fit the following five characteristics. The first characteristic was the willingness to assume responsibility. The answers included Transformational Leadership and Transactional Leadership. The second characteristic was the willingness to serve. Most suggested Servant Leadership as the best fit. The third characteristic was the willingness to challenge the status quo and ask questions. Transformational Leadership was the primary answer. The fourth characteristic was the willingness to participate in transformation. Not unexpectedly, Transformational Leadership was again the most mentioned. The fifth characteristic was the willingness to take moral action, such as quitting a job, if the values of the organization were no longer congruent with personal values. Transformational Leaders, Transactional Leaders, and Leader Member Exchange Theory were considerations. (Each of these theories will be discussed later.)

The group was surprised when I disclosed that the five characteristics I had named were not characteristics of leaders but characteristics of Courageous followers as outlined by Ira Chaleff.[1] Perhaps you are surprised as well to read followers described as having initiative, assuming responsibility, and being willing to challenge leaders. This is not the stereotypical follower that much of the leadership literature describes. In fact, as one ministerial colleague confided, "We need leaders with these characteristics."

49

The greatest impetus to the inactivity of the church and hindrance to participation in the church is the thinking of those who are members of the church. The time has come to uncover the hidden treasure of followers in the church by gaining a new, biblical, and accurate understanding of biblical followers.

Created As Followers

Looking at the first chapters of the Bible we find that God had a plan to create the world and to supervise the activities taking place on the planet. In Genesis 1:28, Adam and Eve were charged by the Creator to "be fruitful and multiply, and fill the earth, and subdue it; and rule over the fish of the sea and over the birds of the sky, and over every living thing, that moves on the earth." Additionally all the "plants yielding seed" were readily available. There was only one prohibition given to these caretakers of God's creation. In Genesis 2:16-17, God says," From any tree of the garden you may eat freely but from the tree of the knowledge of good and evil you shall not eat, for in the day that you eat from it you shall surely die."

Originally, we were all 'wired' to honor God and find fulfillment by following the will of our Creator. Sin entered the world because our first parents refused to follow God's commands, and since that time, the focus of human fulfillment has been myopically placed on one's own personal fulfillment. Rather than reveling in being a follower of the commands of God our sinful natures revel in following the desires of the flesh. But please note, we are always following, because human beings were created to follow.

However, when we are born again, our capacity to follow the will of God is restored. It is not by accident that the 'second Adam,' the Lord Jesus Christ, declares in John 6:38-40 that His purpose was "not to do My own will but the will of Him Who sent Me." Through His perfect life, Christ exemplifies the original human purpose of following the will of God. Christ's specific fulfillment of the will of God was "that of all He has given Me I lose nothing, but raise it up on the last day....that everyone who beholds the Son and believes in Him, may have eternal life...."

As born again believers, our follower purpose is restored. We realize that BEING a follower of Christ is at the very core of who we are. Part of the joy and relief that swells in our hearts is the realization that we not only have the capacity to enjoy an intimate relationship with God through Jesus Christ, but we have also been restored to a correct position under Christ as the 'head' of the Body of Christ and no longer have to struggle to find our worth through self-actualization or trying to be the leader. Our worth is found in being a follower of Christ and loving Him by obeying the commands of Scripture.

Are leaders born or made? From a biblical position the answer would have to be that leaders are made because humans are by nature followers. My fulfillment is found in following the will of God for my life, a will that may include filling the role of leader. But it is important to understand that I can never BE a leader. I can only fill that role. However, I can BE a follower, and as such my primary preparation should be to develop the skills and disciplines necessary to be the very best follower I can be. In addition, I also need to develop the skills and disciplines necessary to fill the role of leader should God's will include, as it often does, leading others to follow Christ. Thus, my primary skill development is on follower skills. My secondary skills are leader skills. I am afraid we have reversed this order in much of our current teaching.

Misconceptions of Followers

The misconceptions of followers which have developed over time in the leadership literature often hinder an accurate understanding of biblical followers. The following examples represent a sampling of such misconceptions.

Sheepness

Perhaps the greatest misconception of followers is exacerbated by the use of the term *sheep*. The New Testament uses this word metaphorically to identify those persons who have believed upon the Lord Jesus Christ and belong to the Father as well as to those who wander "as sheep without a shepherd" (Matthew 9:36).

Throughout the Bible, references are made to the Lord being our Shepherd (Psalm 23) and Jesus referring to believers as, "My sheep" (John 10:27). Such metaphorical descriptions give rise to teachings on how people's actions sometimes resemble the actions of sheep by not having direction, not being able to care for themselves, or even having the inherent need for someone to lead them.

The only problem with such a perspective is that believers in Christ may be His sheep, but they certainly are *not* sheep. They are human beings. We often take the metaphor too far by ascribing a direct equivalency between the characteristics sheep and those of people. The primary teaching point behind using the sheep metaphor is dependence. As followers of Christ we are totally dependent upon Him for our life and our provision.

While teaching my classes, occasionally a pastor may mention he is frustrated because the church people will not change or that many within the congregation continue to make poor decisions. It is not uncommon for someone to jokingly assert, "What do you expect; they're sheep!" followed by confirming laughter. However, I am quick to point out to these students that by consoling ourselves with these assertions, we are forgetting one key truth. Pastors are sheep too.

Such conversations indicate how easily vocational ministers can sometimes begin to think of themselves as better than church members because of their call from God to serve the church. Every vocational minister faces this temptation at some point in ministry. Ministers begin to think that while they may be sheep, they are enlightened sheep. Putting it bluntly, it is as if these ministers are saying, "I may be dumb, but I'm not as dumb as my people." Even worse, what really may be developing is a type of ministerial arrogance in which a call to vocational ministry is accompanied by the belief that the minister is impervious to *sheepness*. It is as if spiritual evolution (if there were such a thing) has made the minister a better sheep than others. If these ideas are left unchecked and ministers carry such ideas forward in working with church people, vocational ministers stand in danger of creating a type of leader aristocracy from which the leaders look down at the followers and show them pity and care for them but never exert the time or energy to equip followers for service. Leaders should be aware that such a condescending attitude is not overlooked by the followers in the church. If such an attitude persists, it may result in fracturing the relationship of trust between the followers and the ministers resulting in eventual conflict.

The danger of conflict already exists because so many in the church perceive pastors and ministry leaders as being better Christians than other people. By adopting a followerfirst perspective pastors and ministry leaders can help alleviate this misconception. When leaders identify themselves as followers, they can embrace their own *sheepness* and dependency on the leadership of the Great Shepherd. Vocational ministers and leaders need to let the congregation know that all followers of Christ, including the clergy, are His sheep. As forgiven sinners, we are all working out our salvation through the process of sanctification toward completeness in Christ. Pastors and/or elders are those in the church called by God to help ALL Jesus' sheep grow toward greater Christ-likeness.

The follower-centric organization evidences what the apostle Paul admonishes all followers of Christ to do in Philippians 2:3-4 and Romans 12:3:

> Let nothing be done through selfish ambition or conceit, but in lowliness of mind let each esteem others better than himself.

> For I say, through the grace given to me, to everyone who is among you, not to think of himself more highly than he ought to think, but to think soberly, as God has dealt to each one a measure of faith.

Nothing in the church is to be done through selfish ambition or conceit. We can have ambition, but it must not be an ambition solely fixed on personal fulfillment. Such a fixation makes the minister conceited. Instead, the minister's ambition should be to make Christ great while showing respect to everyone.

Followers of Christ, His sheep, are to be totally dependent upon Him regardless of what role they play within the church. The pastor's teaching and equipping role is to bring believers from self-sufficiency to Christ-sufficiency, a state of total dependence upon the Lord Jesus Christ.

Subordinates

A second misconception is to consider fellow followers as subordinates. In the business community the idea of subordinates is usually used for those in the organization who are under the direct supervision of others in the organizational chart. In the military, a subordinate is one who is lower in rank than a superior officer. Though church organizational charts sometime reflect a top-down organizational structure similar to those of businesses and the military, in the follower-leader relationship these charts function to outline responsibility, not rank. Within the church there is only one superior-subordinate relationship. Jesus is the superior, and all other believers are subordinate. All other working relationships within the Body of Christ are based upon a willing submission toward one another.

Figure 1: Biblical Subordination

Willing Submission

The organizational diagram (See Figure 1) illustrates how the Bible understands the concept of subordination. Note that Jesus is *the* Head over all within the church. Every person, whether member, deacon, elder, or pastor is subordinate to His rule over the church. Also note that there are distinctions of position and divisions of responsibility within the church. Each group has a distinct biblical outline of responsibilities before the Lord and toward each other. These responsibilities are not carried out through a hierarchy of power and control but rather through a delicate web of mutual submission for each other under the authority of Jesus in obedience to the Word of God. The church does not function in a way that honors God if the members of that church are not willingly submitting themselves to Jesus first and then to those in positions of responsibility within the church. We will explore this concept further in Chapter 6.

Jesus contrasts the incompatibility of power and control through ideas of subordination with the willing submission of followers of Christ by comparing those who lead without Christ as the head with those who lead with Christ as the head. Jesus stated in Mark 10:42-45:

> But Jesus called them to him, and saith unto them, "Ye know that they which are accounted to rule over the Gentiles exercise lordship over them; and their great ones exercise authority upon them. But so shall it not be among you: but whosoever will be great among you, shall be your minister: And whosoever of you will be the chiefest, shall be servant of all. For even the Son of man came not to be ministered unto, but to minister, and to give his life a ransom for many."

It is clear from this teaching that Jesus intended His followers to understand that they are to lead as those under authority. The head of the church, Jesus, has the authority and all under Him are subject to Him. Because Jesus came as a servant (Matthew 20:28), He chose to set an example for us as One who serves, not as one who needs to be served. As one commentator aptly wrote:

> Gentile rulers... lord it over them, dominating and oppressing their subjects, and exercise authority over them, exploiting them. But it is not to be this way with Jesus' followers who are under God's rule. Whoever aspires to become great among you, let him be your (plural) house servant (diakonos), one who voluntarily renders useful service to others. Whoever aspires to be first (lit., "first among you") let him be a slave (doulos), one who forfeits his own rights in order to serve any and all (cf. comments on Mark 9:35-37). A disciple is to serve others, not his own interests, voluntarily and sacrificially.[1]

Jesus is clearly teaching those who would lead the church to have the disposition and behavior of a servant. Being a servant is one manifestation of what it means to be a follower. Servants perform the duties they are commanded to do. They follow what their authority tells them to do. If we are servants of the Lord Jesus Christ, then we are to have the disposition and behavior of a servant, a follower. Such an attitude is evidenced by genuine humility (See Philippians 2:8).

Non-functional

A third misconception within the church is that the term follower is viewed as a devotional concept rather than a functional role. As stated previously, when we talk of followers in the church, most assume we are talking about some aspect of discipleship. I concede that the idea of following may appear to be similar to disciple making. However, upon closer inspection, one can see that the term follower refers to both the *condition* and the *role* of every born-again person in the church. The idea of being a follower is a state of mind that each church member must grasp and a role that each church member is responsible to fulfill. Because we have not investigated the functional role and responsibilities of followers in the church, the vast majority of followers are left to figure out for themselves what role they perform and how to respond to certain situations. Without a biblical understanding of their role and responsibility, the born-again follower only has business models and worldly philosophies from which to respond. This results in schisms and conflicts as the Spirit wars against the flesh within the organization. Another result of not embracing a followerfirst perspective is that followers simply choose the role of spectator and sit on the sideline letting others do the work, an unacceptable follower role as well.

I hope to clarify for leaders and followers what these specific roles are and how the two roles function within the Body of Christ. The follower-leader relationship requires an understanding that the training of followers is an absolute priority in the church. Training will be performed by followers who have that specific (leader) responsibility and the training will be received by followers who have the specific (follower) responsibility of being trained. This may sound a bit convoluted, but hopefully the concept will become clearer.

Follower Characteristics

Because the church has been so preoccupied with developing leaders, we have neglected to investigate the functional characteristics of biblical followers. Preoccupation with leaders has led to a paucity of material from a biblical perspective on the characteristics of biblical followers and their role within the church. In this chapter, I offer a cursory introduction to three of the most often cited authors who have investigated the role of followers within organizations. As you read the various characteristics, I offer some biblical support for how these types of followers respond within the context of a church organization. Hopefully this understanding will give us a preliminary guideline for understanding the biblical role of followers within the church.

Exemplary Followers

In 1988, Robert Kelley wrote an article for the *Harvard Business Review* in which he stated, "Followership is not a person but a role, and what distinguishes followers from leaders is not intelligence or character but the role they play."[2] Kelley further stated, "What distinguishes an effective follower from an ineffective follower is enthusiastic, intelligent, and self-reliant participation—without star billing—in the pursuit of an organizational goal."[3] Kelley's book, *The Power of Followership*[4], provides further insights into the world of effective followers and how important they are to an organization. Kelley attributed four qualities to the effective follower: (a) self-management, (b) commitment, (c) competence and focus, and (d) courage (See Table 1).

Table 1: Kelley's Dimensions of Effective Followers

Dimensions	Explanation
Self-management	The key to being an effective follower is the ability to think for one-self, to exercise control and independence and to work without close supervision. Good followers are people to whom a leader can safely delegate responsibility, people who anticipate needs at their own level of competence and authority.
Commitment	Effective followers are committed to something—a cause, a product, an organization, an idea—in addition to the care of their own lives and careers.
Competence and focus	Effective followers master skills that will be useful to their organizations. They generally hold higher performance standards than the work environment requires and continuing education is second nature to them. It is a staple in their professional development.
Courage	Effective followers are credible, honest, and courageous. They establish themselves as independent, critical thinkers whose knowledge and judgment can be trusted. They give credit where credit is due, admitting mistakes and sharing successes. They form their own views and ethical standards and stand up for what they believe.

RETHINK

How would these dimensions of Effective Followers be applied to biblical followers? Below are some brief suggestions as to how biblical followers might apply these dimensions within a church context.

Self-management

To the biblical follower, self-management, as well as self-discipline, is focused not so much on self as on Christ. The follower's dependence upon the person of the Holy Spirit for the enabling necessary to fulfill the commands of Christ is essential to bringing glory to God. Within the context of the Holy Spirit's leading, each biblical follower is his or her own person. Biblical followers have gifts and abilities that can be used in the fulfillment of the work of the Lord within the church (Consider Romans 12:6; 1 Corinthians 4-11). A spirit-filled follower knows and exercises spiritual discipline and does not need close supervision once a task has been assigned. The biblical follower works through difficulties without the leader's intervention (thus freeing the leader), and is able to gather other followers to participate in the fulfillment of the responsibility.

Commitment

The biblical follower's commitment is not to a cause or an organization but to a person, the Lord Jesus Christ. This is one of the distinguishing characteristics of the Following-Leader we will discuss in Chapter Eight. Because the follower is committed to Christ, he/she will be committed to what Christ is committed. Jesus is committed to the Father. Thus, the follower's focus for each day is the glory of God the Father. Jesus is committed to His church. Thus, all true followers of Christ will be committed to His church, not just universally but locally. Personal ambitions, careers, and advancements take a back seat to the person of Christ and the commands He gives to "love the Lord your God with all your heart, and with all your soul, and with all your mind" (Matthew 22:37-38).

Competence and Focus

The biblical follower is a learner, a disciple. Followers are continually seeking to know more of Christ and His Word. They sharpen their skills and take the necessary time, effort, and resources to find excellence in everything they do. They desire to be "approved unto God" (2 Timothy 2:15). Therefore, they study, read, memorize, meditate, and apply the Word to their daily lives. They take advantage of times of development offered by the church and, if none are available, will seek other sources (internet, colleges, etc.) to further their understanding of what it means to honor God through Jesus Christ.

Courage

A biblical follower is credible. That is, the follower has personal integrity. Their yes is yes, and their no is no (Matthew 5:37). The follower will not talk behind the back of the leader. They speak the truth even at the risk of being misunderstood. Their integrity before the Lord is to love and serve the leader. Loving the leader sometimes means holding the leader accountable and making certain that the leader knows and understands facts, rather than politically motivated spin. Biblical followers will not succumb to the temptation of self-preservation but will make every effort to see that the Word of God is obeyed at all times.

WHY RE INTRODUCE THIS god?

Courageous Followers

Ira Chaleff, author of *Courageous Followership*,[6] identified five characteristics of courageous followers. Describing active followers within an organization, Chaleff suggests that Courageous Followers are an indispensable addition to any organization. By exercising these characteristics, followers engage with leaders in an active leadership process. These Courageous Followers allow leaders to lead with the confidence that the followers are more than willing to accomplish the organizational mission. Table 2 outlines the key ideas for each characteristic:

Table 2: Chaleff's Dimensions of Courageous Followership

Dimensions	Description
Assume Responsibility	Courageous followers assume responsibility for themselves and the organization. They do not hold a paternalistic image of the leader or organization. They do not expect the leader or organization to provide for their security and growth or to give them permission to act. Courageous followers discover or create opportunities to fulfill their potential and maximize their value to the organization. They initiate values-based action to improve the organization's external activities and its internal processes. The authority to initiate comes from the courageous follower's understanding and ownership of the common purpose and from the needs of those the organization serves.
Serve	Courageous followers are not afraid of the hard work required to serve a leader. They assume new or additional responsibilities to unburden the leader and serve the organization. They stay alert for areas in which their strengths complement the leader's and assert themselves in these areas. Courageous followers stand up for their leader and the tough decisions a leader must make if the organization is to achieve its purpose. They are as passionate as the leader in pursuing the common purpose.

Dimensions	Description
Challenge	Courageous followers give voice to the discomfort they feel when the behaviors or policies of the leader or group conflict with their sense of what is right. They are willing to stand up, stand out, risk rejection, and initiate conflict in order to examine the actions of the leader and group when appropriate. They are willing to deal with the emotions their challenge evokes in the leader and group. Courageous followers value organizational harmony and their relationship with the leader, but not at the expense of the common purpose and their integrity.
Participate in Transformation	When behavior that jeopardizes the common purpose remains unchanged, courageous followers recognize the need for transformation. They champion the need for change and stay with the leader and group while they mutually struggle with the difficulty of real change. They examine their own need for transformation and become full participants in the change process as appropriate.
Take Moral Action	Courageous followers know when it is time to take a stand that is different than that of the leaders. They are answering to a higher set of values. The stand may involve refusing to obey a direct order, appealing the order to the next level of authority, or tendering one's resignation. These and other forms of moral action involve personal risk. But, service to the common purpose justifies and sometimes demands acting.

RETHINK

Looking at Ira Chaleff's follower characteristics in Table 2, do Courageous Followers who are believers have a place in our churches? If so, how should we integrate Courageous Followers into the life of the church, and how should these Courageous Followers operate as biblical followers? I offer the following ideas for discussion.

Assume Responsibility

As a biblical follower, each of us has a responsibility. As followers of Christ, it is our responsibility to see that the church fulfills the Great Commission. It is NOT the responsibility of leaders to motivate us out of our mediocrity (as if they could). If we are complacent and mediocre in our service in the church, it is a reflection of our mediocre love for Jesus and/or our lack of understanding our responsibilities before God, not the pastor's inability to lead us. The pastor or elders of the church are not our parents. They may care for us and watch over us, but we are not babies. We are followers of Christ, and as such, we will learn how to feed ourselves, clothe ourselves, and help others do the same. If our leaders are not fulfilling the commands of Christ, this does not give us the right to sit around and do nothing but complain and gossip about how we would do things differently. Our responsibility is to obey Christ. If the leaders don't share the gospel or invite people to church to hear the Word, then we will. If the leaders don't teach people the Word of God, we will learn it and teach it. If the church needs input on how to solve problems, we will give it respectfully and submissively. If our assessment of our church is that it is not doing what it ought to do, **we will not blame the leader(s); we will blame ourselves.** We are followers of Christ. We willingly assume our God-given responsibility.

Serve

God gives the church leaders. If we believe God placed these leaders in their roles of responsibility, we should be committed to serve alongside them and to serve them. In Hebrews 13:17 the writer commands that we submit to those who "rule" over us. As such, we are to let these persons perceive us as a brothers and sisters in Christ, fellow followers who can be trusted to be on the team. We will add our strengths to our leaders' weaknesses without making them feel the lesser or giving ourselves any credit. As followers, we are servants of Christ (John 12:26). As such, our joy is to serve the servants of Christ. Jesus said, "If anyone serves Me, let him follow Me; and where I am, there My servant will be also" (John 12:26). **Followers want to be where Christ is being served.** We will not be a burden to our leaders but will find where we are needed in the organization without waiting to be asked. (Requiring that someone ask me to do ministry in the church often reflects a veiled, pride-filled attitude that becomes an excuse for my own inactivity.) We will stand up for our leaders and stand with our leaders as long as they are following our Leader, the Lord Jesus Christ. By doing so, it will be profitable for us as our leaders are allowed to minister with "joy and not with grief" (Hebrews 13:17b).

Challenge

As followers of Christ we realize our frailties and that the leaders whom God has placed in our lives are human as well. Therefore, we will not expect perfection from them. We will not make our expectations more than the Bible requires. Additionally, we will not let the first time we talk privately with our leader be a challenging conversation. Rather, we will consistently communicate our support and our willingness to help, seeking to be a friend and available to help.

If, however, the leaders move in a direction that directly contradicts the clear teaching of the Bible or lead in such a way that the reputation of Christ might be besmirched, then it is our duty as followers of Christ first, to speak directly to the leader(s). We will not speak to our little group and form an army of sympathizers before challenging the leader(s). This would be gossip and murmuring, and we will have no part in allowing the devil to use us and this verbal mechanism to bring discord and division to the Body of Christ. Instead, each follower should contact the leader and speak respectfully, lovingly, and caringly, in a Spirit-filled manner to point out where there is a potential problem. Like the prophet Nathan with King David (2 Samuel 12:7), each follower should be ready to risk the death of a personal relationship in order to respond biblically and follow the commands of Christ. Followers must be willing to allow the leader(s) to misunderstand them and receive the likely negative emotional response from the leaders at such a challenge. Regardless of the response, followers should seek the unity of the Spirit in the bond of peace (Ephesians 4:3) at all times, never willing to compromise the Word of God or the reputation of *the* Leader, the Lord Jesus Christ, for personal gain.

Participate in Transformation

As followers of Christ we realize that negotiating change within an organization is one of the most time consuming and upsetting events in the life of any organization. We will embrace change and encourage those around us to do the same. We will be open to new ideas. We will trust those who have an informed opinion about a needed change. We will share our insights on what actions can best be taken to help the congregation through the change process, and then we will make ourselves available to enact the needed change. We will focus on the future of what will be rather than look back at the past loss of what was. We will change internally, spiritually, and emotionally. We will not gripe and complain at the changes that have affected us. As the mercies of God are new every morning (Lamentations 3:23), we will have a new and refreshing attitude of seeking to know God and be changed by Him through every context of the day, especially when operating within the church.

Take Moral Action

Followers support God-called leaders in the church. However, if the time comes when we can no longer follow their leading because of immorality or straying from following the Lord by not following the Word of God, we have the moral obligation to challenge the leader and lovingly direct him to the Word and correction according to Matthew 18. Christ specifically states that followers are to confront wrongdoing within the body regardless of the position they hold. The process begins with a personal intervention. If that process is not profitable, then a group intervention is needed. If the wrongdoer continues with his/her ungodly behavior, then the activity needs to be addressed by those in an official capacity within the church and acted upon in a God-honoring manner.

If these interventions are not followed through or the leaders in the church refuse to confront the immoral behavior, followers of Christ have a moral obligation to leave the organization. If the behavior involves a crime such as child abuse or theft, then, before leaving the church, followers should also notify the civil authorities.

Thankfully, such actions are often rarely needed. The primary reason for leaving a church is often not a moral issue but a philosophical one. The leaders of the church may decide to move in a direction in which a person is philosophically opposed. If a person finds himself or herself in a church that is moving in a direction where the person decides, "I just don't think that is a God-honoring direction to take," it may be time to consider leaving rather than cause a split within the Body.

Leaving is the last resort. Followers should do so quietly and without fanfare. When friends ask why we are leaving, give them a substantive, biblical (not personal) reason and no more. Followers should not brag, gossip, murmur, or gather "prayer groups" together to pray for the leader's repentance. Followers do not lead rebellions nor do they play the martyr. Once the decision is made to leave, they follow Christ to another church and submit to the leaders of that Body of Christ to the glory of God.

Post-industrial Followers

Joseph Rost takes a different approach, proposing that leadership be considered in light of a post-industrialized culture.[7] Because the Bible was written in a pre-industrialized society, many of Rost's ideas resonate well with followerfirst thinking. Focusing on the follower-leader relationship in the historic context in which these relationships occur gives us a new perspective on the reality of the interdependence required within this relationship.

Rost suggests five dynamics of a follower-leader relationship:

1. Leaders are Followers

Only people who are active in the leadership process are followers. Passive people are not in a relationship. They have chosen not to be involved. They cannot have influence. Passive people are not followers.[8]

2. Followers Influence Leaders

Active people can fall anywhere on a continuum of activity from highly active to minimally active, and their influence in the leadership process is, in large part, based on their activity, their willingness to get involved, their use of the power resources they have at their command to influence other people. Some followers are very active; others are not so active. Some followers are very active at certain times and not so active at other times.[9]

3. Follower Reciprocality

Followers can become leaders and leaders can become followers in any one leadership relationship. People are not stuck in one or the other for the whole time the relationship exits. Followers may be leaders for a while, and leaders may be followers for a while. Followers do not have to be managers to be leaders. This ability to change places without changing organizational positions gives followers considerable influence and mobility.[10]

4. Follower Flexibility

In one group or organization people can be leaders. In other groups and organizations they can be followers. Followers are not always followers in all leadership relationships.[11]

5. Followers Lead

Joseph Rost summarizes the essential nature of a follower-leader relationship by pointing out that *together,* followers and leaders get things accomplished. Together, those in positions of leading and those who are in positions of following lead the organization to accomplish the goals. Rost said:

> Most important, followers do not do followership, they do leadership. Both leaders and followers form one relationship that is leadership. There is no such thing as followership in the new school of leadership. Followership makes sense only in the industrial leadership paradigm, where leadership is good management. . . . Followers and leaders develop a relationship wherein they influence one another as well as the organization and society, and that is leadership. They do not do the same things in the relationship, just as composers and musicians do not do the same thing in making music, but they are both essential to leadership.[12]

RETHINK

Joseph Rost adds another positive view of what it means to be a follower in a post-industrial organizational context. His five statements may be applied to the church in this way:

Leaders are Followers

One of the keys to understanding biblical followers is the realization that followers are not stagnant but active. Following is an action. The very meaning of the word requires the follower to actively pursue the Lord Jesus Christ. Within the church, followers are actively engaged in the process of seeking out those who are leaders and presenting themselves for service.

Followers Influence Leaders

Biblical follower activity is based upon the freedom the followers have to exercise their gifts, talents and abilities. This level

---

of follower activity is based upon two aspects. First, a follower's level of intimacy with the Leader, the Lord Jesus Christ, determines the level and activity of following within the context of the church. Followers who have a keen desire to know Christ in all aspects of life are usually actively engaged in the process of making Christ known resulting in these followers having a greater degree of responsibility and influence in the church and among the leaders. Next, the titular leaders of the church must establish a permission giving atmosphere in which the follower is secure to initiate activity without fear of reprisal. Leaders do not 'empower' followers. Rather leaders create the structural freedom in which followers can exercise their gifts and abilities. Such freedom results in high follower participation and greater productivity.

Follower Reciprocality

The interdependent nature and the humility required of persons within the biblical follower-leader relationship allow both followers and leaders the freedom to serve within the scope of their giftedness. In a follower-centric organization, position and rank are not highly prized. Therefore, followers and leaders can cooperate with each other under the lordship of Christ without fear of being replaced or being upstaged by someone else. The end result of honoring God by fulfilling His commands trumps any prideful and arrogant thinking of holding on to a title or position. (See the explanation of the Mobius Strip.)

Follower Flexibility

Biblical followers do not see being a leader as better than being a follower. Therefore, the follower is comfortable in whatever position within the organization the providence of the Lord may allow. In one instance the biblical follower may be the titular leader of a business or in a management position within a company. At the same time, this biblical follower may also be a member of a local church. Because of the followerfirst mindset, the biblical follower who may be a leader at work can operate within the church without feelings of resentment because he/she is not a titular leader. In fact, biblical followers hold no expectations that their positions at secular jobs give them any greater influence within the church. The thought process of the biblical follower is never to perceive himself or herself as leader, but rather as a follower in a specific position within the organization. The flexibility of the biblical follower allows the person to respond according to need, notwithstanding title or position.

Followers Lead

Within the follower-centric organization, followers are not viewed as mere necessities in order to accomplish goals, but to use Rost's words, followers are "essential" in the process of leading the church to fulfill her mission. Followers influence others and have an impact on everyone around them. Biblical followers are aware of this awesome responsibility and guard how they respond because the glory of their Leader, the Lord Jesus, is always at stake.

Dishonoring Follower Types

We have spent most of our time examining positive follower types and how they might be evidenced in a church context. Yet, there are some who call themselves followers who do not manifest the characteristics of those who embrace the followerfirst perspective. Unfortunately, these non-followers are the people who discourage leaders and give faithful followers a bad reputation. The following are a few dishonoring follower types who sometime appear within the church.

Angry Followers

Angry followers have become hurt or angry because of a breach of trust or unmet expectations. These followers have violated one of the key rules of being a biblical follower. They have allowed a breach of trust or unmet expectations to form a division between them and the leader. They have not pursued the leader and gotten a definitive answer to the situation. They may have relied upon speculation and even third-party gossip to form unfounded opinions about the leader. These followers need to confess their sin to God, repent, and humble themselves to the leader. They especially need to make right any wrongs (character assassinations) done to the leader through sharing gossip or innuendo with others. If after these actions have been corrected and the follower and leader have not been reconciled, other church leaders may need to intervene at the request of the leader and follower in order to clarify the situation and make any corrections that might facilitate reconciliation according to Mathew 18. Angry, alienated followers are not biblical followers. They are cysts within the Body of Christ and can often become cancerous, spreading their poisonous attitudes and infecting others.

Whatever Followers

'Whatever' followers are those individuals who are not engaged in making a difference within the organization. Their favorite response to someone's suggestion is... "Whatever." They lose credibility because they do not think for themselves. By not thinking for themselves, these 'whatever' followers are not being circumspect in their daily lives. They are not good stewards of their minds. They may have poor self-concepts which evidence a lack of understanding of who they are in Christ. Additionally, these 'whatever' followers usually want everyone to simply get along. Peace at any price is their mantra, whether it is peace at the expense of truth or not. They are not actively engaged and connected with the person of Christ, are not walking in the power of the Holy Spirit, and leave themselves open to being led astray by those who distort biblical teaching (2 Timothy 3:6).

Mediocre Followers

Mediocre followers perform required tasks minimally and look out for themselves. They follow the adage that the one rule of the army is never to volunteer for anything. Thus, they never volunteer or offer themselves for service other than that which is the minimum necessary to maintain status in the group. They are proficient in the politics of church, knowing how to be for and against a particular issue at any given time. They make it a point not to cross powerful people and to be on the winning side of a discussion. In the church, these followers will come, sit, give a little money each week, carry their Bible, sing the songs, and smile with everyone else. They will, however, not honor God by giving their lives in service to Christ. They do not experience the joy of second-mile service (Matthew 5:41). Their desire is never to be challenged or personally extended to the point of relying solely upon the work of the Holy Spirit to get a job done. Their lives are mediocre. The bread of life to them is stale and tasteless.

Maintenance Followers

Maintenance followers lack initiative, require constant direction, and look to leaders to do their thinking. They represent the stereotypical *sheep* that so many believe make up the church. These people do not honor the Lord with their lives and fall short of the Lord's command to deny self, take up their cross daily and follow Jesus. However, what is striking about these followers is that their attitudes and actions may be exacerbated by the leader-centered perspective in the church. When the people are taught that the leaders have the vision, the goals, and the gifts to do the work of the Lord, why should followers think about such things? If all the leaders want is for followers to fulfill the leader's vision, could this be a reason for a lack of initiative? Because these followers have not engaged or perhaps haven't even been consulted regarding their vision, goals, and desires, there is no buy-in to the direction of the church and certainly no participation. These followers have been brainwashed into believing that they are not a vital part of the body and, as a result, become inactive and despondent. They are fully convinced that they are nobodies in the great scheme of things.

Pseudo Followers

Pseudo followers are those individuals who give an outward appearance of following but are actually not following at all. When in the presence of the leader, they give the impression they are the leader's greatest friend and helper. When away from the leader, the pseudo follower degrades and diminishes the character and credibility of the leader. These are the people who say one thing to the leader's face and then the exact opposite to others. Their intention is to wield power over the leader by undermining other's trust in the leader. They cause doubt and confusion. They are a cancer within the organization and unless they are found out, can do irreparable harm.

The Mobius Solution

One of the best symbols I have found regarding the nature of the follower-leader relationship is the Mobius strip (See Figure 2).[13] Taken from topographical mathematics, the unique quality of this geometric shape is that it only has one continuous surface. A twist in the band allows one to traverse the surface of the band without ever crossing a boundary.[14]

Figure 2: Mobius Strip

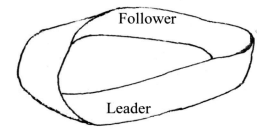

By having only one surface, the Mobius strip is the perfect example of how leading and following take place. A follower may be a leader and a leader a follower in a given context. This is often the case in team meetings in which the leader of the team may be less informed about a matter than another and encourages the other team member to take the lead in the discussion and decision making. With this view, *leadership becomes an intentional, reciprocal, interdependent, dynamic, relationship between a leader and a follower.* Such an understanding of leadership allows for a fluid functioning of the gifts and abilities of positional followers and leaders. It may still fall to the titular leader of the group to make the final decision, but the interplay between the leader and follower usually results in a better decision and more buy-in on the part of the group.

Context is Key

The followerfirst perspective affords both the leader and follower an opportunity to work together with little to no regard to who holds the title leader. The overall purpose and goal of the group trumps any grandstanding or turf protecting. Who leads the group at any one time is determined by the context and need of the group. That is, the person who has the information, credibility, and competence to achieve the purpose and goal is given permission to lead and to act by the titular leader and the group so that the team/group achieves success. Ken Blanchard stated:

> At its best, leadership is a partnership that involves mutual trust between two people who work together to achieve common goals. Both leaders and followers influence each other. Leadership shifts between them, depending on the task at hand and who has the competence and commitment to deal with it. Both parties play a role in determining how things get done.[15]

Understanding the leader-follower relationship from this perspective raises the value of followers within an organization. Leading is not a linear activity like a row of dominoes whereby the leader acts and the followers simply line up and fall into place. The Mobius strip exemplifies that followers play a much more important role in the process of accomplishing goals and objectives than simply fulfilling the wishes of the leaders. In fact, from the descriptions we have investigated, Exemplary, Courageous, and Post-Industrial followers play an integral part in making leaders successful, developing organizational vision, and accomplishing organizational objectives. This is all the more true within churches.

With a followerfirst perspective, every person within the church is given the responsibility to use his or her gifts to fulfill the commands of Christ. Followers who understand their divine role and operate in the power of the Holy Spirit hold the key to accomplishing the world mission of this God-established organization.

Chaleff, Kelley, and Rost, have influenced much of what we know and understand about followers. There is much work to be done to identify specific organizational traits and behaviors of a follower of Christ. However, **willingly following the Lord Jesus Christ with all one's heart, mind, soul, and strength in every circumstance regardless of organizational position** appears to be a good starting point from which we can further explore the treasures of these unique people who make up our unique church organizations.

RETHINK

One of the reasons for writing this book is to give a positive image of what it means to follow and how there is no shame in identifying yourself as a follower, especially a follower of Christ. Rethinking who we are and how the church is designed to be a follower-centric organization affords us an opportunity to look for those who evidence the best follower characteristics. Below are a few questions to ask when identifying followers and overcoming prevailing follower stereotypes:

- Do leaders really want to surround themselves with leaders or rather with faithful courageous, exemplary followers?
- Do you think of followers as being competent or incompetent? Why?
- Do you think a person can choose the role of follower and still be appreciated and respected in your organization?
- In your thinking, is it acceptable to be a follower on purpose?
- Might it be possible to get more people involved in the life of the church if we simply appealed to their role as followers?

Exercise

Have those with whom you work make their own Mobius strip. Cut pieces of paper ½ inche wide and 14 inches long. Have the members of the team write the word LEADER on one side of the paper and the word FOLLOWER on the other side. Then hold the two ends with both hands and bring both ends together to form a circle. Before attaching the two ends together with tape, twist one end one half turn and then attach the ends. This twist creates the appropriate shape.

Once you have created your Mobius strip, have the members put a pen or marker in the center of the strip and draw a line through the center of the strip not raising their markers off the paper. As team members complete the circuit of the strip you will hear comments such as, "How about that," or "Well, what do you know." They will be commenting on the fact that they were able to draw a line along the surface of the strip without a break. As they mark the line through the words LEADER and FOLLOWER, the point is made that the process of leadership involves people serving as leaders and then serving as followers depending on the context.

Point out that the 'twist' in the paper allows the strip to become a single surface. It is this 'twist' that is the CONTEXT that determines who is the leader and who is the follower in the group. Point out that although a person may have the title, leader, he or she operates in the leadership process not with a title, but as a cooperative member of the process.

An additional activity is to have each person disconnect the ends of their Mobius Strip and then reconnect them with other members of the group so that everyone is connected to one another. [Be sure to have the members reconnect to each other with a Mobius and not just a circle.] When complete ask these questions:

1. What was required for you to connect with others?
   Observations:
   - Each person had to be willing to initiate the action (show initiative).
   - Each person had to open themselves up and become vulnerable to another.
   - Each person had to move toward another person and participate in the activity.

- Each person had to give up a part of themselves in order to connect to another (this is reflected in the particles of paper left on the tape when you disconnect the Mobius strip).

2. What was created when all of the Mobius strips were connected?
Observations:
- A delicate chain of interpersonal relationships
- Connections that can be easily broken
- People connected for a common purpose who are unimpressed with who is the leader or follower

Next, take the chain of Mobius strips and place (pile) them on top of an open Bible. What do you have?
Observations:
- A Mess! (This is what organizations really look like and why they take so much work.)
- The CHURCH! (This is the group God uses to change the world; a connected group of leaders and followers whose foundation is the Word of God, working together for a common purpose, the glory of God in the Great Commission.)

I have done this exercise with entire congregations during a morning service. It takes time, the people enjoy the interaction (well most) and the point is made. It gives people a new appreciation for what it means to be the church. At one particular church in the Dominican Republic, over 200 people participated in the exercise. People were laughing and talking. It was a wonderful, chaotic moment as people took links of the 'chain' and moved about the auditorium, making certain to connect all the pieces together. When all the parts were connected, it took several people to bring the 'chain' to the front and place it on the open Bible on the table. The chain spilled over the sides of the table and people kept trying to lift the various loops up onto the rest of the bulk that was resting on the Bible. When I finally declared that what they were looking at was the Church, the people broke out in spontaneous applause and hallelujahs. May God grant your church that same sense of togetherness and freedom.

Part II

Embrace Your Follower Identity

Chapter 3

Life from a Follower Perspective

Enormous amounts of time, effort, and money have been concentrated on leaders, leadership, and leading. As a result, church practitioners, academics, and theoreticians have all but forgotten the followers who faithfully fulfill the work of the ministry and deserve our respect and understanding. My study of follower/leader relationships has brought me to the place where I can confidently say that the church's obsession with leadership has blinded her to a problem she does not want to recognize, because to do so, she has to admit that many current standard operating principles and methods are inconsistent with a *biblical* understanding of how Christ's church should function. Adopting non-biblically based methodologies has resulted in many churches becoming dysfunctional and ineffectively impacting their local communities and the culture at large. Much of the current leadership literature precipitates the acceptance of these aberrant systems by elevating becoming a leader as the optimal goal of the Christian life while forgetting, if not ignoring, the multitude of biblical texts calling for a faithful following of Christ as the primary operating principle. Instead of creating a unique organization with a unique purpose, this concentration on the organization's top few outstanding people creates churches which establish leader-centered organizations functioning in similar fashion to for profit business. What is needed is a way to perform the business of the church without becoming a church business.

I propose that we view the church from the perspective of the follower. When you read the Bible with a follower mindset, you will be astonished to find a large number of scriptures referencing the role and function of followers within the Body of Christ. Whether people find themselves in positions of leading or positions of following, the Bible is quite clear that they are to always think of themselves as followers.

Questioning Leader/Follower Assumptions

In these pages I hope to show that any teaching on Christian leadership that does not contain a followerfirst perspective misses the important follower theme resonating throughout the Bible. The Bible certainly has a few direct teachings regarding leaders and leading. Yet, if we look beyond our ingrained leader-oriented biases, we find the over-arching theme and teachings of Scripture relate to being godly followers who follow the will of God and who relate to one another as fellow followers within a community of followers. This is where our "unlearning" needs to take place.

Examination of the literature espousing supposed biblical leadership teachings reveals that much of this literature is not based in specific, didactic teachings from the Bible but on principles derived from the Bible's historical narrative and anecdotal observations. It is quite telling that many of these observations usually serve to support the author's favorite leadership theory and preconceived idea of what biblical leadership is. In addition, a good portion of the current Christian leadership literature appears to embrace a leader-centered perspective that mirrors what is accepted within secular organizational cultures rather than the follower theme of the Scriptures. Some writers simply take popular business principles regarding leaders and leader theories and impose these theories and principles as a template on the text of Scripture. Scriptures are often cherry-picked and taken out of context to support these principles and make them more palatable to the church. As a result, we have created 'baptized business principles' instead of allowing the Bible to speak. We muzzle Scripture's teaching by reading with a preconceived thought process that places being a leader and becoming a leader as the ultimate goal of the

Christian life. I find no such teaching in the Old or New Testaments. I hope through reading this book you will begin to question your personal leader presuppositions and begin to embrace the position that the ultimate goal of the believer is to be a follower of Christ *first*, and fulfill the responsibilities He gives regardless of organizational position.

There is no question the church needs good leaders. However, leaders need to be taught how to lead from a followerfirst perspective, while followers need to follow from a followerfirst perspective. The church is the most unique organization on the planet. Her Head, the Lord Jesus Christ, is physically absent but present to lead through the accurate understanding of the teachings of Scripture and the indwelling Holy Spirit. The guidelines for church operation are given in the Bible, and our Head expects His church to fulfill them with the singular purpose of glorifying God in all that she does. Yet, it appears that operating with a leader-centered perspective, rather than a followerfirst perspective results in the church experiencing many unintended consequences.

Unintended Consequences

Leaders are a necessary part of the church organization, and these leaders need to know how to lead. But they need to know how to lead from a followerfirst perspective rather than from a leader-centered perspective. To support my argument for a more follower-centered perspective, I offer four specific unintended consequences that appear to have occurred during the past two decades of teaching a leader-centered approach: (a) church ineffectiveness, (b) member non-participation, (c) church divisions, and (d) cavalier biblical interpretations.

Church Ineffectiveness

One of the more popular sayings among leadership enthusiasts is, "Everything rises or falls on leadership." I would have no problem supporting such a statement if people understood that leadership is a process that takes place between leaders and followers.

However, the reality is that when people hear this statement, they do not hear that everything rises or falls on leadership. The people hear that everything rises or falls on *leaders*. The statement implies that if leaders don't do the right things at the right time, then nothing is accomplished. Statements such as this place leaders as the key figures in the organization who ultimately determine the success or failure of that organization. If it is true that everything rises or falls on leaders, then we might assume that the church has benefitted from over three decades of teaching on leadership and how to become leaders. Church statistics, however, do not support such an assumption.[1]

The Southern Baptist Convention is the largest Protestant denomination in the United States. In June of 2013, LifeWay Research, the research arm of The Southern Baptist Convention reported that although the number of churches increased within the denomination, the actual numbers of members within SBC churches declined by more than 100,000. This troubling statistic was coupled with even more disturbing news in that worship attendance declined 3.1 percent and baptisms declined 5.5 percent over the previous year's statistics.[2]

Certainly there are many contributing factors to these disturbing statistics. However, if we accept the idea that everything rises or falls on leadership, then the leaders of these churches are to be held responsible for this decline. Leadership enthusiasts might conclude that leaders in these churches are not leading as they ought and need more training on how to motivate their members to obey the Great Commission. However, what if within the church organizational context everything does not rise or fall with leaders? What if God designed the church in such a way that followers, not just leaders, are held responsible for the growth of the church?

I suggest that the responsibility for this lack of church growth and lack of impact on our communities is not primarily due to a lack of leaders or a lack of leadership skills. To assert that the primary reason for church stagnation rests with the pastor's lack of leadership is to offer too simplistic a view of the problem and also reveals a lack of understanding that the church is composed of followers with specific responsibilities. The church is an organized group of followers. If we are to levy any blame for this apparent stagnation and decline, the blame falls squarely with the followers of Christ within these congregations, whether they have leader positions or not. When Jesus said, "All authority has been given to Me in heaven and on earth. Go therefore and make disciples of all nations, baptizing them in the name of the Father and the Son and the Holy Spirit, teaching them to observe all that I commanded you; and lo, I am with you always, even to the end of the age" (Matthew 28: 18-20), He intended His words to apply just as much to followers of Christ who hold no leader positions in the church as those followers who do hold leader positions. With a followerfirst perspective, followers of Christ within the church do not need someone to motivate them to do what the actual Leader of the church, Jesus, commands them to do. A followerfirst perspective teaches that followers do not have an option of whether or not they obey the commands of Christ. Whether a follower does or does not like a particular pastor, elder, deacon, or teacher who is responsible for them is irrelevant. A followerfirst perspective encourages followers to fulfill the obvious commands of Christ, the Leader, whether the titular leader in the church is appreciated or not. However, such a perspective of following is rarely found in today's church and results in a second unintended consequence.

WHAT IS "THE WORK of THE CHURCH"?

Member Non-participation *HAVE WE CREATED THIS ILLUSION?*

For years the church has operated under the assumption of the 80/20 rule. Twenty percent of the people do [the work] while eighty percent sit on the sideline. There is not a pastor or church worker alive who has not experienced this phenomenon. I am certain those who were teaching leadership principles in the church had the desire to increase the twenty percent and reduce the eighty percent. However, my observations and interviews with church members and ministers indicate that what many think increases the numbers of people participating in the church actually has a numbing effect on the church membership. By emphasizing leaders and everyone in the church becoming a leader, these leader-centered organizations subconsciously teach those *not* in leader positions and those who do not see themselves as ever becoming leaders that they are insignificant. *

When the leaders only train potential leaders, a subconscious self-fulfilling prophesy begins. The leaders teach that leaders get things done and, as a result, those who are deemed non-leaders wait on the leaders to get things done. Unknowingly the leaders create an organization in which followers are reinforced to believe they have no initiative, no input, and no influence to make a difference. Non-leaders are relegated to the pejorative status of *follower*. As followers, these people believe they have no say in any matter and may even develop an entitlement mentality. This belief assumes the church exists and church leaders are chosen solely to meet the needs of the entitled. Leaders perceive these followers as *sheep* and expect them to do what they are told. The role of the follower is diminished to that of a barnyard animal and they just need to submit to their leaders. Similarly, those who have leader responsibilities begin to think that if followers only knew their place and submitted to the church leaders everything would be wonderful. Such an attitude does not comprehend the biblical concept of followers.

As mentioned previously, the greatest impetus to the inactivity of the church and hindrance to participation in the church is the negative thinking of those who are members of the church. Emphasizing leaders and only training leaders with the attitude that leaders are the only ones who count has had little impact on the 80/20 rule. As a result, growing churches still need workers, current workers grow more and more tired, and the vast majority of people become more content to show up, sit for an hour, put a tip in the offering plate, and then head to the restaurant and an afternoon of play. Such actions are commonplace because followers have not been taught the importance of follower responsibilities within the church organization. The vast majority of followers are unaware how they influence those around them either positively or negatively. The continuous drumming of a need for leaders drowns out any occasional appeal to the importance of the body to do the work of the ministry.

Church leaders may be charged with "equipping the saints to do the work of the ministry" (Ephesians 4:11), but the prevailing idea in some circles seems to be that the only saints worth equipping are those the current leaders think will one day become leaders. Who can fault the young follower of Christ for thinking that he or she doesn't have what it takes to really make a difference when they are not tapped for leader training? The result is continued non-participation and the development of a wrong attitude on the part of the follower to let the leaders initiate and maintain all activities, never realizing his/her biblical responsibilities within the Body of Christ and how life can be more fulfilling by collectively obeying the commands of Christ.

Church Divisions

One of the subtle demoralizing aspects of church organization is qualifying people into different categories of service within the church. When we use the word disciple or discipleship in our modern context, we give people the impression that they have to rise to a different level of Christian development.[3] Discipleship is often perceived as a higher level of spirituality. Most Christians do not perceive themselves as being spiritual people. They reserve that attribution for ministers who are called to full-time ministry. Church members determine that somewhere in that calling to vocational ministry these called individuals are somehow better Christians, better disciples, and better followers than the other regular, normal people (I resist the term lay people.) in the church.

In our churches we have come to the place where those who do spiritual things (witness, study the Bible, pray, have a quiet time) are labeled disciples. Those who do not are just Christians. We coin our phrase *discipleship* to identify processes by which Christians become disciples. However, this idea of disciples being substantively different than Christians is actually the reverse order of what we see in Scripture. The followers of Christ, the disciples, were first called Christians in Antioch (Acts 11:26). What was first spoken as a pejorative term toward the followers of Christ has now become the common term for normal, uncommitted, un-called people in the church. *WE HAVE TO LOOSELY IDENTIFIED PEOPLE AS CHRISTIANS IN THE PAST/PRESENT*

We believers are very good at comparing ourselves with ourselves and creating categories of spirituality to make ourselves feel better about ourselves. We don't want to be just Christians. We certainly don't want to be just followers. We want to be disciples. Of course, we leave it to ourselves to assess other people's discipleship standards. We may be prone to think, if you read your Bible as much as me, or pray as much as me, or worship as much as me, you might be a disciple too. Such assessments create division in the Body of Christ and have the potential of harboring pride, arrogance, and thoughts of superiority. Additionally, by creating programs of discipleship we can separate the process of discipleship from evangelizing and make ourselves feel better about our lack of sharing the gospel with others by saying we are not into evangelism (another created term) but are more interested in discipleship. Such terminology creates a divisiveness that permeates the Body. In the same way, choosing to value leaders and devalue followers only exacerbates the division of those who are real go-getters to those who are just the plodders. We inadvertently develop leper colonies of people who are *just followers* because they do not measure up to our standards of what a leader ought to be.

Followers are well aware of their apparent lack of value to leaders. As a result, false divisions of the *haves* and the *have nots* occur, creating a lack of unity and diminishing the corporate impact of the church.

A biblical understanding of following the person and teachings of Jesus Christ alleviates such pseudo divisions. With a followerfirst perspective, because you follow Christ, you study the Bible (John 14:21). If you do not study the Bible, you do not follow Christ. Because you follow Christ, you share Him with others as a natural part of life (Matthew 18:18-20). If you do not, you do not follow Christ. From the follower perspective there is no debate, no caveat, no rationalizing. The church needs to quit qualifying itself into mediocrity. We are either followers of the Person and teachings of Jesus Christ and Scripture, or we are not.

The followerfirst perspective creates an atmosphere in the church where each person, regardless of position or title, recognizes others as fellow followers. Such thinking establishes a common ground of respect and understanding. With a followerfirst perspective, leaders think only of how to follow the Lord by serving and fulfilling their responsibility within the body. Those who are in positions of responsibility over others do not perceive themselves as being better, or special, or of more value than any other person in the Body of Christ. Followers are also aware of their role and responsibility to support their leaders as these leaders follow Christ. There is no jealousy or envy on the part of these followerfirst followers. They understand and submit to the Scriptures and operate willingly under the godly leading of their leaders as together they follow the will of the Head, the Lord Jesus Christ.

Cavalier Interpretations

I have a great deal of respect for those who have written on the important concept of leading in the church. There is a wealth of good material available. However, the church needs to question the axioms, suppositions, assumptions, and principles of what some present as teachings related to biblical leadership. If followers of Christ are not careful, they may partake in a leadership meal composed mostly of a gracious helping of business leader and management principles coupled with a small side dish of Bible verses, many of which are taken out of context. It concerns me when the church does not critically assess the biblical truth of a matter and carelessly consumes philosophies that have no place in the organization and operation of the Bride of Christ. I confess my bias is that although the church is an organization, it is the most unique organization on the planet. The church is operated by people, but these people supposedly have had something life-changing take place within them so that they are not conformed to the world's ways of operating (Romans 12:1-2). The church should be seen as a special organization, with a special purpose, operating with specific guidelines, and led by people transformed through a relationship with Jesus Christ. These characteristics are why the church must not fall prey to the idea that if a principle works within a business environment such a principle should be automatically enacted within the church without first determining the biblical validity of the principle. This is not to say that we cannot learn from extra biblical sources. The principle of general revelation allows us the opportunity to learn from other sources outside the Bible.[4] However, these social science and business sources should never be considered equal with, much less superior to, the authority of Scripture. The church must diligently reject leadership principles that contradict the Scriptures and scrutinize leadership principles based upon Scriptures that are taken out of context.

We can learn much from the way Jesus interacted with people. However, we must be careful not to make the actions of the Savior support any of our own preconceived ideas, especially such banal ideas as leadership. We must not allow the perfect life, death, and resurrection of the Lord Jesus Christ to become merely an "example" for us to follow. Nowhere in the New Testament is there didactic teaching from Jesus about how anyone should lead. All such leadership principles gleaned from His life are merely anecdotal and should be understood as being **descriptive, not prescriptive**.

There is no question that Jesus was the perfect leader and we can learn much from studying His actions. Being a perfect man, Jesus would have possessed every possible leader quality, trait, and style. However, we should be careful not to cherry-pick events in Jesus' life to support our preconceived leader principles. If we look at the life of Jesus we must look at His life as a whole. If Jesus was the perfect leader, and his purpose was to teach His disciples how to lead, then it follows that everything Jesus did with His followers was perfect and should be emulated as a leadership principle. Such a position does pose a problem with some of the more unique actions Jesus took with His disciples. Consider the following three examples.

1. *Call Your Closest Associates Satan.*

Then Peter took Him aside and began to rebuke Him, saying, "Far be it from You, Lord; this shall not happen to You!" but He turned and said to Peter, "Get behind Me, Satan! You are an offense to Me, for you are not mindful of the things of God, but the things of men" (Matthew 16:22-23).

I do not think any of today's leadership authorities would promote rebuking an associate with the words, "Get behind me Satan." This is not to say that we might have, on occasion, thought of such a rebuke. However, note the reason for Jesus' rebuke. Jesus points out that Peter was thinking from a human, selfish perspective, not God's perspective. Jesus' purpose on the planet was to glorify God, and His death on the cross would be the culmination of His life of perfect obedience. If we give Peter the benefit of the doubt we can say that his response was motivated by a love for Jesus, and he did not want to see Him die. However, Jesus could not allow Peter's love to stand in the way of the Father's purpose. Human approval does not trump the will of God. In similar fashion, we cannot allow our study of leadership, or our study of following for that matter, to become a man-centered enterprise that only human beings approve. There must be a solid, exegetical basis for all our teaching, not simply the approval of others or the seeming success of certain leadership principles.

2. *Destroy the Livelihood and Businesses of Your Opponents?*

Now the Passover of the Jews was at hand, and Jesus went up to Jerusalem. And He found in the temple those who sold oxen and sheep and doves, and the money changers doing business. When He had made a whip of cords, He drove them all out of the temple, with the sheep and the oxen, and poured out the changers' money and overturned the tables. And He said to those who sold doves, "Take these things away! Do not make My Father's house a house of merchandise!" Then His disciples remembered that it was written, *"Zeal for Your house has eaten Me up"* (John 2:13-17).

Making a cord and whipping the merchants and money changers out of the temple is certainly not the type of executive behavior we want our church leaders to manifest. Jesus' actions here, although appearing antisocial, were certainly within the will of the Father and consistent with Jesus' one desire to honor God the Father. Perhaps having leaders in the church who know how to recognize deceit, fraud, and manufactured worship is exactly what we need. We need leaders who manifest Jesus' passion for the honor of God the Father so that our churches don't become commercial centers for the selling of the gospel. To date, I have not seen anything written with regard to this particular leadership event in the life of Jesus.

3. *Go to Parties with Scoundrels and Prostitutes.*

Now one of the Pharisees was requesting Him to dine with him. And He entered the Pharisee's house, and reclined at the table. And behold, there was a woman in the city who was a sinner; and when she learned that He was reclining at the table in the Pharisee's house, she brought an alabaster vial of perfume, and standing behind Him at His feet, weeping, she began to wet His feet with her tears, and kept wiping them with the hair of her head, and kissing His feet, and anointing them with the perfume. Now when the Pharisee who had invited Him saw this, he said to himself, "If this man were a prophet He would know who and what sort of person this woman is who is touching Him, that she is a sinner." And Jesus answered and said to him, "Simon, I have something to say to you." And he replied, "Say it, Teacher." "A certain moneylender had two debtors: one owed five hundred denarii, and the other fifty. "When they were unable to repay, he graciously forgave them both. Which of them therefore will love him more?" Simon answered and said, "I suppose the one whom he forgave more." And He said to him, "You have judged correctly." And turning toward the woman, He said to Simon, "Do you see this woman? I entered your house; you gave Me no water for My feet, but she has wet My feet with her tears, and wiped them with her hair. "You gave Me no kiss; but she, since the time I came in, has not ceased to kiss My feet. "You did not anoint My head with oil, but she anointed My feet with perfume. "For this reason I say to you, her sins, which are many, have been forgiven, for she loved much; but he who is forgiven little, loves little." And He said to her, "Your sins have been forgiven." And those who were reclining at the table with Him began to say to themselves, "Who is this man who even forgives sins?" And He said to the woman, "Your faith has saved you; go in peace." (Luke 7:34-50).

Throughout the life of Jesus there are many occasions where He interacts with those who were frowned upon by the more cultured people of society. Such actions on the part of Jesus did not put Him in good standing with many of the proper religious people of His day, and yet, He was constantly spending time with these commoners to the detriment of His own reputation. Why? One explanation is that Jesus was more concerned with following the will of the Father than He was with His own reputation. I wonder if the same can be said of us. Have we become so concerned with being the leader that we have forgotten to follow the Lord and be more concerned with His reputation among men than our own?

Please understand, through the use of these examples, I am not advocating anything other than an examination and re-evaluation of how the life of Jesus is presented as support for some current leadership principles. I strongly believe we must include the whole of Jesus' life in our understanding of how He led others and that Jesus' primary concern was to follow the will of the Father.

What about Moses?

By now you have come to realize that my perspective on leaders in the Bible is substantively different from much of the leadership literature. One person with whom I have a particular problem considering a leader is Moses. Yet, he is probably the most cited person in the Old Testament about whom we are told we can learn how to lead others. My contention is that Moses was a follower holding a leader position. Consider the following:

1. **Moses was told what to do (Exodus 3:10).**
2. **Moses was told what to say (Exodus 3:12-18).**
3. **Moses was told what would happen (Exodus 3:19-22).**
4. **Moses followed the cloud by day and the pillar of fire by night (Exodus 13:21).**

Throughout the story of the Exodus we read where, "Moses and Aaron did just as the LORD commanded them" (Exodus 7:6).

93

Psalms 77: 20 records the most accurate portrayal of the work of Moses by declaring to God, "You led your people like a flock, by the hand of Moses and Aaron." God was doing the leading. Moses was God's "hand." In fact, the only times Moses took the lead was when he got angry and broke the initial set of tablets at the sight of the golden calf (Exodus 32:19) and when he struck the rock twice (Number 20:11-12), an event that cost him his entrance into the promised land. Some may argue that Moses was acting as a leader when, in order to keep his sanity, he took the advice of his father-in-law to divide the people into more manageable groups and set judges over these groups (Exodus 18:13-26). I would argue that this was not so much leadership as management. This action did not give the people a new vision or lead the people in a new direction. It merely allowed for a more efficient caring of the people as they followed the direction of the Lord. In reality, Moses exemplifies the type of follower needed in today's church: one who understands the Word of God and seeks to fulfill it regardless of their position within the organization.

The best reason I can think of as to why these events in the life of Moses as well as the unique leadership events in the life of Jesus are not mentioned in our leadership texts is because these events do not fit the template of what much of the literature portrays leadership to be. However, if we allow the leadership literature to determine what we teach from the Bible, then we must ask ourselves, "Are we teaching what the Bible says, or are we simply proof-texting what we *want* the Bible to say and teaching this as biblical truth?"

From a follower perspective it is clear that all of Jesus' actions have their genesis in a desire to fulfill the will of the Father (John 6:38). Jesus' overwhelming desire to honor His Father and fulfill His purpose on earth was the reason why His actions and responses were sometimes conventional but mostly unique. As followers of Christ, we must interpret Jesus' actions and words from the same perspective He had, the perspective of a follower.

Anti-Follower Bias

I distinctly remember having a conversation with a man several years ago that started badly and rapidly deteriorated into a full-blown confrontation. It seemed that every attempt I made to engage the man in a civil conversation was met with heated resistance. I finally abandoned my efforts at friendship and retreated to the safety of my home and the confidential ear of my wife. As I shared with her my experience, she asked one question that clarified much of what I had experienced. She asked, "Did you tell him you were a pastor?" When I shared with her that I began the conversation by telling him I was a pastor, she informed me that the man had a history of bad experiences with pastors and did not want anything to do with them. With that new piece of information I realized that this man's resistance to my overtures of friendship was not personal in as much as it was the result of an ingrained bias against pastors.

We all have our biases. I am biased against my college Alma Mater's football opponents. I am biased against anchovies. I am biased for followers. Bias is a predisposition either favorably or negatively toward an object or a person usually based upon some past experience. It may be that past experiences with some poorly behaving followers have led to a generalized bias within leadership literature against followers. It may be that some followers have developed a bias against leaders because of some authoritative, over-bearing leaders with whom they have had to deal in the past. We all have our biases.

However, it wasn't until I began to try and understand life and organizations from a follower perspective that I noticed the overt negative bias toward followers in the leadership literature. Many leadership writers concede that everyone is a follower on some level, but the implication is that being a follower is secondary to becoming a leader. Other writers will imply that following is not a priority, much less a privileged position with important responsibilities. The following are just a few excerpts from one writer:

- "Followers tell you what you want to hear. Leaders tell you what you need to hear".[5]

- "Any leader who has only followers around him will be called upon to continually draw on his own resources to get things done."[6]

- "Followers will always weigh the advantage/disadvantage issue in light of personal gain/loss, not organizational gain/loss."[7]

- "Followers need leaders able to effectively navigate for them."[8]

- "The bottom line for followers is what a leader is capable of."[9]

- "Followers simply cannot develop leaders."[10]

JUST 2D HIM, THIS SEEMS LIKE A SUCKER PUNCH!

I believe this particular author did not intend for his comments to be perceived as being anti-follower. However, from these comments it is painfully obvious that the author has a bias against being a follower. But then, this particular author is not alone in his opinion. Leadership books consistently proclaim that it takes leaders to make a difference. Leaders are special. The constant message from the culture is a person needs to aspire to be the leader. Businesses don't spend thousands of dollars teaching employees how to aspire to become followers (although in my opinion they should). Parents do not stand on the sideline of the soccer game and encourage their young player to, "Get in there and be a real follower." Such thinking is not largely accepted in our independently minded, western American culture. Being the leader is the prize position. The leader takes the spotlight in business and the church.

Please understand. I believe the Bible clearly teaches that leaders are a necessary part of any organization, especially the church (Hebrews 13: 7, 17, 24). An emphasis on followers is not a de-emphasis on leaders. It is merely a re-examination of the role and responsibilities of followers and leaders within the unique organizational culture of a church. Every organization has a culture, and I explain some aspects of this in Chapter 9. However, my position is that church organizational culture is different (by divine design I might add) than any other organization on the planet. This uniqueness may be why many within the church refer to the church as an organism, a living entity operating through the power of the Holy Spirit. However we perceive the church, its organizational culture should not revolve around position and rank (power and control) but role and responsibility (submission and obedience). A followerfirst perspective emphasizes this role and responsibility for every follower of Christ.

Short Circuiting the Process

In our zeal to have the church make an impact on the world we have begun teaching about leadership and training leaders without first fully embracing the process by which leaders are established in the church. This lack of understanding short-circuits the church's impact and effectiveness in the world. Although we certainly need leaders and leader training, the emphasis within all Christian organizations needs to be that before we accept the role of leader, we recognize that we are followers first. I do not subscribe to the theory that to be a good leader you first need to learn to be a good follower. Many times when people make this statement they imply that being a follower is a stepping stone toward the ultimate prize of becoming the leader. This is NOT what I am proposing. I propose:

GOOD LEADERS ARE GOOD FOLLOWERS.

A Leader is Born

When we take on the responsibility of being leaders, we don't quit being followers. Christian leaders in all organizations must begin to think of themselves as followers first. Consider Figure 3 and the process by which a follower of Christ assumes a leader role.

Figure 3: A Leader is Born

1. Leader (Christeri)

2. Follower
4. Leader

3. Follower

In the first position (1) is Christ Jesus. Because of the work He has done in our hearts and because He is the Head of the Church, we all follow Him. Christ's position puts all believers in the second (2) position as followers. This relational position is primary in all our affairs. However, over time we may be asked to serve in positions of responsibility over other persons within the church organization. Such a role would mean that we would have followers in position number three (3). The people in position number three, then, would naturally refer to those in position number two as their leaders, position number four (4). In the church, the primary responsibility of those in leader position number four is, as a fellow follower, to lead the followers in position three to follow Jesus.

A subtle temptation occurs, however, when the followers in position two begin to believe what the followers in position three call them (leaders) more than believing what the One in position one (Christ) calls them because Christ calls them who they really are, followers. In the church, if a leader begins to act in the role of a leader without understanding that he or she is responsible for being a followerfirst leader, that leader runs the risk of leading in ways that may not honor the One whom they profess to follow. In the church, if someone seeks to become a leader without first being a committed follower, that person can do grave damage to the relationships within the Body of Christ. Paul may be alluding to this understanding of who you really are in Christ when he tells Timothy not to appoint new believers too quickly to leader positions (1 Timothy 3:5).

By teaching leadership with little to no regard for what it means to be a follower, we are training people to lead without understanding their primary purpose for being a part of the church in the first place: to follow Christ. We teach leaders how to accomplish goals and tasks through people without understanding the primary goal and task of every endeavor is to know God through the person of Jesus Christ and introduce others to Him. Perhaps this is why so often our building projects, special events, and daily routines become endurance exercises rather than opportunities to experience the presence of the Lord. Perhaps the growing number of church splits, conflicts, and ministerial dismissals are the result of our current crop of leaders assuming responsibilities, as taught by the business models, they have no business assuming within a church organizational culture. Perhaps current leadership teaching places responsibilities on church leaders that the Bible does not suggest (i.e. everything rises or falls on leaders). Perhaps the leadership principles being taught to business men and women who make up our church congregations are resulting in an increase of faulty expectations of how pastors should lead within the unique organizational culture of the church. Perhaps it is time for leaders and followers to return to a different position, the position of humility and submission, the position of being a followerfirst.

What Might Happen?

What would happen if the church embraced a followerfirst perspective? What if everyone in the church saw himself or herself as a follower: pastors, pre-school workers, teachers and parking attendants? What if church members recognized the difference between each group as one of responsibility, not of position or worth or calling? With a followerfirst perspective, the pastor understands himself to be a follower of Christ whose responsibility is to shepherd the flock of God:

> The elders who are among you I exhort, I who am a fellow elder and a witness of the sufferings of Christ, and also a partaker of the glory that will be revealed: Shepherd the flock of God which is among you, serving as overseers, not by compulsion but willingly, not for dishonest gain but eagerly; nor as being lords over those entrusted to you, but being examples to the flock; and when the Chief Shepherd appears, you will receive the crown of glory that does not fade away (1 Peter 5:2).

With a followerfirst perspective, pastors understand they have a responsibility to shepherd the flock as they have been told by the Owner of the flock [Jesus owns His flock (1 Corinthians 6:20; 7:23) and is the Lord of the church.] Likewise, pre-school workers see themselves as followers of Christ whose responsibility is to nurture the youngest babies and toddlers for of such is the kingdom of heaven. Bible teachers understand they are followers of Christ with the responsibility to teach accurately the Word of God. Parking attendants see themselves as being followers of Christ with the responsibility of making certain those who attend find a place to park and are greeted warmly.

Gone are the yearnings over rank and title and hierarchy. Titles are understood as designating responsibility before God. A followerfirst perspective understands the beauty and power of submission. A followerfirst perspective trusts in the work of the Holy Spirit and rests in the sovereignty of a living God to protect His Bride. A followerfirst perspective confronts the pew-sitter mentality of many who may simply be attending church for the show.

With a followerfirst perspective, excuses about not fully participating in the church are eliminated. If church members are truly followers of Christ, they have a responsibility to obey (follow) Him. Further, they have a responsibility to discover and then fulfill their important place in the Body of Christ, His church. Just because church members do not have the title leader ascribed to their responsibility does not make their work any less important in God's plan than those who hold titular positions of responsibility. Within a followerfirst perspective Christians do not have to wait to be a leader to make an impact and be influential in the lives of others. As a follower of Christ, influence is a given.

RETHINK

I hope these few chapters will encourage the church to question and rethink some of these preconceived ideas about leading and discover the simple truth that the church of Jesus Christ actually operates best with a followerfirst perspective. I realize that the idea of being a follower is often denigrated as a position with little to no influence and unworthy of respect. As one student recently commented, "If we implement this perspective in our churches it will change the way we have pretty much always thought about how the church operates." I agree. However, if we can implement a followerfirst perspective within the church, I believe a genuine revival of obedience on the part of those who have been inactive for years will result. We will see members giving more, participating more, sharing their faith more, and exemplifying the life of Christ more if we raise the level of our understanding regarding what it means to be a follower of Christ. If Christians begin to understand that pastors are humble followers of Christ (just like they are) who are trying to follow the commands of Christ (just like they are), perhaps believers who have never considered themselves leaders will begin to understand that they don't have to be leaders in order to be influential, faithful, followers of Christ. Perhaps if we can instill in followers the idea that faithfully following the Lord is a worthy occupation, that being a follower is a privilege, and that calling ourselves followers carries with it special responsibilities, we will begin to see individuals whom we would never have dreamed become obedient to the commands of Christ.

Now might be a good time reread some of the church leadership books we have read in the past and read them based upon a follower view of life. As you read consider the following questions:

- How are followers and the actions of followers viewed? Are they even mentioned?
- Is the author true to the text or does he/she "cherry pick" Scripture? Are Scriptures interpreted in context?
- Does the cited Scripture teach what is being proposed or is the Scripture used to support a 'principle' of leadership?
- Is the leader presented as the primary person in the organization?
- Is the author using Scripture to support a favorite leader theory or principle?

A critical analysis of these books may cause us to rethink how we have been living our lives and executing our responsibilities based on what we have believed. Consider these questions for your own self-assessment:

- Have I subconsciously become biased against those who do not want to lead?
- Have I unconsciously pigeon-holed people into a less important status because they do not lead?
- Have I been equipping ALL the saints or just those I think might become leaders?
- Have I inadvertently made people feel inferior by constantly exalting leader positions?
- Do I think more of myself than I ought to think? (Romans 12:3)
- Have I forgotten that my own journey in ministry began as a humble follower of Christ?

EXERCISE

As a personal exercise, how would you respond to the following encounter?

> While teaching in a church, a lady approached me with the following statement: "The real reason this church has been unable to make progress is because we haven't had any real leadership."

Answer the following questions:
- From where does this idea come?
- What has this lady been taught in order to make such a statement?
- What would be her definition of leadership?
- Is there any sense of personal responsibility for the state of her church?
- How would you influence this person to begin to think differently about leadership in the church?

Be Encouraged

Let me encourage you to embrace who you are as a follower. Don't succumb to the fear of not becoming the leader that many teach as the ultimate goal of life. Be the person God has created you to be and then act according to His best interest in the positions of responsibility He gives. In so doing, you will be following the example of the ultimate follower, our Lord Jesus Christ.

Chapter 4

Follower Identity:
The Freedom to Be

After studying the material to this point, it is not uncommon for students to make their way to me after class with questioning grins on their faces, and before they can say a word I say, "That's right." They usually reply, "That's right what?" I respond, "I'm answering your question, because you were going to ask me if, as a follower of Christ, all you had to do was to be who God has created you to be. And all I'm saying is that's right. That's all you need to be." At this point they usually smile and let out a, "Whew." This response is typical of those who have tied themselves up in a knot trying to be *the leader* as outlined by much of the current leadership literature. Their experience was the same as mine. In an attempt to be the very best leader they could be for Christ, they had forgotten that their first priority was to be the person God had created them to be, a follower. The grins usually turn to laughter as a mountain of self-imposed expectations rolls off their shoulders. They become free: free to be the person God called them to be and, ironically, a more effective leader.

These students realize that their identity as a followerfirst makes learning leader skills and developing leader traits much easier. Placed upon the foundation of a followerfirst perspective, leader principles and practices are no longer burdensome. These principles are understood as a means of developing greater influence in the lives of others so that other followers can know the freedom of being a followerfirst. As followers of Christ begin to embrace the idea of being a faithful follower, they begin to develop and embrace an identity which, to a watching world, appears to be extremely paradoxical.

The Follower Paradox

Our God is a God who teaches through paradox. The Scriptures reveal that some of the greatest truths are those that resonate in our minds as paradoxical to our intuitive reasoning. Consider the following examples:

Find Life by Losing It

Matthew 10:37-39
He who loves father or mother more than Me is not worthy of Me. And he who loves son or daughter more than Me is not worthy of Me. And he who does not take his cross and follow after Me is not worthy of Me. He who finds his life will lose it, and he who loses his life for My sake will find it.

It is not by coincidence that Jesus' teaching on how to find and lose your life follows three expressions of what it means to be worthy to follow Christ. Note the three relationships mentioned. The first is the parental relationship. Even those who gave you life and cared for you cannot be the primary aim of a follower of Christ. The second relationship is that of a son or daughter. Here again the emphasis is that a follower's relationship with sons and daughters is secondary to one's relationship with Christ. The third relationship is that of a person who holds an accurate self-assessment. The follower of Christ is aware of the areas of life where a denial of self must take place. The cross is where those who have been leading their own lives meet Jesus and submit to His life-giving forgiveness. For the believer, then, the cross becomes the place of death for any personal proclivity that might take precedence over the follower's relationship with Jesus. Far from a focus on death, the cross actually becomes the door through which the believer finds the resurrection power of Jesus. Therefore, if a follower finds his/her life in the person of Jesus Christ, that follower will think nothing of putting that life on the line. He/she

106

will lose it. As a result of losing it for the sake of Christ, the follower is guaranteed that he/she will find true life, a life in relationship with God the Father, Son, and Holy Spirit.

Be Strong by Becoming Weak

> 2 Corinthians 12:7-10
> And lest I should be exalted above measure by the abundance of the revelations, a thorn in the flesh was given to me, a messenger of Satan to buffet me, lest I be exalted above measure. Concerning this thing I pleaded with the Lord three times that it might depart from me. And He said to me, "My grace is sufficient for you, for My strength is made perfect in weakness." Therefore most gladly I will rather boast in my infirmities, that the power of Christ may rest upon me. Therefore I take pleasure in infirmities, in reproaches, in needs, in persecutions, in distresses, for Christ's sake. For when I am weak, then I am strong.

We read much about becoming a strong leader. However, if we are to lead in the power of the Holy Spirit by the grace of the Lord Jesus Christ, it appears we must be weak leaders (i.e. followersfirst). It is a vital paradox for us to remember that when we are weak, we are strong. A Christian leader cannot allow his/her self-assessment to dictate what will or will not be attempted, what commands will or will not be obeyed, or what he or she can or cannot accomplish. The work of the Lord is not contingent upon the strength of the leader but rather upon the leader's submission and dependence upon Christ. When the leader is most dependent, the leader is most influential, because then God must act if anything of lasting significance occurs. By correctly assessing infirmities and short coming, leaders assess themselves as followersfirst and rely totally upon the enabling power of the Holy Spirit. Followers, who understand their biblical responsibilities, embrace these frailties, pray for the strength to overcome them, and rely upon God to work for His good pleasure through them and in spite of them. This healthy humility precedes God's granting the grace necessary to assume other responsibilities (James 4:6).

Receive by Giving

> Luke 6:37-38
> "Judge not, and you shall not be judged. Condemn not, and you shall not be condemned. Forgive, and you will be forgiven. Give, and it will be given to you: good measure, pressed down, shaken together, and running over will be put into your bosom. For with the same measure that you use, it will be measured back to you.

In rapid succession, Jesus instructs His followers how they are to conduct themselves in relationship with others. To fully understand what Jesus is saying in this passage, the passage needs to be read in context. Jesus' teaching of not judging or condemning but forgiving and giving is shared within the context of loving your enemies. In so many words, Jesus teaches His followers that their actions will be significantly different from those who do not have a relationship with Him. It is our enemies whom we are not to judge or condemn. It is our enemies to whom we are to give, expecting nothing in return. This unreserved trust in the promises of the Lord makes the life of the follower of Christ distinctive. For the follower, there is no place for manipulation, calculation, or reservation, only trust. Giving to our enemies allows us to receive a greater understanding of God's own beneficence toward us who were once "enemies of God" (Romans 5:10).

How do we find life? We lose it.
How do we become strong? We become weak.
How do we receive? We give.
How do we impact the world? We follow.

Is it too strange to consider that within God's divine design the effectiveness of the church may rest with teaching and developing followers who understand and revel in following Jesus rather than focusing on leaders and leading? Is it possible that God has designed the organizational DNA of His church to operate best with follower cultures because leader-centric cultures create mutations within the church DNA that hinder the growth and effectiveness of the church? Should we at least be teaching biblical followers how to act, and how to follow church leaders? Should be we teaching these concepts with as much intensity and commitment as we have for teaching leaders within the church? Such concepts appear to be organizational paradoxes that have the potential of mystifying the business world and showing a world in need of a Savior how different life is with Jesus as the Leader and with His people as followers first.

Personalize the Concepts

Over the past several years, as I have sought to live out a followerfirst perspective, I have tried to simplify my identity as a follower in the body of Christ with the following statements regarding who I am and my responsibility before God. These statements are by no means comprehensive. I offer them as a stimulus to your own thinking in order to discover your own special place as a follower of Christ. I encourage you to read them and contextualize them to who you are and where you are in your relationship with Christ.

IDENTITY
I am a follower of the person and teachings of Jesus Christ and the Bible.

TITLE
I have been given the title, Ambassador of Christ.

MINISTRY
I have been given the ministry of reconciliation.

PLACE
I am a member of the body of Christ.

ROLE
I have a role and responsibility within the body of Christ.

INFLUENCE
I always influence others.

IDENTITY
I am a follower of the person and teachings of Jesus Christ and the Bible.

Being a follower implies action. I am a follower, not a sitter, stander, or sleeper. If I follow I must be actively pursuing Christ. This requires me to learn, read, apply, and humble myself before others.

Saying one is a follower of the person of Christ, is different than when some say they are followers of any other historical person (Gandhi, Mohammed, Buddha) because implicit in the phrase "follower of the person" is the understanding that to follow a *person*, the person whom you follow must be alive. If a leader is buried in a grave, he/she is not going anywhere for someone to follow. Christians believe Christ to have been raised from the dead and that He is with them and intimately involved in their lives through the indwelling person of God the Holy Spirit. Thus, His followers can truthfully say they follow Him as they are directed by the Holy Spirit through obedience to the Word of God.

When I say I am a follower of the teachings of Christ, I acknowledge the authority of the commands of Scripture, both Old and New Testaments, and that they are "God breathed" (2 Timothy 3:16) teachings for all humanity. Followers of Christ have a high view of Scripture. Otherwise, the follower might want to become the leader in deciding what biblical passage is or is not inspired and worthy of accepting. Biblical followers submit themselves to Christ by following His commands, not only the direct commands of Christ, but also the teachings found in the Old and New Testament. Let me be clear. A true follower of Christ is committed to the whole of Scripture.

110

In John 14:21 Jesus stated that followers declare their love for Him by following His commands:

> He who has My commandments and keeps them, it is he who loves Me. And he who loves Me will be loved by My Father, and I will love him and manifest Myself to him.

In this context it is appropriate to consider following as an act of worship. The root meaning of the word 'worship' is to prostrate oneself on the ground. When we bow before the Lord, submitting to His will, His Word, and even His established leaders (Titus 3:1), the follower of Christ yields to the Lord's leading. In this way, the attitude of the follower is one of continuous worship to the glory of God.

TITLE
I have been given the title, Ambassador of Christ.

THIS IS NOT THE any TITLE given...

2 Corinthians 5:20-21
> Now then, we are ambassadors for Christ, as though God were pleading through us: we implore you on Christ's behalf, be reconciled to God. For He made Him who knew no sin to be sin for us, that we might become the righteousness of God in Him.

When we consider the role of ambassador it is obvious that an ambassador is one who represents the authority of another. The ambassador only has the delegated authority to act if the king whom he represents commands him. Ambassadors do not speak for themselves. They only communicate what the king says. Ambassadors usually serve as the representative of the king in a foreign country. It is easy to see the parallel to our being on the planet and away from our citizenship which is in heaven (Philippians 3:20). I sometimes think it would be better if our church members called each other Ambassador rather than brother or sister. There is nothing wrong with such familial greetings. However, if members called each other by their title, ambassador, perhaps it would remind

111

us all of our responsibility to do the work of the King and to follow Him.

MINISTRY
I have been given the ministry of reconciliation.

2 Corinthians 5:17-19
Therefore, if anyone is in Christ, he is a new creation; old things have passed away; behold, all things have become new. Now all things are of God, who has reconciled us to Himself through Jesus Christ, and has given us the ministry of reconciliation, that is, that God was in Christ reconciling the world to Himself, not imputing their trespasses to them, and has committed to us the word of reconciliation.

Followers of Christ are ministers and as such have a specific ministry. In the church we often say that every member is a minister, but our leader-centric organizational cultures prohibit us from actually accepting such a perspective. In the typical church, only the ordained pastor and staff members are considered true ministers. However, in a follower-centric organizational culture, it is natural for all the followers of Christ to accept the responsibility of being ministers of reconciliation. From a biblical perspective, every person on the platform from the pastor to all other staff, as well as every believer in the pew or chair who works and participates in the church, is a minister responsible for carrying out his/her ministry of reconciliation. What is the ministry of reconciliation? Paul states it plainly, "...that God was in Christ reconciling the world to Himself, not imputing their trespasses to them" (2 Corinthians 5:19). In other words, sharing the gospel of Jesus Christ with others is the ministry of every follower of Christ. Every believer in the church, pastors, music leaders, ushers, Bible teachers, nursery workers, Sunday morning worshipers, has the ministry of reconciliation and needs to find an expression of this responsibility through his/her local church. True followers of Christ will be compelled by the Holy Spirit to find meaningful and practical expressions for the hope that is within them (1 Peter 3:15).

PLACE
I am a member of the Body of Christ

> 1 Corinthians 12:12-14
> For as the body is one and has many members, but all the members of that one body, being many, are one body, so also is Christ. For by one Spirit we were all baptized into one body — whether Jews or Greeks, whether slaves or free — and have all been made to drink into one Spirit. For in fact the body is not one member but many.

As a believer in Christ, the Lord Jesus places me in His Body, His Church, and cherishes me as His special possession. I cannot be lost for He is in me and I am in Him (John 14:20). Jesus is my hope and my salvation. Within the church universal and local, my place is to follow Christ. When a child becomes unruly and out of line you may hear a parent say, "Child, you better find your place." Such words are a not so veiled threat for the child to change his behavior and find himself in submission to his parents or suffer the consequences. In the church, when we know our place, we no longer have to jockey for positions of power and prestige. When we know our place, conflicts and contentions subside. Unity within the Body becomes evident as each individual in the Body of Christ knows his/her place with the singular purpose of gaining and maintaining the mind of Christ (Philippians 2:1-7).

ROLE
I have a role and responsibility in the body of Christ.

My role for being on the planet is to know God and Jesus Christ (John 17:3). I come to know God and Jesus as I obey His commandments (John 14:21). This is my responsibility. Often the key to learning obedience is to practice submission. We all have to learn obedience because obedience is not natural. By submitting to the will of the Father, I evidence the same mind as Christ Who humbled Himself by becoming obedient unto death, even death on the cross (Philippians 2). The writer of Hebrews extends this idea even further when he wrote: "Though He was a Son, yet He learned obedience by the things which He suffered. And having been perfected, He became the author of eternal salvation to all who obey Him" (Hebrews 5:8-10).

Whatever position I may have (leader/follower), I must always seek to practice submission. I personally don't have a problem learning submission from God. What I really have a problem with is when God teaches me submission through someone else. It is when I am responsible to obey the command of God by being submissive to another human being that I usually find I am trying to rationalize my way out of being a follower so that I can make up my own mind about a matter. However, the way for me to fulfill my role and responsibility is through submission, and it is through submission that I, as a follower, exercise tremendous influence.

INFLUENCE
I influence others.

A surprising component of followers is the breadth of their influence. Although much of the leadership literature addresses the influence of leaders upon followers, the truth is that leaders and followers influence each other. We all influence each other. We cannot be alive on the planet and not influence each other. I address the influence of followers in the next chapter. However, never presume that followers are powerless to impact lives.

1 Thessalonians 1:6-10
And you became followers of us and of the Lord, having received the word in much affliction, with joy of the Holy Spirit, so that you became examples to all in Macedonia and Achaia who believe. For from you the word of the Lord has sounded forth, not only in Macedonia and Achaia, but also in every place. Your faith toward God has gone out, so that we do not need to say anything. For they themselves declare concerning us what manner of entry we had to you, and how you turned to God from idols to serve the living and true God, and to wait for His Son from heaven, whom He raised from the dead, even Jesus who delivers us from the wrath to come.

The above Scripture tells the story of how the gospel was spread throughout the region by the believers of Thessalonica becoming "followers of us and of the Lord." Turning from idols to serve (follow) the living and true God, these people probably had no idea that their simple act of following the Lord Jesus would have such a world-wide impact. Consider how many millions have read of their following over the course of 2,000 years. How many lives have been changed as a result of their response? It is a question we need to constantly ask ourselves, "How am I influencing others toward Jesus?" If I do not assume the responsibility to follow Jesus every day in every way, then it is likely that my life is influencing others not to follow Christ. There is no neutral ground. As I follow, I influence those around me. I desire to influence others in such a way as they might become followers of Christ.

Following Jesus' Path

Just how does one follow Christ today? An exegetical study of Luke 9:23 outlines a path all followers of Christ take as they enjoy the benefits of following Christ. After hearing Peter's answer that Jesus was "the Christ of God" (Luke 9:20), Jesus begins to explain that He must go to Jerusalem and suffer and die. Matthew records that Peter took Jesus aside and rebuked Him for saying such things. In response to Peter's words, Jesus rebuked Peter saying the famous line, "Get behind Me, Satan." It is after this strong rebuke that Jesus turned to His disciples and said:

> If anyone desires to come after Me, let him deny himself, and take up his cross daily, and follow Me.

This verse of Scripture contains five important concepts that are essential in understanding how we are to follow Christ.

1. If anyone desires

The beginning point for every decision is the follower's will. When we follow Christ, we act according to our will. This requires our will to be consumed with the desires of Christ and not our own personal desires. The Holy Spirit enables the believer to will to follow, and God is glorified by the willing response of His new creation.

2. To come after Me

In the above verse, one might think the terms "come after" and "follow" are the same terms with the same meaning. However, in this verse they are distinct. The use of the word "come after" can be translated *to line up after*. When I was a child, we used to play a game called Follow the Leader. The point of the game is to do everything the leader does. If the leader jumps on one foot you would have to jump on one foot. If the leader jumps over a rock you would have to jump over the rock or be out of the game. Each person lines up after the leader and does exactly as the leader. I believe this is the essence of what Jesus means when he uses the term "come after." His disciples would literally follow Him, listening to every word and observing every act. Even though today it is impossible for believers to physically line up behind Christ, it is possible for followers of Christ to listen to every word and observe every act recorded in Scripture. In this way we can *line up* behind Jesus and apply the words and ways of the Lord Jesus to our lives.

One further insight to the game Follow the Leader is that when we played the game as children, we would always have to determine who would be the first leader. The choice was actually very easy. The leader would be the person in whose backyard we were playing the game. If we went to Chris' house, Chris would be the leader, same for Hank, Greg, or me. You always followed the lead of the person in whose backyard you played the game. The same is true with regard to following Christ. Every person on the planet plays in God's backyard. This is His earth, and we have no right to claim independence in what we will or will not do. We all play the game according to His rules. He is the Leader. We follow Him and no other. If we refuse to follow Him we lose.

3. Let him deny himself

An important aspect of the above phrase is to realize what Jesus did not say. Jesus did not say to deny ourselves things. He invites us to deny self. Jesus makes it clear that the heart of the person (self) is His primary concern (Matthew 23:27). If we follow Christ we must deny self. Our purpose for being on the planet is to be consumed with honoring Him from the heart. Quite simply put, if we follow Christ, we can never put our needs, our desires, and our goals and dreams in the primary position. Christ must be preeminent in all things (Colossians 1:18).

4. And take up his cross daily

Without question, the cross was the cruelest and most humiliating form of execution the Romans could think of for the day. It was the electric chair, the gas chamber, and lethal injection all wrapped up into one excruciatingly painful way to die. This is the cross. It is a place to die. And it is here that we learn to die to self. Our Leader set the example and followed the will of the Father to His cross. We must take up our cross daily and follow Him. The cross is not a one-time opportunity. For followers of Christ, the cross is a daily experience of death to self and reliance upon Christ for our every need.

Think of the multitude of opportunities we have to take up our cross. The workplace is a wonderful place to die to self. How many times are we met with people who want to take advantage of us, treat us poorly, or perhaps advance over us at our expense? It is our responses to these opportunities that reveal whether or not we are dead to self and alive to Christ. The home is another place of opportunity to take up the cross. Any time you have two people in close proximity for extended periods of time you run the risk of conflict. As much as we may not like it, men and women are human and sometimes we act as fallen humanity instead of followers of Christ. On these occasions, it is our response of forgiveness and compassion that allows us to humble ourselves before our spouse and submit ourselves to each other. Finally, the church is a good place to die. There are many hurting people in the church. We sometimes cover up our hurt with a plastic smile and a phony, "I'm blessed," but underneath the façade is a heart that has been broken and emotions that have been wounded. It does not take much to have certain people in the church respond in ways that do not honor Christ. Still, it is the follower's opportunity to die to self in these instances and respond in ways that only the Holy Spirit can empower. The one who dies first is the leader.

5. And follow Me.

Jesus concludes His sentence with the words, "Follow Me." As mentioned before, this is a different Greek word than the word for "come after." This word can be translated "come alongside." Putting the different pieces of the verse together, the picture I have in my mind is a progression of personal intimacy with the Savior. Willing followers line up their lives with the Savior as the Bible reveals His words and actions beginning a journey of walking in the same path with Jesus, following His lead in every endeavor. In the process, the providence of the Lord provides ample opportunity for the follower to experience joys and blessings, as well as endure hardships and disappointments. Each day the follower is given opportunities to die to self and glorify the Lord through every event. It is in this process that the followers one day realize their walk with Jesus is not one of lock-step obedience to His commands but rather a relationship of willing love and abandonment to Him. It is as if the followers are walking alongside the Lord Jesus with His arms around their shoulders, whispering to them intimate details of Himself and His love which compels these followers to love and obey Him even more.

Such is the progression of followers. They take on the persona of the One whom they follow. They are bold, yet humble; strong, yet weak; assertive, yet submissive. In all things they hold their purpose as a treasure, to honor the One whom they love more than life itself, their leader, the Lord Jesus Christ.

Conclusion

As you think about your own journey of following the Savior and developing a biblical follower identity, I share with you the words of G. D. Watson (1845-1924).[2] I first read them as a young seminary student and today these words still challenge me to be the follower of Christ I know I should be. Through the power of God's Spirit and His process of sanctification, let us pray and act in such a way that God will be glorified through our lives.

Others May… You Cannot

If God has called you to be really like Jesus he will draw you into a life of crucifixion and humility, and put upon you such demands of obedience, that you will not be able to follow other people, or measure yourself by other Christians, and in many ways he will seem to let other people do things which he will not let you do.

Other Christians and ministers who seem very religious and useful, may push themselves, pull wires, and work schemes to carry out their plans, but you cannot do it, and if you attempt it, you will meet with such failure and rebuke from the Lord as to make you sorely penitent.

Others may boast of themselves, of their work, of their success, of their writings, but the Holy Spirit will not allow you to do any such thing, and if you begin it, he will lead you into some deep mortification that will make you despise yourself and all your good works.

Other may be allowed to succeed in making money, or may have a legacy left to them, but it is likely God will keep you poor, because he wants you to have something far better than gold, namely, a helpless dependence upon him, that he may have the privilege of supplying your needs day by day out of an unseen treasury.

The Lord may let others be honored and put forward, and keep you hidden in obscurity, because he wants to produce some choice fragrant fruit for his coming glory, which can only be produced in the shade. He may let others be great, but keep you small. He may let others do a work for him and get the credit for it, but he will make you work and toil on without knowing how much you are doing, and then to make your work still more precious he may let others get credit for the work which you have done, and thus make your reward ten times greater when Jesus comes.

The Holy Spirit will put a strict watch over you, with a jealous love, and will rebuke you for little words and feelings or for wasting your time, which other Christians never feel distressed over. So make up your mind that God is an infinite Sovereign, and has a right to do as he pleases with his own. He may not explain to you a thousand things which puzzle your reason in his dealings with you, but if you absolutely sell yourself to be his love slave, he will wrap you up in a jealous love, and bestow upon you many blessing which come only to those who are in the inner circle.

Settle it forever, then, that you are to deal directly with the Holy Spirit and that He is to have the privilege of tying your tongue, or chaining your hand, or closing your eyes, in ways that he does not seem to use with others. Now, when you are so possessed with the living God that you are, in your secret heart, pleased and delighted over this peculiar, personal, private, jealous guardianship and management of the Holy Spirit over your life, you will have found the vestibule of Heaven.

RETHINK

Applying the followerfirst perspective to the church requires us to rethink what we are teaching the people regarding who they are in Christ. Additionally, how does this identity manifest itself in the activities of the church? As you rethink what you have been communicating to those you influence consider the following:

- As members of the Body of Christ, do we really know who we are?
- Are our egos prepared to not be "all that" and humbly accept the mantle of follower?
- Are we trying to increase people's self-esteem by offering a concept of self that is not supported by the Scriptures?
- In our celebrations do we celebrate the obedient follower?
- If people embraced their function as followers, how would this impact the numbers of active people in the church?
- When the followerfirst perspective is embraced by the members, are we prepared to support and equip them?
- Am I willing to lead from a follower position?

Part III

Exercise Your
Follower Influence

Chapter 5

The Follower's Influence

One of the most surprising aspects of followerfirst thinking is the amount of influence followers have within organizations. For the past 30 years many have been teaching that "everything rises and falls on leadership," and such statements have gone largely unchallenged. As previously mentioned, when people hear this phrase they usually hear "leaders" not "leadership." The reason for such uncritical thinking may be that in our western culture we are programmed to believe leaders are better and have the power. This assessment is reinforced through the media, personal experience, as well as much of the literature we read. As a result, the influence of followers is often overlooked as a key component in the process of leadership.

In this chapter, I challenge the prevailing thinking regarding leaders being the *sine qua non* of the organization. Joseph Rost and others (Chapter 2) have challenged the linear aspect of the leader-follower relationship by focusing on the process of leadership and the interdependence of each responsible party in the organization. Understanding leadership as a process between "those who aspire to lead and those who choose to follow"[1] gives a greater understanding of the power that followers have to make or break individuals, processes, and productivity. Highlighting the influence that followers have within an organization can be illustrated by the following two diagrams.

Figure 4 illustrates the normal organizational chart for a simple hierarchical organization. The leader is at the top and everyone else is considered a follower. It is assumed that the leader at the top holds influence over all others in the chart. What the leader does impacts everyone within the alignment. Thus, if everything rises and falls on the leader, as is often preached, then an assumption is being made that the followers are merely responders to the leader and have no initiative of their own. However, what if the follower with the X drawn through the box decides that he or she does not want to play that game anymore? To debunk the "everything rises and falls on leadership" myth, let us turn our attention to Figure 5.

As you can see, the result of the follower's actions turns the entire organization upside down. Unfortunately, churches experience this type of upheaval regularly. The leader may have been a good leader. The leader may have performed his duties in textbook fashion, yet the results are not exponential growth but chaos and confusion. Such a scenario prompts pastors and church leaders to leave the ministry everyday thinking they are failures when they may have been leading exactly as they should have been as faithful followers of the Lord Jesus Christ. The reason for the failure may not have been a crisis of leading but, as in this case, a crisis of following. Everything does NOT rise and fall on leaders.

As a young pastor, I had the privilege of hearing Dr. Charles Stanley of the First Baptist Church in Atlanta give some sage advice that I did not embrace until the latter part of my pastoral ministry. I can't remember the exact quote, but the substance of his remarks was that, it does not matter how good a pastor you are or how good a preacher you are, if the church does not want to grow, it will not grow. This simple fact is the 800 pound gorilla in leadership teaching that few are willing to recognize.

Without question, leaders influence those around them. They have the position and usually the organizational authority to direct the organization. However, these two illustrations graphically illustrate how refusing to recognize the influence of followers can lead to total disarray and confusion.

Figure 4: Normal Organizational Structure

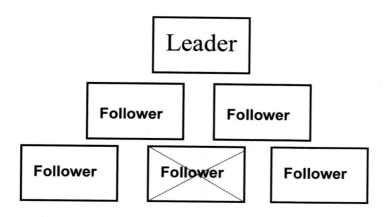

Figure 5: Result of Follower Resistance

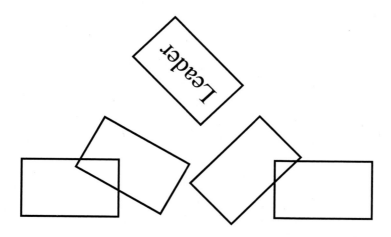

Someone may suggest that if the leader in these figures had been a better leader with better skills the dissenting follower would not have pulled out. Such a contention cannot be proven because leading and following are not the linear, cause and effect scientific process that some leadership literature presupposes. And as we have already seen, there are such people as bad followers. Leadership, to reiterate Joseph Rost, is an interdependent relationship between a leader and a follower in which there must be cooperation or leadership does not exist. This cooperation is the responsibility of both the leader and the follower.

There is no guarantee that good leading will result in good following. It may increase the odds, but followers always have the choice of whether or not they will follow the lead of the leader. A follower has a will that is free to act on its own. Guided by a biblical ethic, followers of Christ can decide whether or not the leader is acting in a God-honoring manner and choose to respond accordingly. By using a leader style that respects the role of the follower, and/or by embracing the Following-Leader style (Chapter 8), leaders can influence followers to participate in the life of the church and become an integral part of the church's mission. The choice, however, remains with the follower.

Leaders and followers need to realize the power and influence followers have within the organization. Followers within any organization and especially the church have tremendous responsibilities to act in ways that preserve the unity of the Spirit in the bond of peace (Ephesians 4:3). Followers need to be taught that the casual word, the off comment to another, the occasional speculation about the integrity of the leader, can be fatal to the overall mission of the church. Consider Paul's teaching to the church when he instructs the church to "quit devouring one another" (Galatians 5:15). From the context it is evident Paul is talking to the followers of Christ whether they are leaders or followers. By finding common ground as fellow followers with different responsibilities, the participants in the church organization can seek to overcome the common principles of leading through authority and power and instead find the freedom to act according to the teaching of responsibility and submission.

Trust

Trust is the heartbeat of any relationship. The quality of a relationship is usually gauged by the level of trust evidenced by the people involved. Without trust there is no leadership. Leaders who do not trust their followers will never lead them. Followers who do not trust their leaders will never follow them. How then can trust be developed in the follower-leader relationship?

Several years ago I had the pleasure of meeting with Jeremie Kubicek, the founder of Giant Impact, to discuss various leadership ideas. As the conversation progressed, he shared with me how leaders can speak to the heart of others in order to influence them. He posited that if the leader does not speak to the heart of the other person then genuine influence is never accomplished.[1] I agreed.

Jeremy shared with me a diagram that basically showed a process of leaders developing character, integrity, competence, and credibility as a means to influence others. As I later mulled over the diagram, I could not get rid of the feeling that something was missing. Finally it hit me. We had been focusing on what the leader could do but had left out the other side of the equation. Leaders cannot influence the heart of followers unless the followers want to be influenced. What must be the conditions necessary in the life of the followers in order for them to receive the influence of the leader? These questions gave rise to the development of the Influence Bridge.

The Influence Bridge

Looking at Figure 6 one can perhaps imagine a suspension bridge. A suspension bridge is used to cross wide expanses in order to transport people, or goods and services. The Influence Bridge seeks to bridge the expanse between leaders and followers in order for information to be communicated. Once the span of TRUST is developed information can be communicated in both directions simultaneously. But how is this bridge built?

The bridge begins with an idea and a desire to speak into the heart of another person. Rather than viewing others as pawns to be

Figure 6: The Influence Bridge

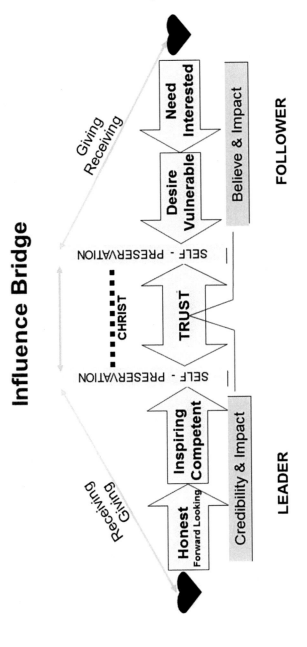

Once TRUST is established the Leader takes on the characteristics of the Follower and the Follower takes on the characteristics of the Leader in a reciprocating process.

manipulated in a game to gain advantage, both followers and leaders desire to influence others based upon a desire for the best interest of others. This "other-centeredness" is a key factor in followerfirst thinking. Where you are on the Influence Bridge is determined by your own context. For many of us, because of our positions where we work, we are both leader and follower at the same time. That being the case, understanding the influence that leaders have and the influence that followers have becomes all the more important. Additionally, understanding what prerequisites are required before influence takes place helps us understand the importance of the roles we assume, whether leader or follower.

Looking at the left side of the bridge, the leader begins the process by having four characteristics. Kouzes and Posner's research on leadership suggests that in order "for people to follow someone willingly, the majority of constituents believe the leader must be honest, forward-looking, competent, and inspiring."[2]

LEADER

Honesty
The idea of honesty comes from an ethical center of speaking and living the truth. An honest person's yes is yes and their no is no. They do not cheat. It is a core value.

Forward-looking
The leader who inspires a vision is the one who is looking to the horizon for the things that can be and the things that must be. They are those who excel in envisioning the future and resonating with others in a shared vision of the future.

Inspiring
Leaders inspire others through their words or actions which create in the follower a desire to act in concert with the leader. They ennoble followers to their best self in pursuit of shared goals and vision.

Competent
Leaders are viewed as competent when they show over time the abilities and/or skills necessary to achieve shared goals. Sharing

knowledge with constituents and encouraging others to do the same creates an environment of continuous learning from one another's experiences.

These characteristics give the leader credibility in the eyes of the followers. Kouzes and Posner assert that, "credibility is the foundation of leadership."[3] The simple definition for credibility is that a person does what they say they will do. It is this credibility that will impact the life of the other person.

FOLLOWER

Need
There is no reason for the follower to respond to anything that the leader has to offer if the follower has no need. It is this self-assessed lack that begins a willingness to be influenced.

Interested
Because the follower is aware of their needs, when they observe that the leader may have a solution to their problem or an answer for their need a level of interest is developed over time.

Desire
As interest increases, the follower develops a desire to receive what the leader is offering. This desire activates the will and moves the follower to engage with the leader.

Vulnerable
At this point the follower is willing to open a part of his/her life and allow the leader to influence them in a way that meets the follower's need. It is a decision of humbling one's self to another.

These characteristics allow the follower to believe that the leader can actually meet their need. Their willingness to believe the leader will not only impact the follower but will impact the leader by allowing the leader to prove his/her credibility.

SELF-PRESERVATION

At this point on the bridge both the leader and follower are met with an impediment to building trust. The leader has evidenced the credibility necessary to influence the follower and the follower has believed that the leader can help meet the need. Still, there is a major act of the will that must take place before the leader and the follower can move toward each other in an authentic manner. Both leader and follower must overcome the desire for self-preservation.

The idea of allowing someone to influence you or even attempting to influence others can be a fearful experience. This fear is the product of the natural desire to preserve self. Just think of the possible consequences for the leaders: (1) They may be rejected out of hand, (2) They could be misconstrued and accused of an improper motive, (3) They could unintentionally say the wrong word or take the wrong action which would make them look foolish to others, (4) You fill in the blank for the reason why you become nervous and fearful when seeking to lead.

Followers are not immune to fear. Consider these possible consequences for the followers: (1) They could trust someone who would take advantage of them, (2) They could reveal too much personal information and make themselves look bad in the eyes of others, (3) They could be led astray, (4) You fill in the blank for the reason why you hesitate and are fearful to trust others.

There is no easy way to address the fear of self-preservation. It is a powerful force within us that constantly reminds us to beware of others. Yet, there is a way.

■ ■ ■ ■ ■ ■ ■ ■ ■ ■
CHRIST

For both leader and follower, Jesus Christ is the unseen scaffolding above the relationship. What might appear to be a leap into the abyss by trusting another person is in reality a stepping out in faith upon the commands of Christ to love one another. There is no fear of being rejected by Christ. There is no fear of being used and abused by Christ. When followers of Christ trust Him, they are free from fear knowing that the Father superintends over the event. Love can overcome fear and a relationship can be established as both leader and follower trust Christ and seek the best interest of the other.

TRUST   _Actually..._

(Not by coincidence) does the link between credibility of the leader and belief of the follower meet at the 'U' in the word TRUST. It is a reminder that trust relationships are maintained by YOU. Whether you are leader or follower, you are responsible to maintain trust. It is the final span in the relationship and without it love cannot be communicated to the other person. Hearts will not be touched.

GIVE & RECEIVE

You will notice that the suspension cables on the bridge actually indicate the direction of the flow of communication. The leader initiates communication and 'gives' it to the follower. Once trust has been established the follower receives the communication. At this point an interesting phenomenon occurs. If the relationship is to be maintained the follower must give back to the leader and the leader receive the communication offered by the follower. The follower actually takes on the characteristics of the leader and the leader must take on the characteristics of the follower. This would make the illustration look like a type of Swing Bridge. On the Influence "Swing" Bridge, TRUST becomes the anchor point and the bridge rotates around that axis (See Figure 7).

Figure 7: The Influence "Swing" Bridge

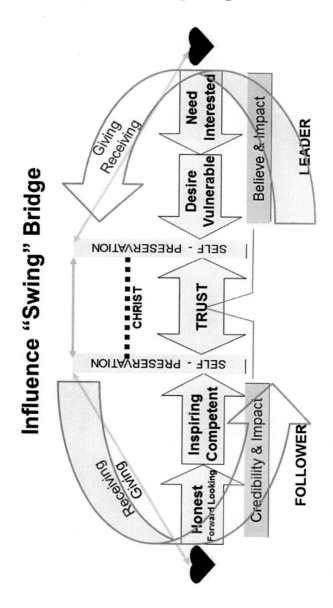

Note in Figure 7 that the Follower has now taken what was the Leader position and the Leader has assumed the Follower position. What the illustration is trying to depict is that once trust has been established between the Leader and Follower, in order for this trust relationship to continue the leader now:

- **Has a Need**: Leaders need followers to respect them and cooperate with them.
- **Is Interested**: In the follower and making certain the follower has what they need to in order to be fulfilled
- **Has a Desire**: That the follower continue to trust them
- **Is Vulnerable**: To the follower in humbly respecting the input of the follower into his/her life

These characteristics now afford the leader the opportunity to believe in the follower. It provides the realization that the leader cannot accomplish leadership alone.

At the same time, in order to maintain trust the follower must be:
- **Honest**: With the leader and be truthful
- **Forward Looking**: Join the leader by being willing to change and embrace new ideas
- **Inspiring**: By their words and actions indicate that they are fully engaged
- **Competent**: Learn the skills necessary and perform them with excellence

Embracing these characteristics, the follower now raises the level of his/her credibility. It allows the follower to gain a greater appreciation for the character of the leader and the responsibilities associated with leading.

INFLUENCE
The constant giving and receiving of information between the leader and the follower establish a consistent cycling of responsibilities between each person. As trust becomes more grounded over time, the reciprocal responses are executed more quickly reflecting a continuous influencing of leader to follower and follower to leader.

When Trust is Broken

So what if someone violates trust? How do we respond? As the diagram explains, the creation of trust involves many aspects that are established over time. If trust is violated, then reestablishing trust will take even more time. Both leader and follower must determine if the breach of trust is fatal to the relationship. Unfortunately, sometimes this is the case. In those instances when the breach is determined not to be fatal the abused party has the opportunity to exercise grace, forgive the offender, and seek reconciliation. These steps, however, take time and effort and continuing communication, which we have seen is the building block of trust and influence.

RETHINK

As you consider influencing others, answer the following questions:

1. What position(s) do I hold on the Influence Bridge?
2. What are my responsibilities?
3. What character traits do I have that would invite a follower to trust me?
4. Do others see me as a credible person?
5. Do I comprehend the amount of influence I have as a follower?
6. How would a leader know that I could be trusted?
7. Do I communicate to the 'hearts' of people?
8. As a leader, how do I communicate my needs to those followers whom I trust?
9. As a follower, how do I communicate my competence to those leaders whom I trust?
10. Am I willing to trust Christ enough to step through my fears and trust others?
11. How does the Influence Bridge relate to the other relationships in my life?
    a. Marriage?
    b. Children?
    c. Friends?
    d. Work Associates?
    e. Fellow Followers in my church?

Chapter 6

The Power of Submission

"You've got to be kidding!" is the usual response I get when I tell people that one of the most powerful actions a person can take is to submit. In today's leadership circles, submission is not considered a power. The prevailing thought seems to be that leaders do not submit; leaders get others to submit to them (or as we like to say, agree to the leader's vision and plan). However, from a biblical perspective, although it appears to be paradoxical and counter-intuitive, submission is *the* way by which the follower of Christ glorifies God and influences others. I am thoroughly convinced that Scripture supports this claim. First, consider how often the Scriptures speak of submitting to God. Next, consider how often the Scriptures address submitting to one another.[1] Submission is so prevalent throughout the Scripture it appears to be the very vehicle by which the will of God is carried out in the world. To consider submission as an occasional action on the part of the follower of Christ, rather than to understand it as the constant attitude of the faithful follower in every event, is to short-circuit the power of the believer to act in the power of the Holy Spirit.

Consider the life of Jesus. As previously stated, Jesus' purpose on earth was to do the will of the Father. His life was a constant example of submission to the will of the Father. His cry in the garden of Gethsemane, "...not my will but Thine be done" (Luke 22:42), resonates in the heart of every true follower. There was no greater act of submission in the life of Christ than His submitting to death on the cross. By being the greatest follower of the will of God, Jesus became the greatest influencer (leader) of all mankind.

Speakers on leadership are fond of quoting a Chinese proverb that says something to the effect, "He who thinks he leads and turning around finds no one following, is only taking a walk." Although on the face of it such a statement would appear to be true, in reality, this Chinese philosopher never knew Jesus.

When I quote this proverb in class there is usually muffled laughter. However, when I ask the class how many of Jesus' disciples walked with Jesus on the Via Dolorosa, the way of suffering, when Christ carried His cross to His death, the laughter quickly turns to soberness. The obvious answer is... no one. Not one of Jesus' closest followers followed Him to the cross. Despite all their grand statements to the contrary, when it was the will of God to die, not one follower followed. The point can be made that it was not the will of God that any of the disciples die but only Christ, for He alone was the substitutionary atoning sacrifice. Also, it fulfilled prophecy that none of Jesus' disciples joined Him in death at that time. However, such an understanding of the purpose of God was only revealed after the resurrection.

What needs to be noted is that, as the perfect follower, when Jesus was carrying His cross to Calvary, if He had looked around, He would have seen *no one* following. Yet, I doubt there are but a few who would say that Jesus was not the greatest influencer of mankind who has ever lived. Jesus was the greatest leader who ever lived and at His greatest influential moment, He had no followers. Of course there was Mary, the mother of Jesus, and the other women, as well as John and quite possibly other disciples standing as observers, but observing is quite different from actively following. The lesson for all followers is this: Jesus influenced the world by walking *alone* in the will of God.

According to some leadership teaching, the ministry of Jesus would be an abject failure. From the prevailing leadership perspective that numerical increase is indicative of ministry success, an assessment of the ministry of the preacher from Galilee might include the following questions: How is it that the greatest leader who ever lived did not have the leader capacity to rally his followers around him at this moment of crisis? Did Jesus fail to be a transformational leader at certain times in the disciples' development? Did Jesus miss an aspect of situational leadership theory where He coached when he should have directed? Should Jesus have been more of a servant leader to His disciples? Sounds ridiculous doesn't it?

Of course, none of these questions are relevant. These questions represent the rationalizations we create when we try and explain the failures of our contemporaries. When a church does not grow or a ministry fails we think, "Surely, there was a leadership flaw somewhere." Yet, to attribute a flaw to Christ, especially at the most important moment of his earthly existence is unacceptable. There has to be another reason.

It is apparent from the Scriptures that Jesus' submission to the will of the Father required Him to follow a path of sacrifice that His followers, at least at that moment, were unwilling to follow. Is it possible that Jesus' example at this moment of His life can give us some insight into what perfectly following the will of God might mean to us as followers of Christ? Consider the following points:

1. As a leader (influencer) of others, submission to the will of God may require us to follow His will *alone.* This act of obedience does not void a leader's influence.
2. The absence of the physical presence of followers does not mean you are not leading (influencing). If leading others is predicated upon the actual presence of followers, then we may be tempted not to follow the will of God if it will cost us our following.
3. One never knows how the Holy Spirit will use a lone act of obedience to influence the lives of observers or even those who might hear of such obedience. One need only look at the lives of the martyrs to gain a greater appreciation for the influence that occurs from following the will of God. Such following does not necessarily have to result in physical death to have significant influence.

4. Self-preservation is one of the biggest detriments to submitting to the will of God. I have observed among leaders that self-preservation largely revolves around one's ego and the desire to protect one's reputation.

If we continue to teach that great leaders are defined by the numbers of their followers, those in positions of influence may never understand that it is through submission to the will of God, regardless of the consequences, that ultimately brings about the greatest influence in the lives of others to the glory of God. Through submission we point the focus of everyone's attention away from ourselves as a leader to Christ before whom we are submitting.

Submission to Christ is one premise Paul taught in Philippians 3:17-19 when choosing whom to follow:

> Brethren, join in following my example, and note those who so walk, as you have us for a pattern. For many walk, of whom I have told you often, and now tell you even weeping, that they are the enemies of the cross of Christ: whose end is destruction, whose god is their belly, and whose glory is in their shame — who set their mind on earthly things.

The word, "following" in this verse is the Greek word from which we get our English word "imitate".[1] The biblical writers were fond of this particular descriptor and used it to encourage believers in their devotion to Christ.

Consider the following verses:

- **1 Corinthians 4:16**
  Therefore I urge you, imitate me.
- **1 Corinthians 11:1**
  Imitate me, just as I also imitate Christ.
- **Ephesians 5:1**
  Be imitators of God, therefore, as dearly loved children....

- **1 Thessalonians 1:6**
  And you became followers of us and of the Lord, having received the word in much affliction, with joy of the Holy Spirit....
- **1 Thessalonians 2:14**
  For you, brethren, became imitators of the churches of god which are in Judea in Christ Jesus. For you also suffered the same things from your own countrymen, just as they did from the Judeans....
- **Hebrews 6:12**
  ...that you do not become sluggish, but imitate those who through faith and patience inherit the promises.
- **1 Peter 3:13**
  And who is he who will harm you if you become followers of what is good?

The idea of imitation is significant in that submission to the Lord is not only an attribute in the heart of the follower, but is manifested through actions. Submissive followers, who serve as organizational leaders, walk according to a particular biblical pattern. Looking at the context of Philippians we can readily see this pattern evidenced:

1. **In the life of Paul (Philippians 3:4-16),**
   If anyone else thinks he may have confidence in the flesh, I more so: circumcised the eighth day, of the stock of Israel, of the tribe of Benjamin, a Hebrew of the Hebrews; concerning the law, a Pharisee; concerning zeal, persecuting the church; concerning the righteousness which is in the law, blameless. But what things were gain to me, these I have counted loss for Christ. Yet indeed I also count all things loss for the excellence of the knowledge of Christ Jesus my Lord, for whom I have suffered the loss of all things, and count them as rubbish, that I may gain Christ and be found in Him, not having my own righteousness, which is from the law, but that which is through faith in Christ, the righteousness which is from God by faith; that I may know Him and the power of His resurrection, and the fellowship of His sufferings, being

conformed to His death, if, by any means, I may attain to the resurrection from the dead. Not that I have already attained, or am already perfected; but I press on, that I may lay hold of that for which Christ Jesus has also laid hold of me. Brethren, I do not count myself to have apprehended; but one thing I do, forgetting those things which are behind and reaching forward to those things which are ahead, I press toward the goal for the prize of the upward call of God in Christ Jesus. Therefore let us, as many as are mature, have this mind; and if in anything you think otherwise, God will reveal even this to you. Nevertheless, to the degree that we have already attained, let us walk by the same rule, let us be of the same mind.

2. **In the life of Timothy (Philippians 2:19-24)**
   But I trust in the Lord Jesus to send Timothy to you shortly, that I also may be encouraged when I know your state. For I have no one like-minded, who will sincerely care for your state. For all seek their own, not the things which are of Christ Jesus. But you know his proven character, that as a son with his father he served with me in the gospel. Therefore I hope to send him at once, as soon as I see how it goes with me. But I trust in the Lord that I myself shall also come shortly.

3. **In the life of Epaphroditus (Philippians 2:25-30)**
   Yet I considered it necessary to send to you Epaphroditus, my brother, fellow worker, and fellow soldier, but your messenger and the one who ministered to my need; since he was longing for you all, and was distressed because you had heard that he was sick. For indeed he was sick almost unto death; but God had mercy on him, and not only on him but on me also, lest I should have sorrow upon sorrow. Therefore I sent him the more eagerly, that when you see him again you may rejoice, and I may be less sorrowful. Receive him therefore in the Lord with all gladness, and hold such

men in esteem; because for the work of Christ he came close to death, not regarding his life, to supply what was lacking in your service toward me.

4. **In the life of Jesus Christ (Philippians 2:1-11)**

Therefore if there is any consolation in Christ, if any comfort of love, if any fellowship of the Spirit, if any affection and mercy, fulfill my joy by being like-minded, having the same love, being of one accord, of one mind. Let nothing be done through selfish ambition or conceit, but in lowliness of mind let each esteem others better than himself. Let each of you look out not only for his own interests, but also for the interests of others. Let this mind be in you which was also in Christ Jesus, who, being in the form of God, did not consider it robbery to be equal with God, but made Himself of no reputation, taking the form of a bondservant, and coming in the likeness of men. And being found in appearance as a man, He humbled Himself and became obedient to the point of death, even the death of the cross. Therefore God also has highly exalted Him and given Him the name which is above every name, that at the name of Jesus every knee should bow, of those in heaven, and of those on earth, and of those under the earth, and that every tongue should confess that Jesus Christ is Lord, to the glory of God the Father.

These verses clearly indicate that the biblical pattern we are to imitate is an undiluted devotion to God and Christ and His commands. The result is a willingness to serve others even to the detriment of ourselves if necessary. We are to follow Him.[3]

People Follow Submissive Leaders

As a practical matter, submission effectively influences people toward you and your position. Surveys indicate that honesty is the number one personal characteristic that influences others to want to follow.[4] From the Scriptures we see how honesty is, at its core, the result of a submissive heart. Honesty results from submitting to the standards of do not lie, do not steal, do not bear false witness (Exodus 20:12-17, Romans 13:9-10).

According to Kouzes and Posner, three characteristics, being honest, competent, and inspiring "make up what communication experts refer to as source credibility."[5] Practicing these characteristics consistently over time gives the person the moral authority to lead.[6] It is not difficult to find these characteristics in the life of Jesus.

I have a friend who likes to use a word game when teaching others about how important submission is in relationships. He will take the word, understand, and write it like this on a piece of paper:

<u>UNDER</u>
STAND

He then goes on to explain that in order to truly understand another person you have to "stand" under them. In other words, humble yourself before them, hear their heart, and seek their best interests according to the word of God. If leaders see themselves as standing over people and telling them what to do, the followers will determine that the leader does not have their best interest in mind and will not enthusiastically follow the leader.

The Enabling of the Holy Spirit

I love the word enable. Embedded in this word is the idea of dependence upon something (or someone) before any other activity can take place. The word depicts the position of every follower of Christ as being totally dependent upon God for everything. A life without the enabling power of the Holy Spirit can only accomplish what human effort can produce.

Asking God to help in time of need is a beautiful expression of our dependence upon Him. Unfortunately, the idea of asking God for help has the potential of mutating into a works-oriented, unbiblical idea of God doing His part and me doing my part, as if I could do something on my own and in my own strength to aid God in accomplishing His will. What needs to be in the forefront of the follower's mind is an absolute dependence on God. For me to do any part in accomplishing God's will requires that I be enabled by His Spirit to act. What actions, gifts, and abilities I employ in obeying Christ's commands are gifts that He gives.[7]

I am concerned that our concentration on leader styles, leader characteristics, and leader behaviors has subtly diminished a dependence on the Holy Spirit. Rather than depending upon the Holy Spirit, we may subconsciously be tempted to rely upon the cleverly devised philosophies of men. Followers of Christ must resist such temptations and constantly rely upon nothing and no one but the Holy Spirit to influence. Failing to recognize our need leads to pride and reliance upon human ability to create change rather than giving all glory to God. Such self-aggrandizement eventually results in nothing short of idolatry.

J. Oswald Sanders wrote, "Spiritual leadership requires Spirit-filled people. Other qualities are important; to be Spirit-filled is indispensable,"[8] Sanders completed his thoughts regarding this essential element of submission by writing:

> To be filled with the Spirit means simply that the Christian voluntarily surrenders life and will to the Spirit. Through faith, the believer's personality is filled, mastered, and controlled by the Spirit. The meaning of "filled" is not "to pour into a passive container" but to "take possession of the mind." That's the meaning found in Luke 5:26: "They were filled with awe." When we invite the Spirit to fill us, the Spirit's power grips our lives with this kind of strength and passion.
>
> To be filled with the Spirit is to be controlled by the Spirit. The Christian leader's mind, emotions, will, and

physical strength all become available for the Spirit to guide and use. Under the Spirit's control, natural gifts of leadership are lifted to their highest power, sanctified for holy purpose. Through the work of the now ungrieved [sic] and unhindered Spirit, all the fruits of the Spirit start to grow in the leader's life. His witness is more winsome, service more steady, and testimony more powerful. All real Christian service is but the expression of the Spirit's power through believers yielded to Him (John 7:71-39).[9]

It is only when we are dependent upon God and enabled by His Spirit that we are able to exercise the power of submission when interacting with others. The Holy Spirit enables us to "stand under" others and seek to understand them so that we can be used of God to meet their needs. Such actions are often considered foolish by those who do not embrace the commandments of Christ.

In fact, one of the distinguishing characteristics of followers of Christ is their willingness to follow the will of God even though it may appear that such obedience is not in their own self-interest. We see this in the life of Jesus when on several occasions He purposefully chose a path that would be more difficult if not more dangerous in order to fulfill the will of the Father.

- When informed that His words were offending the religious leaders Jesus continued His assault of their hypocritical actions by calling them "blind guides of the blind" (Matthew 15:14).
- He continued to heal even though He knew the religious leaders would seek to destroy Him (Mark 3:1-6).
- At the end of His ministry Jesus willingly chose to go into Jerusalem even though there were people there who wanted to kill Him. This was Jesus' choice because He knew this is where He must die (Matthew 20:17-19, Mark 10:32-34).
- The night He was betrayed, surely He could have chosen to hide away and not leave the upper room. Yet He chose to go to the garden, as was His practice, to pray, knowing full well

that Judas would lead the arresting mob to Him (Matthew 26:47).

- At His trial before Pilate, instead of defending Himself to the accusations of the chief priests Jesus chose not to say a word. An action about which Pilate was amazed (Matthew 27:13).

After Pentecost we see the disciples evidencing this same fearless submission to the will of God.

- After the Holy Spirit had come, Peter stood in the very city that just a few days previous had killed his Savior and preached a bold message accusing these people of the death of the Christ, calling them to repentance (Acts 2:14-40).
- Having already been jailed, Peter and John declared before the religious leaders that they could not help but speak what they had seen and heard (Acts 4:13-20).
- The Apostles defied the order of the religious leaders and were jailed, yet they continued to preach knowing full well that these people would plot to kill them (Acts 5:33).
- They chose to be scourged rather than be released (Acts 5:40). After the beating they rejoiced that "they were counted worthy to suffer shame for His name" (Acts 5:41).
- When on trial for blasphemy, Stephen refused to compromise the Gospel and declared Jesus to be the Christ (Acts 7:55-56).

It was these disciples who turned the world upside down (Acts 17:6). They used no guns, no financial resources, and no powerful positions. What they possessed was an unrelenting dependence on God and the Holy Spirit in order to live in the power of submission.

Prayer: The Activity of the Submissive

When we look at the life of Jesus, we see that prayer is a priority (Luke 6:12; 9:18, 29; 11:1, Mark 1:35). As the perfect follower, Jesus knew that in order to fulfill the will of the Father He had to be in constant communion with God. The motive behind the activity was a keen awareness of His dependence on the Father. He was a man under authority. As we have mentioned in a previous chapter, Jesus always acted as one who understood His submissive position to God the Father.

> For I have not spoken on My own authority; but the Father who sent Me gave Me a command, what I should say and what I should speak. And I know that His command is everlasting life. Therefore, whatever I speak, just as the Father has told Me, so I speak (John 12:49-50).

> Do you not believe that I am in the Father, and the Father in Me? The words that I speak to you I do not speak on My own authority; but the Father who dwells in Me does the works. Believe Me that I am in the Father and the Father in Me, or else believe Me for the sake of the works themselves" (John 14:10-11).

This awareness was evidenced in His prayers. Jesus walked the earth as a man in constant, submissive communion with the Father. In this way He modeled the power of submission.

Consider Jesus' model prayer (Matthew 6:9). The opening lines address the Father, His holiness, and His kingdom purpose. This is followed by a list of needs: bread, forgiveness, and protection. One implication of this prayer is that followers of Christ are to submit themselves to God as their provider. The prayer also acknowledges that we are on the earth to fulfill God's will. We desire to see God's will done on earth as it is in heaven. We recognize that we are God's instruments through which His will is performed on earth.

I have already mentioned Christ's prayer in the Garden of Gethsemane, "O My Father, if it is possible, let this cup pass from Me; nevertheless, not as I will, but as You will" (Matthew 26:39 Mark 14:36, Luke 22:42). Here, in the most excruciating moments of His life, Jesus chooses to submit Himself to the will of the Father. One can almost see the strength pouring into His submitted heart as He rises from the ground, gathers His disciples, and meets those who will arrest and crucify Him. Jesus' life can be summed up in four simple words, "Thy will be done."

Conclusion

I hope you have been able to see that by exercising the power of submission followers of Christ have influence whether they are identified as leaders or followers. There is never a time when we are not influencing others. This is why it is crucial that everyone in the church knows and understands his or her biblical follower responsibilities. The interdependent relationships that are the basis of decision making within the church depend upon followers of Christ who are enabled by His Spirit, submissive to the will of God, responsive to His commands, and sensitive to those around them.

Those identified as leaders must also understand that living out a followerfirst perspective may require them to make difficult decisions that at times may result in many followers, if not all, refusing to follow. At these times, the followerfirst leader is called to persevere and trust the promises of God. Through the power of submission, the primary objective is to perform the will of God. Through a prayer-filled heart submitted to God and actions to match, faithful followers can be used of God to influence many.

RETHINK

As you consider influencing those around you, use the following questions to determine if you are employing the power of submission in your relationships and organizational responsibilities:

1. Is my heart submitted to the will of God in every area?
2. Am I a humble person?
3. Am I honest?
4. Am I inspiring?
5. Do I have source credibility with others?
6. Do I truly seek to understand people by standing under them?

---

7. Is my life filled with constant prayer?
8. Am I dependent upon the Holy Spirit?
9. Am I willing to follow the will of God alone?
10. Am I willing to be misunderstood and taken advantage of by others in order to do the will of the Father?

An Illustration

An illustration you might try in order to show how follower submission can move a leader in your direction is to designate yourself as the follower. Then, have a person stand facing you designated as the leader. Next, have the person hold their hands over their head, palms facing toward you. You take the same position and put your palms together. Slowly, each of you move your feet backward until the weight is evenly distributed between you, forming an arch, and are both dependent on each other to keep from falling flat on your faces. Reaching this state of interdependence is crucial. At that moment, as the follower, release the pressure by pulling your arms toward you and the other person will take a step toward you. They will have to take a step forward or fall flat. I use this illustration in class as a way of showing that acts of submission, not power and control, are the crucial influence in an interdependent relationship. The same illustration can be used to show how leader submission can move followers in their direction as well. What is clear from the Scriptures is that an attitude of submission to Christ and the Bible needs to permeate the follower-leader relationships within the church. The Holy Spirit enables us to be submissive. Others may take advantage of us on occasion. This is to be expected. However, even then, as we submit ourselves to God's Word and live submitted to the power of God's Holy Spirit, our actions will ultimately redound to the glory of God.

"The Golden Rule of Leadership: ask others to do only what you are willing to do yourself."[10]

Chapter 7

Who Gets to Tell Who
What to Do?

It is by design that this chapter follows the study on the power of submission. All discussions of authority and power need to be conducted within the context of the Bible's clear teaching regarding our dependence and submission to God and to one another.

A key question in the follower-leader relationship is why do leaders want to lead? What is it about being the leader that is attractive? The responses vary widely from the altruistic, "I believe I can help," to the dominating, "I want to be the one in charge."

As we have noted in the discussion of the Mobius Strip, the followerfirst perspective recognizes that followers become leaders, and leaders become followers depending on the context of the organizational need and purpose. All followers need to be prepared to assume the leader role. However, before becoming the leader, especially a leader in the church, we need to ask ourselves the hard "why" questions regarding our personal motivation for assuming this responsibility lest we embrace the prevailing philosophies of power and control.

Friedrich Nietzsche

Through the study of history we can learn the origins of our ideas. Origins do not always tell us whether an idea is right or wrong, but they certainly are important in helping us analyze the validity of an idea.

In the 19th century a particular thinker by the name of Friedrich Nietzsche became quite influential in the way that people believed businesses and education should be run. A German philosopher, Nietzsche was an atheist who is best known for declaring the death of God. That is, that we humans had progressed to the point where we no longer need a god figure as a means to plug in the gaps of our understanding with how the world operates. He believed God was merely a construct created by human beings to try and add meaning to the world. Nietzsche was highly influenced by the teaching of Charles Darwin, the person to whom we attribute much of the teaching of biological evolution and the process of natural selection.

What Nietzsche's perspective did was eliminate value and morality and all meaning. Without God as the anchor for these, there is no ground for morality. Thus, all the constructs that human beings place value in no longer have intrinsic value. In Nietzsche's view, even human beings held no intrinsic value. The Judeo-Christian perspective of God giving value to human beings was no longer considered to be valid. According to Nietzsche, all of these value concepts were human constructs.

Nietzsche considered that there were two types of morality: (1) Master Morality – Power Over and (2) Slave Morality – Jewish and/or Christian thinking. Nietzsche replaced the ethics of humility with the ethics of power. This is the basis for the phrase, "might makes right." This perspective supports the idea that whoever is in charge determines what's right, and they exercise their power over people in order to make them conform to their idea of what is right. Thus, the person in power makes up their own morality and their own values and imposes this on everyone else. So, morality for Nietzsche is nothing more than power.

The concept of "power over" is the logical consequence of Darwin's idea of the survival of the fittest. Nietzsche believed the fittest individuals desire not just survival but power over others. Nietzsche's "Will to Power" refers to a person's superior abilities and the use of force to suppress others. Therefore, once this is completed, the person in power makes up the moral rules and then imposes them on others as a means of control.

In conjunction with "Will to Power," Nietzsche also developed the idea of the "superman." The superman rises above the herd and moves beyond good and evil creating his own set of values. He towers over and has utter contempt for the herd, condemning its weak slave morality consisting of the virtues of meekness and pity, the Christian virtues. Nietzsche held the teachings of Christianity in contempt, considering it to be a way to conciliate the masses, the herd, even though they were being oppressed by others. There is no clearer manifestation of the outcomes of Nietzsche's thinking than to look at the atrocities perpetrated on humanity by the Third Reich. Nietzsche was Adolf Hitler's favorite philosopher.[1]

Nietzsche's perspective still impacts the thinking of many within businesses, education, and unfortunately, the church. The education system used to be the realm where the discovery of truth, the way things are, was sought. Once truth had been discovered, one would align his/her life with that truth in order to live consistently with the way things are. Today, in many circles, education is no longer a means to truth because truth does not exist except that truth which you form for yourself. Education is a means of obtaining power. Education is perceived as being something that can be obtained in order to have power over other people, to lift yourself up and over those less educated and informed.

Many businesses adopt Nietzsche's view of power by creating a "dog-eat-dog" environment among competitors and many times within its own organizational personnel. The person left standing after the carnage is the "big dog," and from that point forward gets to call the shots until someone else comes along to defeat him/her. The primary aim of the victor becomes putting down any opposition or challenge for fear of losing his/her position of power. An organizational culture of competition is created rather than a culture of cooperation.

Sneaky Nietzsche

Those who oversee the church especially need to realize that the members of the church are living and trying to cope with these philosophical realities every time they enter the work environment.

155

Believers in the world of business are constantly immersed in an ocean of power seeking thinking. Perhaps this is why so many members are quick to say, "Pastor, that teaching on being a servant and all might be fine in the church but it will never work in the real world." Such words reveal a subtle acquiescence to a world perspective that is in direct contradiction to the teaching of Christ. These dear believers have embraced a false, ungodly teaching of "power over" regarding what is real rather than trusting the teaching of Scripture. The question we need to ask ourselves is how far has this model crept into our thinking with regard to how churches operate? These business men and women are the leaders and followers in the church. Vocational ministers are also not exempt from believing this insidious perspective. As leaders in the church, are we unwittingly exercising this "power over" thinking in our attempts to get people to do what we want them to do?

What Does Jesus Say?

In direct contrast to "power over" thinking, Jesus modeled the truth of the power of His Kingdom by donning a towel and washing the feet of His disciples (John 13:4-17). Jesus taught that his followers were not to be like the Gentiles who "lord [their authority] over them" (Matthew 20:25). Instead, they were to think of themselves as servants.

The human desire for power is as old as the Garden of Eden where our first parents succumbed to the temptation to "be like God," that is, all powerful, answering to no one. Our fallen human nature revels in false ideas of autonomy, setting our own values, and controlling others to do our bidding. The source of this thinking comes from our enemy, Satan. When Jesus confronted the Pharisees for not believing the truth He was teaching, He boldly told them, "You are of your father the devil…" (John 8:44). Nothing has changed.

Jesus establishes a different value system than that accepted by those who are not His. Once again, the seeming paradox between the two world systems is evident with Christ's kingdom exalting servants and the world system exalting the powerful. Christ's kingdom espouses virtue and holiness. The "power over" system revels in usury and control. This is a battle that will continue until Christ comes. Ours is not to grow weary in proclaiming the truth of the Scriptures in the midst of these warring philosophies.

Followerfirst Thinking

When you implement a followerfirst perspective within the church you will have leaders emerge from the group of followers who are willing to take on different levels of responsibility within the church. The distinction with these leaders is that within their own thinking, they will come from the substantively different place of kingdom thinking rather than the vain power and control thinking of the world philosophies. These leaders will resist teachings such as:

- If you are the leader then you have the power.
- If you have the power then you have control.
- If you have control then you can influence people.

Followerfirst leaders understand that control is a fiction. They realize that the only person they can control is themselves, and that often poorly. They understand that their positions of authority within the organization may provide them with a certain degree of potential power and that this potential power needs to be wielded in concert with the teaching of the Word of God, gently and carefully. I say potential power because followerfirst leaders are aware that though they are given a position of authority, the amount of actual power, the power to influence others, is contingent upon the willingness of followers to be influenced.

Followerfirst leaders realize that individuals are only influenced by that which they value. As a follower, if I value honesty, I will follow those who are honest. If I value money, I will follow those who can make me money. Who I follow reveals what I value.

This understanding is all the more important for those in the church. Determining the actual core values of the congregation is invaluable in determining how to influence others. What needs to be realized is that congregational unity is a product of shared values. People who value following Christ above all things will be unified in their purpose and mission.

Power

Power is defined as "the capacity or potential to influence."[2] As we have previously noted, people are only influenced by that which they value. The following types of power reveal how power can be wielded productively or destructively within an organization.[3]

Types of Power

Reward Power

Reward power is usually addressed from the perspective that the leader has an ability to reward the compliance of followers. I would quickly add that followers also have reward power in rewarding leaders with their following. Reward power establishes a type of exchange relationship or a transaction whereby the leader agrees to offer a certain reward in exchange for the compliance of the follower. As in all sources of power, the follower may agree with this reward or may choose not to comply.

In the church, reward power may be positively manifested through the leaders acknowledging individuals for jobs well done or showing appreciation for service within the church. It has been my observation that consistently showing gratitude to those who work within the church both at a paid and especially at a volunteer level is gravely lacking. Additionally, I have seen churches in which followers rarely, if ever, show any appreciation for their leaders except once a year when the newly established pastor appreciation month rolls around. Followers would do well to embrace Paul's admonition in 1 Timothy 5:17-19, "Let the elders who rule well be counted worthy of double honor, especially those who labor in the word and doctrine. For the Scripture says, 'You shall not muzzle an ox while it treads out the grain,' and, 'The laborer is worthy of his wages'." Showing appreciation to pastors and other leaders who consistently serve the Lord by ministering and serving the Body of Christ never dishonors God.

Senior pastors can follow these same guidelines. First, senior pastors and every staff member need to remember to appreciate their spouse. There is no more important person than your spouse. Guard

158

this relationship and constantly show your spouse your appreciation for all they do to support you. Additionally, except for their spouse, there are no more important people to a senior pastor than those who work in fulltime ministry positions alongside him and those who serve in administrative areas of service. Take the time to appreciate your staff. Go to meals together. Find the time to recreate together. Support them and serve them. Reward their loyalty by being loyal. Keep confidences. Be a friend. These followers who follow Christ and you do not require much except your love. Give it to them.

For all the positives rewarding people may have, there are negatives. These occur when the leader chooses to withhold rewards or extend rewards for the purpose of manipulating people to comply with requests. This type of exchange system establishes an implied contract in which the leader only rewards behaviors that comply with the leader's stated desires. Such theories of leadership are firmly rooted in business organizations in which paychecks are used as rewards for services rendered. Such actions may not be as overt in the church, but contingencies can be established between leaders and followers, especially with regard to funding special projects within the church. For example, if a member decides to help the pastor with a project with a large sum of money, there may be an implied expectation that in the future that member would be rewarded with some special favor. On these occasions, gifts ostensibly given to the Lord through the church actually become bribes for future favors. As followers of Christ, we must seek to alleviate doing business in this way. We will address this *quid pro quo* relationship later.

One important aspect for followers and leaders to remember is all such rewards are but temporal expressions. The spiritual reality is that the greatest and most precious reward a leader or follower can give to another is faithful service to the Lord Jesus. As pastors accurately teach and preach the Word of God, as elders humbly oversee matters of the church, as followers willingly follow, trusting the leading of the Lord through their leaders, the church is blessed, healthy, and able to fulfill its mission and vision of making disciples of all nations.

Coercive Power

Coercive power is based upon the leader's ability to punish followers for non-compliance with requests. This may be the type of power the Lord Jesus spoke of when He said in Matthew 20:25-28,

> You know that the rulers of the Gentiles lord it over them, and their great men exercise authority over them. It is not so among you, but whoever wishes to become great among you shall be your servant, and whoever wishes to be first among you shall be your slave; just as the Son of Man did not come to be served, but to serve, and to give His life a ransom for many.

In this text the phrase "lord it over" has the idea of control or subjugation.[4] It is clear that Jesus does not want His followers assuming they can coerce people into obedience.

Many times within the church, coercive power is implemented in order to cajole people into certain behaviors. Leaders may sometimes use guilt manipulation in sermons to try and emotionally move the people to comply with what the Bible commands or, even more egregious, to get the church to agree with their particular plan for the church. It is sometimes too easy for leaders to succumb to using language that implies, "If you don't stand with this plan, you will be standing against the will of God." Even more destructive is for the leader to begin thinking that those who disagree with his plan must be of the devil. Such thoughts and actions are not those of a leader, but a manipulator, and an authoritarian. Characteristically, in Ephesians 6:5-9, Paul identifies a coercive leader-follower relationship as that between a slave owner and a bond slave and instructs both to cease from such destructive behaviors:

> Bondservants, be obedient to those who are your masters according to the flesh, with fear and trembling, in sincerity of heart, as to Christ; not with eye-service, as men-pleasers, but as bondservants of Christ, doing the will of God from the heart, with goodwill doing service, as to the Lord, and not to men, knowing that whatever good anyone does, he will

receive the same from the Lord, whether he is a slave or free. And you, masters, do the same things to them, giving up threatening, knowing that your own Master also is in heaven, and there is no partiality with Him.

Astute followers have the capacity to perceive coercive behaviors and to choose not to comply. Taking up the courageous follower mantle, followers need to address coercive behaviors with the leader, individually, privately, and gently. It may be that the leader is unaware of his/her manipulative tendencies. However, in the case of the leader who intentionally uses coercive power, followers can put him/her on notice that they are aware of what he/she is doing and will not respond positively to continuous coercive techniques.

Although coercive power usually resides in the person who holds the position of leader, followers also have a degree of what I call passive coercive power by choosing to respond or not to respond. As we have already shown, follower response can either make the leader or break the leader. If followers use their responses as manipulative weapons to try and direct the actions of the leader, they are using a form of passive coercive power to move the leader in a desired direction. Such actions produce nothing but conflict. Personal relationships in the church usually suffer while productive ministry ceases. Open communication between leader and follower without speculation or assumption on either party's part is necessary for the church to remain healthy and vibrant.

Expert Power

Expert power rests with those who may have a particular expertise. Some pastors have a gift of preaching. Others may have a gift of administration. It is through these gifts, and others, that the pastor can influence those around him. Followers as well have a form of expert power. As I have observed decision making in the church, coming to a decision is vested with a small group of individuals to the exclusion of the larger church body. Although I recognize the functional benefits of such a decision making system, at the initial stages of the decision making process, the followerfirst perspective encourages leaders to include as many minds as possible. By seeking the genius of the whole, the expertise of one who could really make a difference may be added to the decision making process. Whether leader or follower, expert power needs to be held with an attitude of humility if it is to be honoring to God. The expertise must be understood as a stewardship from God for His glory and the benefit of the Body of Christ. Such expertise should be used to influence others toward greater obedience to God and not used to aggrandize self or for personal advantage.

Referent Power

This type of power rests with the charisma of the individual leader or follower and is based on the person's character and integrity. Trust is built between the leader and the follower as each exercises integrity and competence over time. The trust formed through this mutually interdependent relationship creates a powerful dynamic that allows both leader and follower to operate at high levels of performance and productivity. Both follower and leader are to be persons of the highest character and integrity. In other words, as a followerfirst, both leader and follower are to manifest the character and integrity of Christ basing all decisions on the core values found in the Scriptures.

Structural Power

Structural power "results from the nature of the organizational social system rather than from attributes of an individual."[5] That is, the structure of the organization determines who has the authority to make the decision. It is the structure that determines a person's specific tasks and responsibilities and thus, lends the commensurate power and authority for carrying out those prescribed tasks.

Within the church there is specific structure with regard to bishops, pastors, elders, and deacons. Leaders who hold these offices within the church are bound by Scripture to fulfill the responsibilities given to them by the Lord, who is the Head of the church. As previously stated, officers of the church need to perceive that they are followers of Christ and obedient to His prescribed duties and responsibilities. The officers need to be aware of over-stepping their place within the church structure so as not to assume power and authority not specifically given by the Scripture.

Although rarely recognized, persons who hold the position of follower within an organization have a type of structural power. The hierarchical structure of most organizations is built upon a foundation of followers. Any engineer knows that a structure is only as stable as its foundation. In the church, the Lord Jesus Christ serves as the "chief cornerstone" upon which the entire body rests (Acts 4:11). As the perfect follower, Jesus establishes His church upon the expectation that those who believe in Him will follow His Word and obey His commands. To have hierarchical positions within the church organization and have people in those positions who do not follow Christ is to sabotage the very purpose for the existence of the church. The church was established to follow Christ. Structural power without following Christ becomes an exercise of human aggrandizement that scandalizes the name and character of Christ before the world.

Resource Power

Resource power resides with the person who has access to resources (money, relationships, technology, etc.) needed by the ministry in order to fulfill its mission. It is likely that a new pastor entering a congregation will have some resource power. However, it is more likely that members of the congregation or longer term staff members will have more of this type of power.

The ministry is filled with horror stories of the abuse of this type of power. There may be a wealthy person within the church who uses his resources to influence decisions within the church either through giving gifts or withholding them. Other persons may have access to individuals whom they believe can help the church with its mission, but such help is only forthcoming with conditions of advancement or recognition. Such abuses of this type of power are expressly prohibited within the church as written in James 2:2-9:

Suppose a man comes into your meeting wearing a gold ring and fine clothes, and a poor man in shabby clothes also comes in. If you show special attention to the man wearing fine clothes and say, "Here's a good seat for you," but say to the poor man, "You stand there" or "Sit on the floor by my feet," have you not discriminated among yourselves and become judges with evil thoughts? Listen, my dear brothers: Has not God chosen those who are poor in the eyes of the world to be rich in faith and to inherit the kingdom he promised those who love him? But you have insulted the poor. Is it not the rich who are exploiting you? Are they not the ones who are dragging you into court? Are they not the ones who are slandering the noble name of him to whom you belong? If you really keep the royal law found in Scripture, "Love your neighbor as yourself," you are doing right. But if you show favoritism, you sin and are convicted by the law as lawbreakers.

The correct use of resource power would be for a person to realize that he/she is a steward of all that God has given. Church leaders especially need to recognize that serving the church is a stewardship. As Paul relates in 1 Corinthians 4: 1-5:

Let a man so consider us, as servants of Christ and stewards of the mysteries of God. Moreover it is required in stewards that one be found faithful. But with me it is a very small thing that I should be judged by you or by a human court. In fact, I do not even judge myself. For I know of nothing against myself, yet I am not justified by this; but He who judges me is the Lord. Therefore judge nothing before the time, until the Lord comes, who will both bring to light the hidden things of darkness and reveal the counsels of the hearts. Then each one's praise will come from God.

Resource power can be a tremendous blessing to the church when exercised in humility. All church ministries need resources. Those whom God has blessed with financial resources are a blessing to the church. For the person with resource power, giving becomes a way for them to honor the Lord Jesus by following Him. In this respect, all members of the church can have the joy of giving to the Lord regardless of how much or how little they give. Jesus is honored by the followers' desire to give. God is the one who sees the true gift of the heart.

Information Power

Similar to resource power, information power exists because there are those within the organization who may have knowledge about important matters that others within the organization do not. Such knowledge can, in many cases, mean the difference between success and failure. Access to this type of knowledge is crucial in decision making. Therefore, it is important to identify those who wield this power within the organization. Many times such knowledge may abide with those who have been with the organization for long periods of time. The willingness to share such information with a new leader is a tremendous asset and blessing to the leader.

Because of its similarity to resource power, those with information power must guard against being deceptive with the information they possess. The rationalization of what are termed white lies, and/or not telling all the truth about a matter are serious threats to the integrity of any organization, especially the church. The church operates on the basis of truth, both the truth of the gospel and truth speaking to one another. Paul emphasizes speaking this gospel of truth in Ephesians 4:11-16:

> It was he who gave some to be apostles, some to be prophets, some to be evangelists, and some to be pastors and teachers, to prepare God's people for works of service, so that the body of Christ may be built up until we all reach unity in the faith and in the knowledge of the Son of God and become mature, attaining to the whole measure of the fullness of Christ. Then we will no longer be infants, tossed back and forth by the waves, and blown here and there by every wind of teaching and by the cunning and craftiness of men in their deceitful scheming. Instead, speaking the truth in love, we will in all things grow up into him who is the Head, that is,

Christ. From him the whole body, joined and held together by every supporting ligament, grows and builds itself up in love, as each part does its work. [6]

It is inconceivable that using information to gain an advantage over others would be acceptable in the church. This is why James said that you should "let your yes, be yes, and your no, no; so that you may not fall under judgment" (James 5:12).

AUTHORITY

The concept of authority is often misused and misunderstood in the church. This confusion results from misunderstanding the biblical teaching regarding authority, who has it, how it is distributed through the church, and the limits of authority within the church organization. An in-depth study of the concept is outside the purview of this book. However, I encourage you to study it further. [7]

From an organizational perspective, authority is a person's legitimate power "to influence others because of the position within the organization that person holds." [8] Persons within the organization agree to recognize that the person occupying a particular position within the organization has the right to influence others solely because of the position held. Organizational authority has the following characteristics:

1. *It is vested in a person's position.* An individual has authority because of the position he/she holds, not because of any specific personal characteristics.
2. *It is accepted by subordinates.* The individual... can gain compliance because he or she has a legitimate right.
3. *Authority is used vertically.* Authority flows from the top down in the hierarchy of an organization. [9]

A biblical perspective understands that all authority is vested in God. His authority is intrinsic, unconditional, and absolute (Psalms 29:10; Isaiah 40:1). [10] As God in the flesh, Jesus introduces the Great Commission with the words, "All authority has been given to Me in heaven and on earth" (Matthew 28:18). In the text the word authority translates the Greek word *exousia* which in other texts is translated power.[11] This authority is emphasized by the Apostle Paul when He wrote in Colossians 2:8-10:

> Beware lest anyone cheat you through perspective and empty deceit, according to the tradition of men, according to the basic principles of the world, and not according to Christ. For in Him dwells all the fullness of the Godhead bodily; and you are complete in Him, who is the head of all principality and power.

All human or organizational authority is derived from God and historically recognized through certain societal constructs:

Governments

Romans 13:1-7
Let every soul be subject to the governing authorities. For there is no authority except from God, and the authorities that exist are appointed by God. Therefore whoever resists the authority resists the ordinance of God, and those who resist will bring judgment on themselves. For rulers are not a terror to good works, but to evil. Do you want to be unafraid of the authority? Do what is good, and you will have praise from the same. For he is God's minister to you for good. But if you do evil, be afraid; for he does not bear the sword in vain; for he is God's minister, an avenger to execute wrath on him who practices evil. Therefore you must be subject, not only because of wrath but also for conscience' sake. For because of this you also pay taxes, for they are God's ministers attending continually to this very thing. Render therefore to all their due: taxes to whom taxes are due, customs to whom customs, fear to whom fear, honor to whom honor.

Bondservants and Masters

Ephesians 6:5-9
Bondservants, be obedient to those who are your masters according to the flesh, with fear and trembling, in sincerity of heart, as to Christ; not with eyeservice, as men-pleasers, but as bondservants of Christ, doing the will of God from the heart, with goodwill doing service, as to the Lord, and not to men, knowing that whatever good anyone does, he will receive the same from the Lord, whether he is a slave or free. And you, masters, do the same things to them, giving up threatening, knowing that your own Master also is in heaven, and there is no partiality with Him.

Parents

Ephesians 6:1-4
Children, obey your parents in the Lord, for this is right. "Honor your father and mother," which is the first commandment with promise: "that it may be well with you and you may live long on the earth." And you, fathers, do not provoke your children to wrath, but bring them up in the training and admonition of the Lord.

Elders

Hebrews 13:7 & 17
Remember those who rule over you, who have spoken the word of God to you, whose faith follow, considering the outcome of their conduct. 17 Obey those who rule over you, and be submissive, for they watch out for your souls, as those who must give account. Let them do so with joy and not with grief, for that would be unprofitable for you.

It is important to realize that a person's position of authority does not necessarily mean that the person has power to influence others. This reality stems from the fact that,

Power is not an attribute of a particular person. Rather, it is an aspect of the relationship that exists between two (or more) people. No individual or group can have power in isolation; power must exist in relation to some other person or group. If A has power over B, it is, in part, because B is willing for that to be an aspect of the relationship between them. If and when B no longer desires that to be part of the relationship with A, A will no longer have power over B and no longer be able to influence B's behavior. Thus obtaining, maintaining, and using power are all essential to influencing the behavior of people in organizational settings.[12]

One key point from the above quote is that power is not granted because of position. Power is **obtained** through a relationship between the leader and the follower. Although a person's power may be legitimized because of their position of authority, that person's authority to tell another person to perform a task does not guarantee they have the power to make the person perform the task.

How Much Authority Does an Ordained Church Leader Have?

Pastoral authority is a concept that derives its merit from the biblical injunction for the members of the church to be submissive to those who have oversight of the church (Hebrews 13:17). The construct gives biblical authority to a pastor of a local church to equip the saints so that the members of that church follow his lead with regard to how the church should function and operate in fulfilling God's purpose according to the Scripture. This concept is more common in churches with congregational polity as opposed to those with elders. There is some debate regarding the operation of such authority within the church. However, I mention it here as a means to show how a followerfirst perspective enhances the position of the lead pastor of a church without the pastor having to rely upon this authority construct. In my experience, those pastors who focus on their pastoral authority often extend the scope of such authority beyond what Scripture allows. Such an expansion usually results in: (a) the congregation assenting to the desires of the pastor, (b) the congregation rebelling against the desires of the pastor, (c) the congregation half-heartedly complying with the desires while a growing dislike of the pastor simmers within the body making the life of the pastor and his family extremely difficult, or (d) the extra burden of assuming responsibilities not outlined in the Scriptures becomes unbearable and the pastor leaves the ministry.

Most members of a church would not debate the clear teaching that Jesus is the head of the church (Colossians 2:10). Where the difficulty is sometimes evidenced is when the pastor, elders, or similar individuals within the church, claim authority that has not been scripturally given to them.

The Bible makes it clear that the primary concern for leaders in the church is that the leaders have godly character. Pastors/elders are never to "lord" (Matthew 20:25) their position over the members of the congregation. This is made clear by James Means when he wrote,

> Never are church leaders to think of their status as lordship, but as servant-hood. Leaders are not selected so that they might have dominion over the body of believers, but that there might be guidance in spiritual matters by qualified, godly individuals under the lordship of Christ. Therefore, however we interpret the words rule, direct, obey and submit, they cannot be interpreted in a way that gives leaders the kind of authority that the rulers of the Gentiles had, or that officials exercise in the secular world.[13]

Aubrey Malphurs suggests it is the ability of the pastor to follow that gives the pastor insight into how authority is exercised within the church. Malphurs stated,

> A primary requirement for a leader in the church is the ability to follow; that is, following Christ by following other God-given authorities...As the church develops leaders, it must observe how emerging leaders respond to authority. The ability to be under authority should drive who emerges as

leaders and when they emerge...The assessment of this quality is important for leaders at every level....[14]

Malphurs supports the followerfirst perspective by reminding leaders it is who they follow and how they follow that determines the influence one has, especially within the church. Pastors must understand they are under the authority of the Lord Jesus Christ and the Scriptures and regularly communicate this understanding to the members of the church. The pastor's humility and submission to Christ will communicate a followerfirst perspective that will act as a catalyst to the church body, resulting in a corporate submission to Christ.

Even though the pastor operates within the church in a position of organizational authority, he cannot hope to lead (influence) others solely from this position. Pastoral authority cannot simply be understood as a function of position in the church. The pastor's sense of authority must be geared toward the spiritual aspects of intimacy with Jesus. Robert Clinton addressed this authority when he wrote,

> Spiritual authority is not a goal but rather a byproduct. It is a delegated authority that comes from God. It is the major power base of a leader who has learned God's lessons during maturity processing. Leaders have various power bases that give credence to their ability. Spiritual authority comes out of experience with God. A leader does not seek spiritual authority; a leader seeks to know God. Maturity processing enhances this desire to know God. Spiritual authority results from a leader's experience with God.[15]

Although the pastor is responsible before God as one who will give an account for those under his charge, the pastor will only give an account of his personal faithfulness in carrying out the **biblical** duties and responsibilities of the pastor. As I have researched the Scriptures, I find four key responsibilities for those who hold an overseeing type of office within the church:

(1) Teach/preach the Word of God (2 Timothy 4:2)
(2) Do the work of an evangelist (2 Timothy 4:5)

(3) Equip the saints for the work of the ministry (Ephesians 4:12)

(4) Shepherd the flock of God (1 Peter 5:2).

Note that the underlying similarity with each of these responsibilities is the teaching/preaching of the Word of God. In other words, when the person holding an oversight office in the church is teaching the Word of God, that is the time and place where the office holds biblical authority. The pastor/teacher assumes delegated authority from the Word with the full expectation that those who hear the Word will submit themselves to the Word and obey. This clarifies the writer of Hebrew's admonition that followers "obey those who have the rule over you" (Hebrews 13:7).

In contrast, it is important to note that biblical authority does not extend to an expectation that the people in the church are *biblically compelled* to follow the pastor or elders in any and every project or ministry endeavor. It may be controversial to say, but followers are not required by God to obey pastors as they lead in building programs, or paying off debt, or any number of good and worthwhile projects and plans. Such actions are ancillary to the primary role of oversight and do not carry biblical authority.

When I am teaching this section, I will ask the class to imagine I am their pastor. I then hold my Bible over my head as a symbolic representation of my submission to the authority of Christ and the Word of God. While holding my Bible over my head, I will then inform them that their duty as followers is to listen and heed the authority of what I say as pastor, as long as I am speaking the "thus says the Lord" of the Word of God. I will then move the Bible from over my head and hold it out to the side. At this point I tell the class that from this position I no longer hold biblical authority but, taking my place as a fellow member of the church, serve as a consultant to the Body of Christ. My training, expertise, and experiences may help the church fulfill her purpose, but at this point I do not speak "thus says the Lord," and the church is not required to listen or heed what I say. I might also add that, as the pastor of the church, God does not hold me responsible for the obedience or disobedience of the individual members of the church or the corporate actions of the church regarding these programs or plans. As a pastor, God will hold me responsible for how I equipped the saints to do the work of the ministry. Each follower of Christ is responsible before God for the responsibilities God has assigned to him or her in the Word. It may not be good English, but it makes sense: *I am only responsible for what I'm responsible for.*

This understanding serves to free the pastor from self-imposed pressures brought about by some leadership teachings that imply the pastor is solely responsible for the growth of the church. Paul's admonition to Timothy was, "Preach the Word..." (2 Timothy 4:2) and "[equip] the saints" (Ephesians 4:12). As we have studied, faithfully preaching the Bible and equipping people for works of service in the church do not always result in church growth. In fact, if the follower capacity of the members of the church is low, faithfully preaching and teaching the Bible may result in anger, disunity, and stagnation. The world may view such a church as having poor leadership. However, in the eyes of the Lord, such a pastor has remained faithful in fulfilling his biblical responsibilities. Whatever our place of responsibility within the church, let us always remember Paul's words in 1 Corinthians 3:5-9:

> What, after all, is Apollos? And what is Paul? Only servants, through whom you came to believe-as the Lord has assigned to each his task. I planted the seed, Apollos watered it, but God made it grow. So neither he who plants nor he who waters is anything, but only God, who makes things grow. The man who plants and the man who waters have one purpose, and each will be rewarded according to his own labor. For we are God's fellow workers; you are God's field, God's building.

Let me at this point direct an important caveat to those with leader responsibilities in the church who are not fulltime ministerial staff. Although the pastor/elders operate as consultants to the church when planning events, outreaches, buildings, etc., it is important for the members of the church to realize that these pastors and staff members eat, drink, sleep, and die a thousand deaths trying to figure out ways for the church to fulfill her mission. I think I can speak for many pastors when I say that it is extremely disheartening after having planned and prepared for months to present a plan to the church leaders to have it rejected out of hand by those who are not at the church every day of the week, are not constantly pressed by the needs of the ministry, and often do not have a big picture of the need for certain actions. This is not to say that church members should have no say in decisions that are made. The pastor/elders should outline an understandable rationale (big picture). What I am suggesting is that those members who serve on decision making committees or boards prayerfully seek to understand the heart of their pastor and not approach such decisions as merely another business transaction.

As I have stated previously, there is no biblical mandate stating that church members are required to agree with every plan the pastor or leader team presents. However, I would urge every member to realize that cavalier attitudes and/or devising power plays in order to show the pastor who is in charge, as well as other worldly expressions of power and control are extremely dangerous to those who might play these political games and damaging to the church.

As followers realize their power to act or not act, it is wise to listen carefully to those who are your spiritual leaders even when they are speaking outside the realm of their biblical authority. Many pastors have read, studied, and prepared themselves to act in the best interest of the longevity and viability of the church. What they present may be new to you, but I can almost guarantee that the plans and ideas are not new to them. They have been prayed over, cried over, and sweated over all for the sake of seeking to know the will of God in the matter. A spirit of mutual respect is highly recommended. Be certain that if you have reservations regarding following your pastors, that you present your reservations with the same prayed over, cried over desire to know the will of God. With a mutual desire to follow the will of God, and rejecting political infighting and power plays, much can be accomplished through the follower-leader relationship.

God holds the pastor/elder responsible for the accurate teaching, shepherding, and equipping of the saints in the Word of God. Followers are responsible to respect and open their hearts to be persuaded by those who hold positions of biblical authority within the church as these people carry out their God-given responsibilities. Followers are responsible to have teachable hearts for the Word of

God. Followers are to join with the pastor/elders in making disciples of all nations. Followers are to make themselves available to be equipped for the work of service, and they can do this work as unto the Lord and not as unto men. It is here that followers can let the leaders lead with joy because the end result will be a benefit for all.

Sad but true, many a young or uninformed pastor has made his life and those around him miserable thinking that his pastoral authority is what is going to influence others. Such ideas are tolerated only for a short period of time before the congregation begins to resist. Pastors/elders need to understand that influence is the result of relationships.

Role and Responsibility

Figure 8 illustrates how important it is for those who hold office in the church and the followers who are members of the church to understand the role and responsibility dynamic that is explicitly stated and implicitly understood in the biblical order and functioning of the church.

Moving from top to bottom, the figure outlines how various offices of the church work in harmony with those who are members of the church. Jesus serves as the Head of the church and offers eternal life to all who believe Him. The gift of eternal life is much more than a commodity that is experienced when a believer dies. Eternal life is defined by Jesus as knowing "You the only true God, and Jesus Christ whom You have sent (John 17:3). Whereas previous to conversion it was impossible for a person to be brought into right relationship with God, at the moment of conversion, the believer is given the capacity to know God intimately and brought into a right, submissive, relationship to Him. Thus, eternal life is experienced at the moment of conversion and continues through physical death into eternity. This life is experienced most fully as believers learn and obey the Word of God (John 14:21). The order in salvation is that we are first converted to become followers of Christ and then through learning the Word of God we become His disciples.

Figure 8: Role and Responsibility

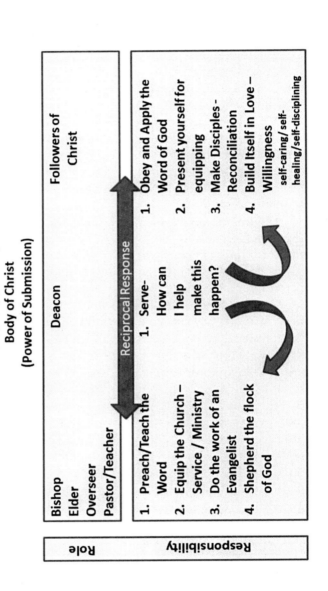

These converted followers of Christ who are seeking to learn more of Him are universally understood to be the Body of Christ, the Church. When believers organize themselves into groups for worship, learning, and ministry, a local church is formed. The prevailing attitude of those within the local church is that of submission to Christ, His Word, the established order outlined in the Bible, and to one another. Without this commitment to submission, the local church becomes dysfunctional.

The diagram is intentionally designed to show the non-hierarchical organizational structure of the church. This emphasizes the point that the church is not to be a power and control organizational culture but rather an organizational culture based on submission to those who hold specific roles and have specific responsibilities.

The first line of the diagram outlines three specific roles within the organized local church: (1) Bishop, Elder, Overseer, Pastor/Teacher [Your particular church may recognize some, or all of these designations.], (2) Deacon, and (3) Followers of Christ, those without office but have important organizational function within the local church. Below each group is a list of specific responsibilities. Those who hold positions of oversight have explicit, biblical responsibilities. Those who hold the roles of Deacon and Follower have implicit responsibilities that are the reciprocal responses to those who have oversight.

Given that each person listed has met the biblical character qualities of those who hold office within the church, reading the illustration horizontally from left to right one can readily see the 'flow' of responsibilities within the church.

1. **Preach/Teach the Word**

    "Preach the word; be ready in season and out of season; reprove, rebuke, exhort, with great patience and instruction" (2 Timothy 4:2).

    Those who hold teaching the Word responsibilities in the church are charged with an awesome privilege. Speaking forth the Word of God accurately and understandably is a task that God takes very seriously. To be sure, those who teach the

Word will incur a stricter judgment (James 3:1). It is a task that is not to be taken lightly and requires hours of study time and effort. Constant learning and sharpening of communication skills is the life-long pursuit of the Bible teacher. Those who teach are the first to obey the Word and grow in a vibrant relationship with Christ.

Serve

Deacons are students of the Word as well. They present themselves to be taught the Word in order to grow in their faith. Their personal walk with the Lord causes them to ask the question, "How can I help the teacher and the listener to be prepared to hear and obey the Word?"

Obey and Apply the Word of God

Followers have a responsibility to present themselves to be taught the Word of God. They need to have minds prepared to be renewed by the Word (Romans 12:2) and hearts prepared to obey. They must also give their teachers time and resources to study. The greatest gift they can give the teacher is to apply the Word to their lives and continue to grow in Christlikeness.

2. **Equip the Church – Service/Ministry**

   "And He gave some...for the equipping of the saints for the work of service, to the building up of the body of Christ;..." (Ephesians 4:11-12).

   When those who hold oversight are seeking to equip the Church for service/ministry it is important that we do not apply an anachronistic point of view to this responsibility. Pastor/Teachers are not biblically responsible for equipping people within the church to do Small Group, Preschool, Student, or Parking Lot ministry, even though they may choose to do so. These may be important organizational steps to take if a church is seeking to reach others with the Gospel. However, these 'ministries' are not the 'ministry' with which overseers are to concern themselves. To make this application would be to place a modern understanding of ministry upon the historical context of the teaching. When Paul commanded those with oversight responsibilities to equip the saints for the work of ministry, he was not speaking organizationally. Paul's command was based upon his understanding that every person who follows Christ has a particular ministry, the ministry of reconciliation (2 Corinthians 5:18-20). In order to fulfill their responsibilities before God to "equip the saints" the overseers must make certain that the followers of Christ are exercising their roles as "Ambassadors of Christ" even as they are exercising this role.

Serve

Deacons also present themselves for equipping in order to fulfill their ministry of reconciliation. There may be certain organizational tasks given to the Deacons to ensure the smooth operation of the church, but these tasks should not supersede the primary ministry of each Deacon to be a reconciling Ambassador of Christ. Fulfilling their ministry of reconciliation the Deacons ask themselves, "How can I help the pastor and the people become the ministers of reconciliation we should be?

Present Yourself for Equipping

Followers have the responsibility of presenting themselves for equipping. Those with oversight will be unable to fulfill their ministry without followers willing to be equipped. Therefore, faithful followers step forward in order to become the ministers of reconciliation that God has given them. They are willing to begin living as "Ambassadors of Christ" sharing the good news that "God was in Christ Jesus reconciling the world to Himself" (2 Corinthians 5:19). Other organizational tasks may be accepted by the follower, but the primary objective is to become a minister of reconciliation.

3. Do the Work of an Evangelist
"…do the work of an evangelist, fulfill your ministry" (2 Timothy 4:5).

When those with oversight are responsible for doing the work of an evangelist, they are actually commanded to make sharing the Gospel a natural part of their lives. Talking about Jesus should be an easy conversation to have when the opportunity presents itself. In this way they model before the congregation a heart's desire to see others come to faith in Christ. When others do come to Christ these overseers continue the relationship by teaching them and growing the new believers in the knowledge of Christ.

Serve
Deacons also share the gospel. They present themselves to be equipped in order to make sharing the Gospel a normal part of their everyday living. They too, embrace new believers, sharing with them their knowledge of the Savior. By living the life of a ready evangelist and disciple maker the Deacons ask, "How can I encourage the Pastors and Followers to make sharing the Gospel a lifestyle?"

Make Disciples – Reconciliation
"Go therefore and make disciples of all nations…" (Matthew 28:19)

Followers present themselves to be equipped in how to share their faith in Christ. As the Overseers and Deacons model a lifestyle of sharing, Followers embrace the same desire and fulfill the Lord's Great Commission by sharing the Gospel and making disciples of all nations. There is no division between evangelizing and disciple making. Each Follower of Christ, regardless of his or her role, is responsible to the Lord to share the Gospel and when someone responds, disciple them to become a growing, disciple-making follower of Christ.

4. Shepherd the Flock of God

"...shepherd the flock of God among you, exercising oversight not under compulsion, but voluntarily, according to the will of God; and not for sordid gain, but with eagerness; nor yet as lording it over those allotted to your charge, but proving to be examples to the flock" (1 Peter 5:2-3).

Shepherding the flock of God is a specific command using the metaphor of a shepherd. The metaphor points out the primary task of the shepherd being the feeding of the flock. The shepherd cares for and protects the flock primarily by teaching sound doctrine so that they are not "carried away by every wind of doctrine..." (Ephesians 4:14). Churches sometimes place this responsibility second to their own need to be cared for. Thus, oversight becomes a function of making sure that the people are well, visited, and cared for. This is not to say that Overseers should not be concerned with the physical wellbeing of those who make up their "flock." They should make themselves available to pray for the sick (James 5:14). However, the biblical priority of caring for the flock through accurate teaching needs to be kept at the forefront of their responsibilities.

Serve

Deacons understand the biblical priority placed upon the overseers and willingly participate to care for the physical needs of the congregation. We see the early church doing just that in Acts chapter 6 when the physical needs of some of the people became a distraction to the expansion of the Gospel. Seven men were chosen to serve tables because the Apostles said, "It is not desirable for us to neglect the word of God in order to serve tables (Acts 6:2). Thus, Deacons are prepared to be an active shepherding arm of the church asking, "Is there a need I can meet?"

Build Itself in Love – Willingness

Followers realize that the primary function of the overseers is to make certain that sound doctrine from the Word of God is taught to those who make up the Body. To that end, followers are not clamoring for attention from the overseers. Through the teaching of the Word, followers understand that,

"...speaking the truth in love, we are to grow up in all aspects into Him, who is the head, even Christ, from whom the whole body, being fitted and held together by that which every joint supplies, according to the proper working of each individual part, causes the growth of the body for the building up of itself in love" (Ephesians 4:15-16).

Followers are the "joints" that supply the "fit" to the Body. Each follower must find his or her specific "individual part" to play within the Body. This individual responsibility on the part of the followers allows for the Body to build itself up in love. There is no sense of a total dependence upon the overseers to do this work. In fact, the Body is to be a **self-caring** organism.

If there is a need, the individuals within the Body are to meet the need and not wait for permission from the pastors. In a church where I was a guest preacher I noticed in the bulletin it said, "If you know of anyone with a need, call the church office." When I rose to speak I suggested a change. I said, "If anyone knows someone with a need, *meet the need*." There is no need to wait for permission to meet another's needs.

The Apostle Paul wrote the Corinthian Christians that as a body, the members should have the same care for one another.

But God has so composed the body, giving more abundant honor to that member which lacked, that there should be no division in the body, but that the members should have the same care for one another.

And if one member suffers, all the members suffer with it; if one member is honored, all the members rejoice with it. Now you are Christ's body, and individually members of it (1 Corinthians 12:24-27).

In this same way the Body is to be a **self-healing** organization. Whether physical or emotional, the Body of Christ, through the power of prayer, has the capacity to be healed. James 5:13-15 encourages the Body to call for the elders to come and anoint the one who is sick and to pray for them. This appears to be an extreme case because the person is unable to go to the elders. However, the following verse is where much healing in the Body could take place, "Therefore, confess your sins to one another, and pray for one another, so that you may be healed" (James 5:16). Through forgiveness and confession with intercessory prayer the Body is made whole.

Building itself in love also requires the Body to be **a self-disciplining** organization. Followers take it upon themselves to hold each other accountable to the commands of Christ. Matthew chapter 18 outlines a procedure of discipline within the Body of Christ that begins with a brother in Christ having a private conversation with a fellow brother in Christ who is believed to have committed a sin. This is followed by further conversation until such time as the perpetrator is brought before the church to be disciplined. All of this activity is initiated and carried out by the followers, not the overseers. It is not until the very last stage of the process that the overseers are involved. Followers realize that the pastor does not need to be the "Principal" of the church. The pastor does not need to be the one to whom the people turn to say, "What are you going to do about this?" Followers understand this as their responsibility. The pastor is protected from these additional burdens up until the time that the sin becomes public knowledge and directly impacts the effectiveness of the church to fulfill her mission.

The attitude of the followers is to willingly respond to the teaching of the Word of God and take an active role in building up the Body of Christ. Followers see themselves as active participants in the work of the Holy Spirit through the Body of Christ.

Reciprocal Response

With every role and responsibility within the church there is a reciprocal response. The previous explanations of roles and responsibilities mention this process. The following description briefly outlines this reciprocal process more explicitly.

1. Preach/Teach the Word

Those with oversight roles teach the Scriptures to those faithful followers who then will reciprocate by teaching others also (2 Timothy 2:2). It is apparent that followers who hear and obey the Word of God are those whom the Lord leads into roles of teaching others. At the same time, those with oversight roles are constantly seeking to gain more and better knowledge of the Scriptures by presenting themselves as learners. Only by learning and applying more of the Word to their lives can leaders within the church maintain their role and lead others to follow Christ.

2. Equip the Church – Service/Ministry

Those who equip others should do so to the point that the equipped become the equippers. When followers present themselves for equipping it is not simply for personal gain but for the purpose of learning to equip others. At the same time, those who initially equip others also must present themselves to be equipped in order to further hone their God-given abilities for further service and ministry.

3. Do the Work of an Evangelist

When leaders perform the role of evangelist, new believers naturally come to faith in Christ. These new believers are equipped to share the Gospel with others. They then seek to evangelize their family, friends, and associates. They also become disciples who are learning more and more of Christ. At the same time, those who perform the role of evangelist are continuing to learn and grow in their relationship to Christ. In this way there is no division between the activities of evangelizing and making disciples. Both leader and follower are involved in this ongoing activity.

4. Shepherd the Flock of God

Those with oversight are charged with caring for those within the church. As these leaders care for others, they model behaviors that should be imitated by those being cared for. Thus, when followers see a need, they can readily care for others without having to rely upon the leader to be present or even involved in the caring process. In this way, the church becomes the self-caring community for which it was designed. At the same time, those who hold a shepherding role build relationships with those in the Body and recognize their own need for care from the Body. In this way those who shepherd the flock are also care for by the flock. (Don't be tempted to take the shepherding analogy too far. Remember, within the Body of Christ, we are all sheep.)

A Dependent Organization

Looking at the church from a followerfirst perspective one can see that the church is designed to be totally dependent on God. Without the power of the Holy Spirit enabling the followers of Christ within the church to submit to Christ and to one another, the organization does not function in the way it was originally designed. Certainly, as with any organization, we can apply specific organizational principles within the church and *make* it work. But such an action would kill it. It would become a static institution without a heartbeat. Organizational principles and job descriptions and rules would become the mechanistic life support system. Gone would be freedom, joy, love, and passion. She would be present in the community, but not able to lead anyone to life.

By focusing everyone's attention on a common dependence on Christ, the church breathes with life only when she is submitted to Christ as the Head. This fellowship of the Spirit is manifested through an ever present effort to regard other persons as more important than self. This "other-centeredness" creates an atmosphere and organizational climate of mutual respect and common purpose.

In addition, being mutually dependent upon the Scripture and each other creates an environment where the will of God can be discerned more clearly. The three most dangerous words in the English language are "God told me." If a person truly believes this, they will not listen any further to human reason and can act in ways that are not consistent with Scriptural teaching. Thus, as a part of the church we are instructed to humble ourselves to the Scriptures and to one another in order to gain counsel when applying the Scriptures to our lives. Our mutual dependence protects us all from error.

Quid Pro Quo

One of the most destructive philosophies operating in the church today is the idea of the *quid pro quo*, a Latin term for "what for what" or "something for something".[16] The basis of the phrase is to give something of value for something of value. Colloquially, we might speak of, "one hand washing the other," or, "I'll scratch your back if you scratch mine." As a pastor, I was often confronted by this type of thinking when dealing with business men and women. The reason for this is that the business world operates on the idea of the exchange. The thought is, "I'll do for you and then you can do for me." As a young pastor, I was somewhat naïve about all this and found myself confronted by some who had hard feelings towards me because I would not return the favor at a later time. They would remind me about votes that were taken in meetings and behind the scenes dealings on my behalf so that my agenda could be passed, and now it was my turn to do what the giver of the favor wanted me to do for them. When I was unable to comply with their request because it would have hurt the church, I was accused of not "playing the game."

Such exchanges within the church are the antithesis of the grace of God which was given to purchase and establish the church. Grace, God's *unmerited* favor, requires nothing on the part of the recipient. When God gives, He gives not as a result of our merit/works or even our future merit/works. God gives because He chooses to. It is this organizational culture of grace in which the church must operate if it is to accurately communicate the glory of God to the world. Unfortunately, and to the great peril of the church, leaders have adopted this ungodly perspective of pay to play by which deals are struck and decisions are made. Grace is forgotten and a favor-based system of power, persuasion, and bribery takes its place. There is no longer a, "Yes." There is a, "Yes, if you will do this for me." The 'what have you done for me lately' perspective begins to warp the very foundation of the church and decisions are no longer based upon biblical criteria but rather a sense of entitlement and self-centeredness. Concerns for Jesus and His kingdom work are undermined for the present obtaining of temporary power and privilege. The organization devolves into a political system in which power brokers influence for their own cause, their own group, or even for their own personal benefit. We cannot allow such thinking or actions to permeate the church any longer.

What will it take to change the prevailing *quid pro quo* culture? Change will require followers of Christ willing to be misunderstood and even taken advantage of by those operating within this system. It will require followers willing to confront ungodly practices within the church and possibly be ostracized by others. It will require courageous followers with a spiritual integrity and love for Christ that cannot and will not be compromised. It will require followers of Christ who cannot be bought. A popular adage within the business world is, "everyone has their price." At what price have we sold the church culture of grace for a business culture of conditions and exchanges? Those followers of Christ who wish to recover the culture of grace will surely pay a price by being misunderstood and even thought a poor leader. Are you willing?

Responses

Regardless of the power that is exerted in the follower-leader relationship, we must never forget that each person in this leadership dance has the power of his or her own decision. There are three basic responses that can occur within this relationship, resistance, compliance, or commitment.[17]

Resistance

Resistance is not an uncommon initial response when influence is exerted upon another. The seasoned pastor is all too familiar with the 'cold water' committee whose job it is to pour cold water on any new idea. However, it might be of some comfort to know that an initial, "No," to an idea is not necessarily a permanent, "No." When moving through change, it is important to understand that, "No," is normal. (Notice that the first two letters in the word normal are "n-o.") This resistance works both with the leader's influence upon the follower and the follower's influence upon the leader.

One of the most unproductive conclusions that can be drawn from resistance is to conclude that such resistance is a sign of spiritual immaturity, or even worse, begin believing that those who resist are of the devil. Pastors often bemoan the fact that their people are not spiritually mature and do not have enough faith to step out and believe. Similarly, members sometimes bemoan the fact that their pastor will not step out in faith and support the ministry they want to implement. Such drawing of assumptions only serves to create unspoken barriers between the two groups that taint further conversations and lead to further discord and doubt and lost productivity.

Although playing the spiritual maturity card may be initially unproductive, I need to quickly add that a lack of spiritual maturity may actually be what is hindering the church from being productive. My advice would be not to jump to the conclusion of spiritual immaturity, but to observe actions overtime. Is there eventual movement in a direction or does the status quo[18] prevail? Are people willing to continue in dialogue or are they content just to let the idea die a natural death through neglect?

If there is movement in the conversation, then it may be that people simply need more time to digest the idea. If there is no movement and no continued dialogue, then it may very well be that those whom you are attempting to influence do not have the spiritual maturity necessary to act on the idea. If this is the case, then it is the influencer's responsibility to love these persons, whether follower or leader, and seek to help them build a more intimate relationship with the Lord Jesus. As people know and understand the love of Christ, they are moved to action. The Apostle Paul said, "...it is the love of Christ that compels us" (2 Corinthians 5:14). It is not our love for Christ, but rather, an understanding of the overwhelming love of Christ for us that moves us and motivates us. Growing a person's understanding of the existence and attributes of God and the love and character of the Son is the greatest motivator. Remember, the dynamic aspect of leadership involves the working of the Holy Spirit. Seek Him and the glory of God and wait to see if resistance is reduced over time.

Compliance

Compliance appears to be the prevalent response in most follower-leader relationships. Follower compliance may be defined as perfunctory obedience to the request of another but only because of the leader's legitimate position of authority. When a leader is compliant to the followers, such a response may be due to the fact that the followers hold certain amounts of influence or power over the leader. At best, compliance is activity without the whole heart. It is a pseudo-commitment that often covers itself with the trappings of loyalty and obedience, but in reality is full of guile.

Pastors and church leaders are often too willing to accept compliance as an affirmation of actions and a vote of confidence to continue full speed to the next project. Remember, just because the people are agreeing to act does not necessarily mean they have a full commitment toward a project. Do not be fooled into thinking that just because the members are doing what they have been requested to do and the ministry is working just fine that the church is actually functioning as a unit.

Be forewarned. Compliant responses, over time, carry the seeds of disillusionment and possible rebellion.[19] Compliant activity is an indicator that some type of coercive power may be impacting the people. There is no joy in compliance; there is only duty and legalistic adherence to a perceived requirement. The wise leader or follower needs to investigate the true motives of the people to determine why compliance is the predominant response and then teach them the freedom that comes from knowing how to follow the Lord Jesus Christ with a whole heart.

Commitment (Obedience)

Commitment is the response of faith, hope, and love. Commitment requires the whole heart. Jesus outlined our commitment to God and to our neighbor when in Mark 12: 29-31 He said,

> The first of all the commandments is: 'Hear, O Israel, the LORD our God, the LORD is one. And you shall love the LORD your God with all your heart, with all your soul, with all your mind, and with all your strength.' This is the first commandment. And the second, like it, is this: 'You shall love your neighbor as yourself.' There is no other commandment greater than these.

With an intimate commitment to God and Christ, the follower is able to trust God through the direction of a God given leader, and the leader is able to trust God to do His work through God given followers. Commitment is a response that is not so much directed at the leader or the follower but at Christ, the Head of the Church.

When leaders trust and are committed to their followers, followers are free to act more courageously, take on more responsibilities, and add to the vision and productivity of the ministry. When followers trust and are committed to their leaders, they can make the leader's leading a joy which embeds a culture of celebration within the church. There is no bickering, fighting, or positioning for power. There is a mutual commitment to follow Christ, and this mutual commitment results in a church that is spiritually empowered to accomplish the will of God. All of this unity and productivity is predicated upon each person's commitment to follow Christ first.

Commitment requires integrity.

The trustworthiness of both follower and leader can be established by each being persons of godly integrity. We need to find our wholeness in Christ and then live out the life of Christ in every detail of life. Integrity has been defined as who you are in the dark when nobody sees you. This is a good definition. Followers of Christ must maintain their integrity even though those around them may not. This requires the follower of Christ to respond differently than what may be commonly expected. Consider what Paul said in Romans 12:17-21:

> Repay no one evil for evil. Have regard for good things in the sight of all men. If it is possible, as much as depends on you, live peaceably with all men. Beloved, do not avenge yourselves, but rather give place to wrath; for it is written, "Vengeance is Mine, I will repay," says the Lord. Therefore "If your enemy is hungry, feed him; If he is thirsty, give him a drink; For in so doing you will heap coals of fire on his head." Do not be overcome by evil, but overcome evil with good.

"Repay no one evil for evil...live peaceably with all men...do not avenge yourselves...overcome evil with good." How strange a place the world would be if the followers of Christ actually practiced such admonitions. How wonderful a place the church would be if the followers of Christ could at least follow these guidelines toward those within the church.

Commitment requires a price.

Maintaining a good conscience within and without the church by upholding the testimony of the Lord Jesus Christ is worth any personal price that occurs as a result of obeying His commands. If we wish to follow Christ we must respond in obedience regardless of peer pressure, political correctness, or loss of position or prestige. Christ's reputation must take priority over our own. As our behaviors change, those with whom we once associated will not understand, and they may (will) speak evil of us (1 Peter 4:4). As followers of Christ we need to always remember Paul's admonition in 2 Corinthians 4:7-11:

> We are hard-pressed on every side, yet not crushed; we are perplexed, but not in despair; persecuted, but not forsaken; struck down, but not destroyed — always carrying about in the body the dying of the Lord Jesus, that the life of Jesus also may be manifested in our body. For we who live are

always delivered to death for Jesus' sake, that the life of Jesus also may be manifested in our mortal flesh.

Such a following would, however, come at a personal price. Practicing such actions will cause some to call you foolish. Others will take advantage, but what of it for the sake of the glory of Christ? Any price we pay for following the Lord pales in significance to that which has already been paid by the Lord Jesus.

Commitment requires faithfulness.

One of the key characteristics of committed followers of Christ is faithfulness. All followers of Christ, whether in positions of following or leading, have been given a stewardship of the gospel of Christ, and it is required of stewards that they remain faithful (1 Corinthians 4:1-2). As we have already mentioned, those followers in positions of leading are responsible for carrying out their biblical responsibilities of teaching, caring, and equipping, and those followers in positions of following are responsible for honoring, respecting, and being obedient to these leaders. For each area, faithfulness is not so much directed toward people as it is directed toward the Savior. He is our ultimate Head, and we all follow Him faithfully by carrying out our assigned responsibilities within the Body of Christ.

Commitment requires humility.

Like Christ, the commitment about which I am speaking is a commitment to the will of another, God the Father. The hallmark of the follower of Christ is his or her humility to Christ and to others. In Philippians, Chapter 2, Paul outlines the mind of Christ with regard to His own humility. Paul instructs us that once Christ was found in appearance as a man, He humbled Himself by becoming obedient to the point of death, even death on the cross. The essence of living a life of humility is to commit oneself to the will of another – willingly and not under compulsion. This humility usually manifests itself through a total dependence upon Christ and His Holy Spirit. When we deny self we can embrace the will of God and respond obediently to the events that surround us. In fact, not only can we respond but, in the power of the Holy Spirit, we have the opportunity to initiate actions that bring glory to God.

RETHINK

Power from the Follower's Perspective

It is sometimes assumed that power is something leaders have and followers do not. Upon closer inspection we can see that followers do indeed have power within organizations and this is even more pronounced in churches. The following is a recapitulation of some of the ideas previously mentioned regarding how followers can understand their influential role within the church. As you read them, perhaps you can ask yourself how these types of power have been evidenced in your church and what may need to change in the process of leadership.

Reward Power

Each time a follower decides to do something a leader suggests, the follower is rewarding the leader with his or her own life. Followers can reward leaders with speaking the truth, sharing information, being available when needed, being responsible for activities, and most everything else you can think of that a leader would do.

Coercive Power

Coercive power is characterized by the ability to punish non-compliance. When viewed from a follower perspective, if a follower knows that a leader must have a project finished, the follower can punish the leader by not completing work, misdirecting effort, or not telling the truth. This may result in the follower being punished but the damage will have already been done. To think that followers have no coercive power is naïve.

Expert Power

Followers can be experts at anything. Unless respected and appreciated, followers may simply remain quiet about their expertise. If the follower knows that he or she will not be given credit for an idea or a solution, he or she may decide to keep the expertise to themselves. Conversely, followers who seek to follow and honor

God will give their expertise to projects without thought of seeking glory for themselves.

Referent Power

The integrity and character of a follower has tremendous impact upon the leader. Leaders need those whom they can trust. By speaking the truth to the leader, the follower can become indispensable to the success and productivity of the church.

Structural Power

The essence of the church is based upon the corner stone of Jesus Christ and His following the will of the Father. Followers are the source through which every ministry of the church is accomplished.

Resource Power

Followers with resources can be a great help to the ministry. Understanding their role as a steward of that which God has given, followers can give so that others might benefit. Resources are not necessarily financial but can be a wide range of important resources to the leader and the church. By withholding resources, followers can short-circuit the efforts of any leader and may be able to do so without the leader even knowing. Positively, the follower with resource power and the right attitude to exercise it can be a great help.

Information Power

Follower lines of social interaction are vast and varied within the organization. In most situations, because of the title and position of the leader, there is little interaction with the *normal* people in the organization. Yet, it is these people who interact and cooperate with one another to make certain the organization continues to function smoothly. Followers hold vast knowledge of people within the organization. Giving and withholding information important to the leader or giving partial or errant information to the leader can do grave damage to the effectiveness of the church. With such power, it is important for followers to remember the words of Paul in Philippians 2:3-4, "Let nothing be done through selfish ambition or conceit, but in lowliness of mind let each esteem others better than himself. Let each of you look out not only for his own interests, but also for the interests of others."

Unless and until leaders understand the inherent power that followers have within the organization, they will never be able to fully utilize the vast resources, expertise, information, and personal integrity available through the followers. To put it more bluntly, if all leaders seek to do is develop people into leaders because they, the current leaders, think certain people have the qualities it takes for being a leader and leave the vast numbers of followers in the organization alone, the leaders, the churches, and other organizations will lose. If there is no change, 20% of the workers will continue to do 80% of the work because the followers, the other 80% of the people, have not been respected, equipped, and taught the responsibilities of being a follower of Christ.

Recruiting Leaders

On the practical side, the church may need to rethink how leaders are recruited to positions of responsibility. Remember, that the members of the church who are going to fill the leader roles of the church are constantly bombarded with a system of thought that is antithetical to a biblical view of how to operate within the church. Many are immersed in power and control organizational cultures that, if allowed to operate within the church, will cause division and conflict.

I was reminded of this fact when confronted by a member of a church during a rather tumultuous time. This member said to me, "Pastor, my view of the church is like this. I see you as the CEO. We deacons are the Board of Directors, and the church members are the stockholders. If the stockholders have a problem with the CEO, or the business is not growing, it's up to the Board of Directors to make whatever changes are necessary." Don't be surprised if you have some of these same people with similar ideas in your church.

This makes the selection of leaders all the more important. If there is a leader position available, it might be wise to ask potential leaders how they view the use of power. How would they exercise it? What would it mean to them to have the position? These questions and others would serve to determine if a person is prepared to face the temptations of having an authoritative position.

There appear to be two extremes when recruiting for leader roles. First, you have the executive. Here is a person who has all the right credentials and experience leading in the business world. It is important to remember, however, that having business expertise does not necessarily translate into being able to function in the organizational environment of a church, especially a follower-centric church. Sometimes these persons may think more of themselves than they ought to think and become a constant source of conflict. On the other hand, if the executive evidences a humble heart and a desire to serve in any capacity, and also understands the use of power, their addition to a position of responsibility can be a great benefit to the church.

Second, you have the person in the church that has never held an actual position of responsibility anywhere. They are the "low man on the totem pole" at work and have rarely been given much respect. When these people enter into leader roles they may be tempted to think more of themselves than they ought to think and become prideful of their new position of respect and authority. Such a response could cause great damage within the Body of Christ. On the other hand, because they have not had the opportunity to be responsible for others, these followers may be ripe for equipping to serve the church from a humble heart. It may require a time of apprentice ministry, but with a correct view of power and service, these persons can greatly impact the church and others.

There is no guarantee that thinking correctly about your position before God as a follower will put you in a leader position. The providence of God determines much of what our actual places of service will be. (Consider the life of Joseph for more insight on this subject.) The activities God desires for us to fulfill are contingent upon His desire for us to know Him more fully and His knowledge of what we need in order to be most fulfilled in Him. Focusing our thoughts and ambitions on Him will relieve a great deal of anxiety and give us the courage and persistence to faithfully carry out our responsibilities.

Chapter 8

Following-Leaders:
The Exercise of Influence

Those who embrace the followerfirst perspective are not dependent on titles or positions in order to gain a sense of identity and worth. They understand that good leaders *are* good followers. They realize that being a faithful follower of Christ enables them to influence everyone with whom they have contact. This influence is not based upon status or rank within the organization. It comes as a natural byproduct of being a followerfirst. Those who embrace a followerfirst perspective are committed to Christ, not a cause or an organization. Those who make up the church should only follow leaders who follow Christ. In other words, the church is to be led by Following-Leaders.

With all the other leadership styles and theories available, I submit that the Following-Leader is the primary leader style for the church's unique organizational structure and purpose. At first glance, the idea of a Following-Leader appears to be oxymoronic. How can a person be following and leading at the same time in the same position? The answer to the question lies in understanding the definitions of following and leading.

**We follow the Leader
in order to
lead as followers.**

Following Defined

We have defined the followerfirst perspective as *a system of thought according to which one willingly follows the Lord Jesus Christ with all one's heart, mind, soul, and strength in every circumstance regardless of organizational position while submitting to fellow followers so that all might fulfill their God-given responsibilities.* The follower may or may not have a recognized position of responsibility in the organization. However, one's position does not determine the passion and integrity of the followerfirst follower. First, these followers understand their primary submission is to the Lord and His commands. Second, followers willingly submit to those whom the Lord has given oversight for them as long as these leaders are fellow followers of Christ. Third, followers willingly submit to every human institution in order to give a good testimony to those who do not follow Christ. Followers are who they are, and following the Lord is what they are called to do.

Leading Defined

Leaders may be defined as those whom followers follow. More precisely, leaders are the persons in most definitions of leadership who exercise influence. Peter Northouse defines leadership as "a process whereby an individual influences a group of individuals to achieve a common goal."[1]

Influencing others appears to be a primary function of what it means to be a leader. Although there are certainly other aspects, this ability to influence is a key element of leading others. It may also be said that anyone exercising influence over another person could be understood as leading others whether this person holds a recognized leader position within the organization or not. Thus, with this understanding, biblical followers may be considered Following-Leaders regardless of their title or organizational position. Perhaps a more apt, but bulky, description is to call them following-influencers.

As we have mentioned, Joseph Rost, Ira Chaleff, and others recognize that the follower-leader relationship is not based upon a cause-effect linear relationship in which the leader acts and the follower responds. We have already seen that the interdependence between leader and follower is much too complicated to rely upon the idea that "everything rises or falls on leadership." Chaleff suggests that leaders and followers revolve around a common purpose in the organization. Within a church context, the follower and leader revolve around a person, the Lord Jesus Christ (See Figure 9). It is this interplay between a designated leader and a follower that allows the leader to follow at certain times within certain contexts and the follower to lead at certain times in certain contexts. The followerfirst perspective is unique in that throughout the leader-follower relationship the idea is never lost that both leader and follower are always following the Lord Jesus. We can see this same relationship illustrated through the Mobius Strip in Chapter 2.

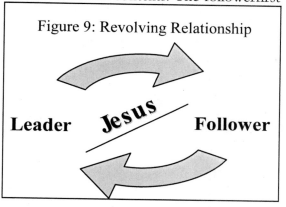

Figure 9: Revolving Relationship

Leader   Jesus   Follower

Being a Follower

Recalling the 'A Leader is Born' diagram from Chapter Three, one can see that followers always consider themselves followers (see Figure 10). When followers assume responsibility over others, the follower is often called a leader. Thus, wherever followers are within an organizational hierarchy, whether they are the custodian or the president, the followerfirst perspective requires the follower to assess himself or herself as a followerfirst. One of the unique aspects of being a Following-Leader is that those who embrace the followerfirst perspective only need be who they are within the organization and, by default, they become Following-Leaders. That is, there is no need to concentrate on *becoming* something other than who they already are. By being followers of Christ where they are within the organization, with a leader title or without, the followers' actions and responses influence those around them. They are being Following-Leaders.

Figure 10: A Following-Leader is Born

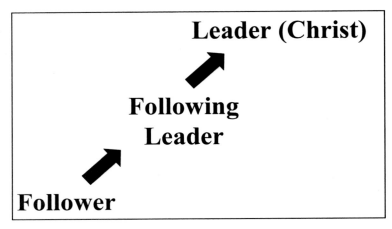

The influence of the Following-Leader increases when he or she is given responsibility over others within the organization. As a follower with a leader title, the follower has the opportunity to influence and to lead others in a way that glorifies God. However, it bears repeating that one of the subtle temptations within organizations is for followers to begin thinking of themselves as leaders first rather than followers first. The Following-Leader construct can be a corrective way of thinking for the leader and an accurate way for followers to think about their leaders.

A Way of Thinking for Leaders

One way of defining success in life is finding what God wants you to do and accomplishing it in the power of the Holy Spirit. If I could add anything to this definition I think I would add that success in life is finding who God wants me to *be* and *being* that person in the power of the Holy Spirit. The reason I make the change is because, if I am the person I am called by God to be, then I naturally will seek to do the things I am commanded by God to do. It is through a submissive relationship to the Savior that I find fulfillment.

Eternal Life is Knowing Christ

My relationship to Christ became clearer to me when on a hunting trip I was confronted by the question, "What is eternal life?" As I thought about the answer, I worked through the simple definitions. Eternal life is life eternal, or as the young people at church might retort, eternal life is living forever. Some might think that heaven is eternal life, but heaven is actually the place where we live out eternal life. Then I stumbled upon John 17:3 where Jesus actually defines eternal life:

> "And this is eternal life, that they might know Thee, the only true God, and Jesus Christ whom Thou hast sent."

According to Jesus, eternal life is knowing God and Jesus Christ. Leave it to the Savior to give such a precise definition. However, I was then confronted with the question, "How do I know God and Jesus Christ?"

I gain eternal life when I intimately know God through a relationship with Jesus Christ. I increase my intimate knowledge of Jesus as He reveals Himself to me as I follow His commands. I experience eternal life daily as I become the person He wants me to be and recognize every event of every day as an opportunity to revel in my personal relationship with God through Jesus Christ. When God provides an opportunity for the follower to lead, He is opening an opportunity for the leader to know Jesus more intimately. The position does entail more responsibility over others. However, let us never forget that *the purpose of the follower of Christ being in a leader position is so that God can honor Himself through the Following-Leader, and so that the Following-Leader can experience eternal life through greater dependence upon Jesus.*

Dependence is gained through obedience to the commands of Jesus. Jesus said in John 14:21, "He who has My commandments and keeps them, it is he who loves Me. And he who loves Me will be loved by My Father, and I will love him and manifest Myself to him." As the believer becomes more and more dependent upon Christ through obeying His commands, Jesus promises to reveal (manifest) himself to the believer. Thus, the one who follows the commands of Jesus becomes a follower who has an intimate relationship with God and with Jesus. Through this intimacy a greater love for God is created which begins a process of falling more in love with Jesus, which produces greater obedience to His word, which allows Jesus to reveal more of Himself to the follower, which creates a greater love for God, which produces a greater love for Jesus, which produces greater obedience, etc. This process continues as long as the follower is obedient to the commands of Christ or until the follower dies and goes to be with the Lord.

Why is it important to understand this process? If we think that leading others is just an exercise in being successful, or being the best me I can be, or fulfilling my destiny, or growing an organization, or making an impact, or doing what others cannot do, then we miss the very point of being a Following-Leader. We are robbed of the very purpose for living out our eternal life on this earth. If I do not know the purpose behind being a follower and a leader, then all the success in the world goes for naught. However, if I think correctly about who I am and that God has me in the positions in which I function in this life so that I might know Him in all His fullness, then life, and struggle, and hurt, and pain, and joy, and relationships take on an entirely deeper meaning. As a result, I experience "life, and that abundantly" (John 10:10). Following and leading are ultimately *not* about following a leader or leading others. **Following a leader and leading others are about knowing God.**

A Way for Followers to Think About Their Leaders

If leading others is about knowing God, then why follow? Following is about knowing God from a different perspective. When we find ourselves in an organization and there are leaders placed over us, our first concern is to determine if the leader is a Following-Leader. One way to determine this is to ask the leader what or who he or she is following. Their answer will reveal whether the person is is a follower of Christ first or a follower of something or someone else. Who our leaders follow determines whether or not this is the person under whom you can serve.

As a follower within the church, I am not looking for perfect leaders. I already have one in the person of Christ. My desire is to honor God and obey the Lord's commands by supporting my human leaders as much as I am able. As long as these leaders are leading me into intimacy with the Savior, I can support them. However, if the time comes when the leaders act in immoral or unbiblical ways, I am required to confront them, gently correct, and if there is no change, remove myself and my family from the influence of these leaders who no longer, by definition, are Following-Leaders.

One thing that needs to be kept in mind is that followers of Christ who do not hold positions within an organization can still be effective Following-Leaders. The fact that you do not hold a title or position does not prohibit you from acting consistently with the Scriptures in your daily activities and influencing (leading) those around you to greater obedience to the commands of the Lord. In fact, Following-Leaders influence others wherever they are.

When the current leadership literature offers guidance on identifying potential leaders, what these authors are really identifying are the characteristics of Following-Leaders. One writer suggests looking for the following characteristics when looking to recruit leaders:

Character	Evident Gifts
Influence	Proven Track Record
Positive Attitude	Confidence
People Skills	Self-Discipline
Communication Skills	Discontent with *Status Quo*[2]

Do any of these traits look familiar? They do because they are the very same characteristics of a person who lives his or her life with a followerfirst perspective. What the leadership literature does not admit is that when leaders are looking for people to serve with them, they are not *really* looking for leaders but followers who have consistently lived a followerfirst perspective. Think about it. How does anyone get recognized for additional responsibility? They fulfill the requests of others in ways that evidence integrity, credibility, competence, and humility. They exhibit the characteristics of a person who knows who he or she is and acts according to core values that are congruent with the organization. Leaders don't need more leaders. There can only be so many chefs in the kitchen. Leaders are really looking for Following-Leaders.

Developing as a Following-Leader

If, as a follower of the Person and teachings of Jesus Christ, I am already a Following-Leader, how might I become a more committed follower and more effective influencer of others? As I understand it, this is a lifelong process of denying self, taking up my cross daily, and following the Lord. I have listed some practical applications of how that process may be completed. These applications are not intended to be comprehensive or prescriptive, but merely suggestions from my own journey as a follower.

1.   Love the Perfect Follower

As a believer, the primary benefit for leading others is coming to know more intimately the perfect follower, the Lord Jesus Christ. This requires the Following-Leader to spend more time with the Lord in prayer and study of the Bible. This requirement is crucial in the future readiness of the Following-Leader to lead others, especially when the will of God begins to require personal sacrifice.

Jesus' own disciples expressed this point clearly, when after Jesus had spoken a difficult teaching, the people began to leave the ranks. Jesus asked His disciples if they too would leave. The answer was spoken by Peter in John 6:68-69, "Lord, to whom shall we go? You have the words of eternal life. Also we have come to believe and know that You are the Christ, the Son of the living God." Jesus has the words of eternal life. These are the words that are not only good for salvation from sin but for living out the abundant life of Christ on earth. Additionally, Jesus is the Christ. He is not just an ideal or a good idea. These men staked their eternal souls on the belief that Jesus was the Christ, the Messiah. According to tradition, most of Jesus' true disciples died a martyrs' death.[3]

One practical means by which the Following-Leader can grow in a relationship with Jesus is through prayer. There are many good books regarding prayer, but one in particular is Andrew Murrays' classic, *With Christ in the School of Prayer*. Murray wrote:

The place and power of prayer in the Christian life is too little understood. As long as we view prayer simply as the means of maintaining our own Christian lives, we will not fully understand what it is really supposed to be. But when we learn to regard it as the highest part of the work entrusted to us — the root and strength of all other work - we will see that there is nothing we need to study and practice more than the art of praying.[4]

2. Apply God's Word

The Bible is the Following-Leader's major textbook for understanding how to act and respond in life situations. He/she must thirst for the Word. Deep within the follower there must be a need to hear from God through the Word of God. As an example to others, the Following-Leader applies teachings from the Word which others may call foolish or naïve. Even though the world system may play by a different set of rules, the Following-Leader refuses to compromise and is willing to be defrauded rather than besmirch the character and reputation of Christ. Without question, this application of the Word in life, business, and family may result in being taken advantage of by others. Still, obedience to the Word of God is paramount in maintaining that which is primary to the Following-Leader, a continuing intimacy with the Lord Jesus Christ.

For Following-Leaders, the Bible establishes both their ethic and worldview. The Bible determines their core values which in turn affect how they make decisions, the direction and goals for their life and ministry, how to resolve conflicts, as well as set priorities for themselves and the ministry.[5] Knowing the Bible and applying its teachings to life is the daily practice of the Following-Leader.

3. Love and Seek to Understand People

One of the sweetest expressions of care in the New Testament is seen when Paul sends Timothy to the church at Philippi because "I have no one else of kindred spirit who will genuinely be concerned for your welfare. For they all seek after their own interests, not those of Christ Jesus" (Philippians 2:20-21). Paul often shared his heart of love and concern with the churches. Consider Paul's words when He wrote the Thessalonians in 1 Thessalonians 2:1-12:

But we were gentle among you, just as a nursing mother cherishes her own children. So, affectionately longing for you, we were well pleased to impart to you not only the gospel of God, but also our own lives, because you had become dear to us. For you remember, brethren, our labor and toil; for laboring night and day, that we might not be a burden to any of you, we preached to you the gospel of God. You are witnesses, and God also, how devoutly and justly and blamelessly we behaved ourselves among you who believe; as you know how we exhorted, and comforted, and charged every one of you, as a father does his own children, that you would walk worthy of God who calls you into His own kingdom and glory.

Even though he has spiritual authority as an apostle, Paul's self-perception is not as a supervisor, leader, or authority figure, but as a nursing mother and a caring father. Paul understood that the church, with all her faults, is still the Bride of Christ who must be cherished and nurtured.

Paul could write these words because of his deep understanding of the love of Christ (2 Corinthians 5:14). Paul had been a recipient of the compassion and love of Christ, a gift which he never forgot or took for granted. Following-Leaders emulate this same type of compassion for others.

In Matthew 9:35-38 when Jesus saw the people as sheep without a shepherd, Matthew shares that Jesus was "moved with compassion."

Then Jesus went about all the cities and villages, teaching in their synagogues, preaching the gospel of the kingdom, and healing every sickness and every disease among the people. But when He saw the multitudes, He was moved with compassion for them, because they were weary and scattered, like sheep having no shepherd. Then He said to His disciples, "The harvest truly is plentiful, but the laborers are few. Therefore pray the Lord of the harvest to send out laborers into His harvest."

The word "compassion" can be literally translated "moved in the bowels."[6] Put in everyday language; the word compassion conveys the idea that when Jesus saw the plight of the multitude, such an emotional experience literally made His stomach hurt. If we are to follow Jesus, we, too must demonstrate similar compassion.

Following-Leaders realize that everyone in the church is broken in some way. God has populated His church with persons whom the world system designates as losers. Consider what Paul says in 1 Corinthians 1:26-31:

> For you see your calling, brethren, that not many wise according to the flesh, not many mighty, not many noble, are called. But God has chosen the foolish things of the world to put to shame the wise, and God has chosen the weak things of the world to put to shame the things which are mighty; and the base things of the world and the things which are despised God has chosen, and the things which are not, to bring to nothing the things that are, that no flesh should glory in His presence. But of Him you are in Christ Jesus, who became for us wisdom from God — and righteousness and sanctification and redemption — that, as it is written, "He who glories, let him glory in the LORD."

Jesus points out in Luke 14:21 that it is "the poor, and the maimed, and the lame and the blind" who will be invited to the banquet table of His blessing. All of us who populate the church fall into this category. We are nothing special in ourselves. God has extended His grace toward us and we must never forget from where we came. Additionally, if we would lead a church of the foolish and the weak, does it not follow that the leaders would be the weakest and the most foolish of all?

4. Develop Integrity

As we have already mentioned, some of the most highly prized values that researchers contend are essential to good leaders are clearly taught in the Scriptures.[7] Some of these values are:

(a) Honesty - "You shall have honest scales, honest weights" (Leviticus 19:36).
(b) Integrity - "The integrity of the upright will guide them but the perversity of the unfaithful will destroy them" (Proverbs 11:3).
(c) Justice - "You shall do no injustice in judgment. You shall not be partial to the poor nor honor the person of the mighty. In righteousness you shall judge your neighbor" (Leviticus 19:15).
(d) Humility - "Humble yourself in the eyes of the Lord, and He will lift you up" (James 4:10).

Following-Leaders need to examine their personal beliefs and values to determine the basis for their decision making. Moving away from biblical core values may be subtly incremental. However, over time these subtle actions are extremely detrimental to achieving the overall purpose of the church.

The essence of the word integrity is wholeness. As followers of Christ, we are complete in Him (Colossians 2:10). However, if we allow compromise to enter our decision making process at the level of our core values, we run the risk of losing our influence in the lives of others. The essence of the Following-Leader's personal integrity is pleasing God in all we say and do. 1 Thessalonians 2:1-6 outlines Paul's personal integrity:

> For you yourselves know, brethren, that our coming to you was not in vain. But even after we had suffered before and were spitefully treated at Philippi, as you know, we were bold in our God to speak to you the gospel of God in much conflict. For our exhortation did not come from error or uncleanness, nor was it in deceit. But as we have been approved by God to be entrusted with the gospel, even so we speak, not as pleasing men, but God who tests our hearts. For neither at any time did we use flattering words, as you know, nor a cloak for covetousness — God is witness. Nor did we seek glory from men, either from you or from others, when we might have made demands as apostles of Christ.

The Following-Leader speaks, "...not as pleasing men, but God who tests our hearts." Being sensitive to the promptings of the Holy Spirit, the Following-Leader speaks the truths of the Bible even when unpopular with the hearers. This does not mean there will never be a time when the Following-Leader misspeaks. However, being sensitive to the Holy Spirit, the Following-Leader will humble himself or herself before others and make the needed correction so that truth might prevail.

5. Develop Avenues of Influence

The primary desire of the Following-Leader is following the will of the Lord and is evidenced through many different leader styles. Certain leadership theories lend themselves well to the Following-Leader perspective. Space will not permit a full explanation of these theories. However, below is a brief overview of some of the more pertinent leadership theories and styles that are congruent with a followerfirst perspective:

Leader-Member Exchange

The Leader-Member Exchange theory (LMX)[8] focuses on the interactions between leaders and followers. It is "the only leadership approach that makes the concept of the dyadic relationship the centerpiece of leadership process."[9] The theory posits that within organizations, leaders build relationships with *in-group* persons (those who take on greater responsibilities and build relationship with the leader) and with *out-group* persons (those content with a more formal, job description-driven relationship to the leader). These relationships are built upon an exchange where the leader does more for those followers who are in the in-group than those who, because of their lack of involvement in the leader-follower relationship, become the out-group.

It is not uncommon for persons to consider certain aspects of the Courageous Follower and Exemplary Follower theories to be expressions of the LMX Theory. At first glance, such a comparison does lend itself to consider courageous followers to be those in the in-group and all other follower types to compose the out-group. However, such an observation fails to consider that the LMX theory considers the activities of the leader toward the follower as the one building the relationship rather than the follower initiating the relationship and supporting the leader. This distinction is important when considering the LMX theory in relation to the followerfirst perspective.

The followerfirst perspective perceives the in-group relationship as one that the follower is responsible to build rather than depending and waiting on the initiation of the leader. The follower understands his/her role as being the one who moves close to the leader and seeks to meet the leader's needs.

Additionally, the followerfirst follower understands that the quality of the relationship between the follower and the leader is not built upon a desire for exchanges offered by the leader. These potential benefits offered by the leader to the follower are inconsequential as the biblical follower seeks to fulfill his/her duty to the leader. The basis for the relationship is not built upon what the follower can *get* from the relationship as much as what the follower can *give* to the relationship. This attitude of an "unprofitable servant" (Luke 17:10) carries over into all aspects of the follower's role and responsibility within the organization.

Charismatic Leadership

Although not used in the theological sense of a person having the spiritual gift of speaking in tongues, charismatic leaders were initially defined by Max Weber[10] as those who have special personality characteristics that give a person superhuman or exceptional powers reserved for a few, are of divine origin, and result in the person being treated as a leader.[11] This view resonates with those who hold to leaders being born with certain traits that propel them into leading roles within organizations.

Robert House[12] suggested that charismatic leaders display six specific behaviors:

1. They set a strong role model for the beliefs and values they want their followers to adopt.
2. They appear competent to followers.
3. They articulate ideological goals that have moral overtones.
4. They communicate high expectations for followers.
5. They exhibit confidence in followers' abilities to meet these expectations.
6. They arouse task-relevant motives in followers that may include affiliation, power, or esteem.[13]

Those Following-Leaders who are gifted to communicate may find this ability allows them to build trust with their fellow followers as they seek to accomplish the church's goals. One aspect of this leadership style that needs to be guarded is that followers may have a tendency to become so enamored with the leader they begin to follow without question. This unquestioning acceptance may need to be diverted away from the human leader and toward the person of Jesus Christ. Additionally, the charismatic leader is prone to begin seeking power through other people rather than following the Lord Jesus. This *gift* then becomes the cause for many being led astray from an intimate relationship with the Lord in exchange for a temporary relationship with the leader.

Transformational Leadership

Introduced in 1978 by James MacGregor Burns,[14] the transformational leadership theory sought to link the role of leaders and followers. Transformational leadership may be defined as,

> a process whereby a person engages with others and creates a connection that raises the level of motivation and morality in both the leader and the follower. This type of leader is

211

attentive to the needs and motives of followers and tries to help followers reach their fullest potential.[15]

Bernard Bass[16] extended the work of Burns by arguing there are four distinct factors involved in the transformational leadership process:

1. **Idealized Influence**

   It describes leaders who act as strong role models for followers; followers identify with these leaders and want very much to emulate them. These leaders usually have very high standards of moral and ethical conduct and can be counted on to do the right thing. They are deeply respected by followers, who usually place a great deal of trust in them. They provide followers with a vision and a sense of mission.[17]

2. **Inspirational Motivation**

   This factor is descriptive of leaders who communicate high expectations to followers, inspiring them through motivation to become committed to and part of the shared vision in the organization. In practice, leaders use symbols and emotional appeals to focus group members' efforts to achieve more than they would in their own self-interest.[18]

3. **Intellectual Stimulation**

   It includes leadership that stimulates followers to be creative and innovative and to challenge their own beliefs and values as well as those of the leader and the organization. This type of leadership supports followers as they try new approaches and develop innovative ways of dealing with organizational issues. It encourages followers to think things out on their own and engage in careful problem solving.[19]

4. **Individualized Consideration**

   This factor is representative of leaders who provide a supportive climate in which they listen carefully to the individual needs of followers. Leaders act as coaches and advisers while trying to assist followers in becoming fully actualized. These leaders may use delegation to help followers grow through personal challenges.[20]

The Following-Leader may take on the characteristics of a Transformational Leader as he or she seeks to inspire his or her followers to achieve even greater things to the glory of God. The Transformational Leader style is preferred over the Transactional Leader style because Transactional Leaders rely upon a negotiated exchange relationship with the follower in which the leader agrees to provide certain benefits when the follower fulfills the wishes of the leader. The Following-Leader seeks to raise the level of the leader-follower relationship to one in which both leader and follower are responding based upon a common desire to honor God. The Following-Leader also understands that it is the role and responsibility of the Holy Spirit to inspire (John 6:44; John 15:5). All appreciation or adulation from others is quickly deflected to the ultimate leader, the Lord Jesus Christ.

Servant Leadership

Introduced by Robert Greenleaf in 1977,[21] the servant leadership model has become quite popular within the church. Greenleaf developed his theory after reading Hermann Hesse's novel, *Journey to the East*, a story about a group of people on a spiritual quest. Greenleaf determined that a great leader is first experienced by others as a servant. Thus, the greatness of a leader rests with his or her willingness to serve others.

Such a concept is well received by many Christians because of Jesus' emphasizing His role as a servant when He said in Matthew 20:28, "...the Son of Man did not come to be served, but to serve, and to give His life a ransom for many." Additionally, Jesus emphasized the servant role His disciples should take when He said in Matthew 20:26, "Whoever desires to become great among you, let him be your servant."

Larry Spears, President and CEO of the Spears Center for Servant-Leadership (www.spearscenter.org), has extracted a set of ten characteristics of servant leaders:[22]

1. *Listening:*
   He or she seeks to listen receptively to what is being said and not said.

2. People need to be accepted and recognized for their special and unique spirits.

3. *Healing:*
   Although this is a part of being human, servant-leaders recognize that they have an opportunity to "help make whole" those with whom they come in contact.

4. *Awareness:*
   General awareness, and especially self-awareness, strengthens the servant-leader.

5. *Persuasion:*
   The servant-leader seeks to convince others, rather than coerce compliance.

6. *Conceptualization:*
   Servant-leaders seek to nurture their abilities to "dream great dreams."

7. *Foresight:*
   Foresight is a characteristic that enables the servant-leader to understand the lessons from the past, the realities of the present, and the likely consequence of a decision for the future. It is also deeply rooted within the intuitive mind deserving of careful attention.

8. *Stewardship:*
   Robert Greenleaf's view of all institutions was one in which CEOs, staffs, and trustees all played significant roles in holding their institutions in trust for the greater good of society.

9. *Commitment to the growth of people:*
   Servant-leaders believe that people have an intrinsic value beyond their tangible contributions as workers.

10. *Building community:*
    Greenleaf said: "All that is needed to rebuild community as a viable life form for large numbers of people is for enough servant-leaders to show the way, not by mass movements, but by each servant-leader demonstrating his own unlimited liability for a quite specific community-related group."

Another scholar, Kathleen Patterson, understands servant leadership as a virtuous theory by which the servant leader's focus is follower-focused rather than primarily focused on organizational objectives. Patterson suggests that there are seven virtuous constructs present in the process of servant leadership.[23] They are:

1. Agapao – A Greek term for moral love that seeks to do the right thing at the right time.
2. Humility – The trait of keeping one's accomplishments and talents in perspective.
3. Altruism – A concern for the welfare of others.
4. Vision – The capacity to see others as worthy and seeks to assist each person in reaching that state.
5. Trust – An essential component of the follower/leader relationship built upon mutual respect and integrity.
6. Empowerment – Giving power to others.
7. Service – Giving of oneself.

Figure 11 illustrates Patterson's model by which servant leaders influence others. By leading with Agapao, the leader exhibits humility and altruism. These two constructs interact with vision and trust ultimately resulting in empowering others. The ultimate goal of this empowerment is service.

Figure 11: Patterson's Servant Leadership Model[24]

Perhaps the followerfirst perspective can best apply to servant leadership as an answer to the questions posed by Peter Senge in the afterward of Greenleaf's, *Servant Leadership*. Senge inquires:

> What does it take to cultivate a genuine desire to serve? I can't think of any more important question. What keeps us from accessing, realizing, and acting from an innate desire to serve? I do not think these questions have simple answers. But I do think they are the right questions. The answers have to be personal. They also have to be situational. But this is where the journey starts.[25]

What does it take to cultivate a genuine desire to serve? The followerfirst perspective would say it takes a life made new by the Lord Jesus Christ. What keeps us from accessing, realizing, and acting from an innate desire to serve? The Bible makes it clear that our basic sinfulness, our selfish desires to be served rather than serve others, is the greatest hindrance to being true servants to others. Senge is correct. The answers do have to be personal, but they are not situational. The followerfirst perspective of Following-Leaders operates from a pan-cultural perspective. Following-Leaders are who they are regardless of the situation. Their motivation, purpose, and desire do not change from context to context. This sense of stability gives the Following-Leader the integrity he or she needs to face the challenges of influencing others, and it gives followers the consistency they need to trust and be trusted by their leaders.

Because Following-Leaders base their leading on a followerfirst perspective, they may embrace many leader styles. The leader style of the Following-Leader is contingent upon the personality, giftedness, training, and spiritual maturity of the particular Following-Leader. In one instance the Following-Leader may manifest more service orientation and in another he/she may evidence more inspiration. Following-Leaders understand that God superintends over each follower-leader context and through the Holy Spirit will enable them to perform in a style that best brings glory to God. Thus, Following-Leaders seek to concentrate on being who they are in Christ and leading from this position.

Following-Leader Responses to Following-Leaders

Following-Leaders make the best responders to other Following-Leaders who are in positions of authority. These Following-Leaders recognize that the person in authority has responsibilities and that the followers will play a crucial role in the success or failure of the one in authority. Therefore, because Following-Leaders who lead are clear with regard to whom and what they follow, it is easy for Following-Leaders who follow to respond positively to the leader. These followers take the lead in responding to the leaders and give joy to the leader. This, "How can we help?" and "How can we serve?" attitude creates an atmosphere of mutual respect and trust.

To the Charismatic Following-Leader the follower responds positively to his/her beliefs and values because the follower's values are congruent with that of the leader. Followers rally to the charismatic Following-Leader because their ideological goals and morals are shared thus creating a dynamic of mutual high expectation and confidence to meet these expectations. Followerfirst followers do not idolize these leaders, but they do enjoy their company because of their mutual love for and expressions of love to the Lord Jesus Christ.

To the Transformational Following-Leader, the follower responds in ways that help accentuate the leader's style. **Idealized Influence** is recognized through the modeling of the leader and because this modeling is exactly how the follower acts and responds, a positive follower response serves to reinforce the moral and ethical conduct of the leader. Open communication between follower and leader allows the vision of the follower and the vision of the leader to be respectfully shared, discussed, and implemented. The **Inspirational Motivation** of the leader is matched by the inspired motivation of the follower. Because the follower shares the high expectation of the leader, little is needed by way of symbols and emotional appeals to motivate the follower to action. The humility and selflessness of the follower often inspires the leader to greater acts of selfless leading and serving. **Intellectual Stimulation** is a reciprocal relationship. Because neither the leader nor the follower considers himself or herself to be *the* authority or expert on a matter, there is always an atmosphere of openness to new ideas and mutual encouragement to learn. Creativity by all is embraced with enthusiasm and new ways of dealing with situations are celebrated as long as they adhere to biblical teaching. Followers embrace the **Individualized Consideration** of the leader and understand that he/she has strengths and weaknesses. Follower acceptance of personality quirks and not demanding that the leader be perfect allow the leader to embrace his/her humanity and become more authentic before the followers. This, in turn, creates a greater level of trust and respect resulting in greater productivity on the part of leader and follower.

To the Servant Leader, followers readily embrace and reciprocate the desire to serve. Followers exemplify all ten of Sperry's traits and contextualize them toward the leader. Followers listen to leaders, have empathy for them and their positions, are aware of their power to make or break the leader, use persuasion rather than demanding when dealing with the leader, are able to conceptualize the big picture of their part in the leadership process, have foresight to think beyond the moment, understand their role within the organization as a steward, are committed to the growth of the leader and other followers around them, and build community within the organization by following biblical principles of giving, loving, and serving one-another. This servant spirit is even more manifest when those served respond in similar fashion to the one serving. Leadership scholar, Bruce Winston, accentuates this point by expanding Patterson's servant leadership model to include a reciprocal response from the follower to the leader. Of this response Winston stated:

> The second half of the story occurs when the leader's service results in a change in the follower's sense of love. The follower's Agapao love results in an increase in both the commitment to the leader and the follower's own self-efficacy. The higher levels of commitment and self-efficacy result in a higher level of intrinsic motivation that lead to a higher level of altruism toward the leader and the leader's desire to see the organization do well. This leads to higher levels of service to the leader.[26]

This "second half of the story" of the follower's response closes the loop on the servant leader/follower relationship. Winston's expanded model takes into account the influential role of the follower responding to the Servant Leader. Winston understands this interaction as a cause-effect relationship between the servant leader upon the follower. The followerfirst perspective would suggest that rather than a linear cause-effect relationship, follower responses are the result of inherent biblical follower characteristics responding to the needs of the Following-Leader who is manifesting Servant Leader characteristics.

Leading Where You Don't Want To Go

Following-Leaders are known not so much for their gifts, talents, or abilities, as for their hearts that beat with the same desire for the glory of God as that of the Lord Jesus. This is never truer than when the providence of God allows the Following-Leader to enter the crucible of trial. The Bible is replete with references to the difficult plight of the early Christian church and the numerous trials the people went through for the sake of Christ. James wrote that various trials test our faith and produced patience (James 1:2-4). Peter wrote that our trials were a testing fire of the genuineness of our faith (1 Peter 1:6-9). Paul wrote that through a great trial of affliction the Corinthian church gave liberally (2 Corinthians 8:2). The writer of Hebrews recalls:

> Others were tortured, not accepting deliverance, that they might obtain a better resurrection. Still others had trial of mockings and scourgings, yes, and of chains and imprisonment. They were stoned, they were sawn in two, were tempted, were slain with the sword. They wandered about in sheepskins and goatskins, being destitute, afflicted, tormented — of whom the world was not worthy. They wandered in deserts and mountains, in dens and caves of the earth (Hebrews 11:35-38).

Persevering through trial is the hallmark of the faithful believer. Following-Leaders accept the path set before them by the Lord and seek to glorify God with their responses, all the while seeking to influence others to do the same. This is never more true that when the Following-Leader fills the role of pastor in a local congregation. It is not uncommon for some within the congregation to become disenchanted with the pastor. This process may begin with a perceived snub or a lack of ministry to a family member or dissatisfaction with the Sunday morning messages. More egregious is the person who, because of fear that they will lose power in the church, begins to sabotage the work of the pastor. Regardless of the origins, these detractors begin a process of whittling away the pastor's reputation. This ungodly act of character assassination serves to undermine the pastor's credibility, and if the lies and slander are believed by enough people, the pastor may be asked to resign or even fired.

Within these tempest-filled environments, the pastor, as a Following-Leader, has an opportunity to witness to the sovereign supply of the Father. When those employing these despicable tactics expect a similar ungodly response, the pastor can glorify God by not responding in kind, but by blessing those who stand against him. Rather than defend himself, the Following-Leader is willing to:

(1) Place himself in the hands of the Father,
(2) Assess whether or not there is some truth to the charges,
(3) Make appropriate changes to behavior,
(4) Remain faithful to the task at hand.

The Following-Leader understands that ministry is difficult and there are no guarantees that faithful service will be rewarded with human gratitude.

Additionally, fellow Following-Leaders serving with the pastor (staff members and members of the church) have the opportunity and responsibility to put down rumors and backbiting. As the Apostle Paul wrote in Ephesians 4:29-32:

> Let no corrupt communication proceed out of your mouth, but that which is good to the use of edifying, that it may minister grace unto the hearers. And grieve not the Holy Spirit of God, whereby ye are sealed unto the day of

redemption. Let all bitterness, and wrath, and anger, and clamor, and evil speaking, be put away from you, with all malice: and be ye kind one to another, tenderhearted, forgiving one another, even as God for Christ's sake hath forgiven you.

In this passage, as well as others (2 Corinthians 12:20; Colossians 3:8; Titus 3:2; James 4:11; 1 Peter 2:1), it is clear that those who follow the Lord Jesus and the teachings of Scripture will need to be Following-Leaders when it comes to putting down wrath and anger within the Body of Christ. Following-Leaders (I am not talking about pastoral staff here), humbly willing to risk rejection by fellow members will need to confront others of their error for the sake of the unity of the church. In the followerfirst perspective, church discipline is a function and responsibility of the *whole* body. The pastor is not perceived as the spiritual principal to whom every infraction of biblical deportment is brought. Each Following-Leader has the responsibility to immediately address the infraction and gently lead the person in error to confront their sin, repent, and be restored. There may be occasion when the infraction is so egregious within the church body that the Pastor needs to be informed and he and the others leaders need to act. However, Following-Leaders are responsible for addressing common mistakes before they have time to grow into larger problems. Let me quickly add that this responsibility does not create a type of spiritual police state in which some take it upon themselves to police everyone and become someone else's 'Holy Spirit.' On the contrary, within the organization with a followerfirst perspective, all responsibilities are carried out with a spirit of humility, love, and gentleness. The power of submission is exercised and the church operates with an atmosphere of love for the Lord, love for others, and submission to the authority of God's Word (see Chapter 6 on the Power of Submission).

I sometimes tell my ministerial students that I have an idea as to why they are in class being tormented by me and why they are currently serving in difficult situations. The reason is, like me, they prayed a prayer once that went something like this, "Father, I want to be more like Jesus." Now, here we are, serving in difficult situations, being talked about poorly, having people lie about us, gnash their teeth at us, sabotage our plans, and call us just about everything we can imagine. Does that sound a little like how Jesus was treated? Rejoice; we haven't been whipped, beaten over the head with rods, had a crown of thorns placed on our heads or been crucified...at least not yet.

Still, as Following-Leaders, we have been called to serve the Lord Jesus regardless of the circumstances. Jesus said,

> "Truly, truly, I say to you, unless a grain of wheat falls into the earth and dies, it remains by itself alone; but if it dies, it bears much fruit. He who loves his life loses it; and he who hates this life in this world shall keep it to life eternal. If anyone serves Me, let him follow Me; and where I am, there shall My servant also be; if anyone serves Me, the Father will honor him" (John 12:24-26).

If we are to serve Jesus, we are to follow Him. Where He is, there will I, His servant, be. Following-Leaders are servants of the suffering servant. It is little wonder that we should be mistreated because the spirit of those who refused to follow Jesus still remains in some within the church. We have given our lives in service to the Lord. It is His prerogative where He should lead. My role, my honor, is to follow. He may lead me in paths where I would prefer not to travel. Still, the life of the Following-Leader is not directed by preference but by obedience. If it be the will of God, the Following-Leader will serve the Lord in obscurity. He will eschew the cries of friends and family that he is much more worthy of a larger pulpit or a larger responsibility within the church. He will cast aside his own desires that might cry out for recognition from peers, colleagues, or the media. The Following-Leader understands that he is guaranteed one honor, and his recognition will come from only one source, and it is enough to make life worth living. Jesus said, "If anyone serves Me, the Father will honor him." The Following-Leader assumes the same role as that of Paul (Romans 1:1; Galatians 1:10; Titus 1:1), James (James 1:1), and Peter (2 Peter 1:1) who took the appellation "bondservant."[27] These Following-Leaders understood their role was to do the will of their Master, the Lord Jesus Christ. As bondservants they surely followed the same guidelines as those actual bondservants whom Paul instructed to:

> ... obey in all things your masters according to the flesh, not with eyeservice, as men-pleasers, but in sincerity of heart, fearing God. And whatever you do, do it heartily, as to the Lord and not to men, knowing that from the Lord you will receive the reward of the inheritance; for you serve the Lord Christ (Colossians 3:22).

As followers of the Lord Jesus Christ, these bondservants have a reward. Their reward, as for all who follow the Lord Jesus, is the, "Well done" (Matthew 25:21) they will hear from the lips of God the Father.

Empower, Enable or Ennoble

In many leadership books you will read how leaders are to 'empower' those around them. The term usually refers to leaders delegating some of their perceived 'power' to others in order for them to accomplish a task. It is not a term that is often used in the followerfirst perspective because the idea of power is actually centered in the person of Christ. All believers are 'empowered' by the Holy Spirit to obey Christ and the Scripture.

The term, empower, also carries with it an imbedded slight toward followers. The idea of empowerment can sometimes be a subtle way of identifying the 'haves' and the 'have nots.' Someone may think, "Because I am the leader, I have power. You are just a follower and are dependent upon me to allocate some of my power to you." Such thinking would obviously be a cynical view of the term. Still, it is not unlikely that some would use the idea of empowering others in this way.

In a more generous (and perhaps more accurately intended) interpretation, the idea of empowering is a way of expressing how leaders build up their followers in order for the followers to gain a greater sense of confidence and accomplishment. We can see this idea evidenced in the transformational leader theory. Still, Following-Leaders are not focused on the idea of 'power' and thus the term is not one that I would suggest be used in a role and responsibility type of organizational culture.

The term enable may be a better way of expressing how Following-Leaders influence those around them to accomplish the common purpose. The idea of enabling reflects an idea of the leader being 'able' and the followers needing the leader to make them 'able.' This can be understood when the leader provides the training and tools necessary for followers to become 'able' to accomplish a task, thus giving the followers a greater sense of accomplishment.

Within the followerfirst perspective, all believers are enabled to follow Christ by the Holy Spirit. He gives gifts to those within the Body of Christ and simultaneously empowers the willing believer to follow the will of the Father. All of the skill in the world will not benefit the church in the least without a Spirit-led willingness to use these skills to the glory of God.

The best use of the term 'enable' is when Following-Leaders seek to find ways to increase their own skill sets and abilities as well as those around them. Rather than seeing themselves as enablers, Following-Leaders understand their own need for improvement and dependence upon the Holy Spirit to work within the hearts of others. Following-Leaders resist the temptation to 'fake it till you make it.'

Thus, 'enabling' is a realization that every person in the leadership process needs constant and continuous improvement. Openness in the leadership process allows those in leader roles to recognize and admit their needs and for followers to recognize and admit their shortcomings. This mutual recognition of dependence results in a cooperative effort to gain the skills needed to accomplish the task.

Even when interpreted in its best sense, the terms empower and enable do not grasp the entirety of the Following-Leader's roll in the life of followers. Therefore, I suggest the term ennoble. When Following-Leaders seek to ennoble others, they focus first on the dignity of each person as having worth as a human being. This realization provides the basis for understanding that although people will have different talents, personalities, and skills, all are worthy of respect and time. Following-Leaders establish systems whereby all within the Body of Christ are equipped to serve according to their gifts.

Second, Following-Leaders ennoble others by focusing the attention of the person on who they are in Christ. As we have already said, followers must understand and embrace their identity in Christ (see chapter 4). By realizing who they are in Christ, followers develop a self-confidence that is actually a Christ-confidence. This confidence manifests itself through followers exercising the power of submission and developing a positive attitude toward the challenges they face.

Third, when followers understand their worth to God and gain a dependent Christ-confidence, Following-Leaders can then join them in a search for more information on how to accomplish the will of God. This information may take the form of developing systems to release people to do the will of God without the bottle-neck of administrative bureaucracy. It may take the form of further instruction on specific tasks from subject matter experts. Whatever the form this information takes, it serves to produce a *self-efficacy*[28] within the thinking of both the Following-Leader and the followers.

A biblical understanding of self-efficacy understands that God does not work around persons but through persons to accomplish His will. People are not an impediment to God but rather the privileged 'instruments' He has chosen to be led by His hand to accomplish His will. Personal self-efficacy suggests that with every capacity of our being (through what we have to bring to his service and even what we do not have) we have worth and value and ability to accomplish God's will through a synergistic relationship with God the Holy Spirit.

Ennobling others to follow Christ allows the Following-Leader to avoid directing, commanding, or demanding. By growing *with* those they influence, Following-Leaders effectively build trust and are able to walk life's journey together with those they lead.

Conclusion

The followerfirst perspective understands every position within the church as being of extreme importance in the fulfillment of the will of God. Following-Leaders understand their influence is not based upon perceived authority or position within the organization but upon their personal obedience to follow Christ and the Word of God in every endeavor. Gone are the self-assessed excuses for not participating in the life of the church because, "I'm just a layman," or, "I'm just a volunteer." With a followerfirst perspective permeating the church, gone are the self-defeating self-perceptions of inadequacy. It may be true that a particular follower does not have as much talent, personality, or capacity when compared to another. Gratefully, the followerfirst perspective renders this comparison moot because Following-Leaders follow with the talents God has given, influence through the personality God has given, and operate within the church with the capacity God has given. There is no longer any need to look for potential. As one coach for whom I played said, "Potential sits on the bench. I need someone who can play now." Following-Leaders are those who embrace Christ's commands *now*. There is growth to be had emotionally, intellectually, and spiritually. Yet, Following-Leaders act, respond, and obey in the now. They do not wait for when they think they are ready. When God provides the opportunity, they respond. The call is to follow. The response is immediate.

As recognized leaders in the church, Following-Leaders understand that their influence may be manifested through various leadership styles. It will take study and time to sharpen their capacity for influencing others. Still, these leaders recognize the fulfillment of the church's mission is primarily contingent upon those Following-Leaders who serve with the recognized leader. Developing leader styles is important but is secondary to followers developing the character, integrity, and consistency of being a biblical follower. It is when these spirit-filled, God-fearing, Christ-loving, followers act in obedience to the word of God they actually live out what it means to be Following-Leaders.

RETHINK

As leaders and followers are developed within the church, the following steps may be helpful in first changing the thinking and then changing the behaviors of those within the church:

1. Take a survey of the church to determine how the people define leadership.
2. Include in this survey questions regarding the people's view of the responsibilities leaders.
3. Teach a series of lessons on the followerfirst perspective, correcting errant thoughts revealed through the survey.
4. Begin to place an emphasis on followers of Christ. Make this term the preferred descriptor of both leaders and followers within the church.
5. Introduce the term, Following-Leaders. Explain how followers of Christ operate within this framework.
6. Ask the question, "Who am I seeking to ennoble?"
7. Find your leader style and encourage others to find theirs as well. This may be accomplished through teaching the styles presented in this chapter.
8. Celebrate the obedience of those who are seeking to act as Following-Leaders.

Part IV

Develop a Follower Culture

Chapter 9

Embedding a
followerfirst Culture

As any young pastor would be, I was thrilled to pastor my first church. I had gone through the candidate process along with my new wife, and the search committee and the church asked me to be the pastor of a new start-up church. I was told by several that the choice was made not so much because of me, but because of my talented and beautiful wife. I have no doubt this is the case.

I was fresh out of seminary and ready to bring the world to Christ. The church was a new mission start and had already suffered some setbacks. The church and I began our journey together amicably enough. The people were supportive and tolerated my new ideas with grace. Of course, being a Baptist church, every decision had to go through a committee of some kind and this slowed decision making to a crawl. Still, we plodded along and the church grew. Finally the day came when I suggested something far outside the congregation's comfort zone.

Growing churches need space, and usually space is a premium. The room in which we conducted our worship services was the largest space in our building, and because we had pews, we could not have any other function in that space. My suggestion was to sell the pews and buy padded, interlocking chairs we could stack during the week and hold mid-week children's events in the same space. Then the fun began. I held meeting after meeting with the church body (about 80 people at the time) explaining the benefits of ministering to others by using the space for more than Sunday worship. Although those in opposition were not vicious, they did have very strongly held opinions and reservations. What will this do to the sanctuary? What about a center aisle for weddings? Won't this have more wear and tear on the carpet? Who will be responsible for moving the chairs? We have never worshipped in chairs before.

Working through the questions, the decision was finally made to sell the pews and purchase chairs. For my remaining four years at the church the chairs functioned exactly as predicted. They were comfortable, functional, and as the church grew, we simply bought more chairs. After five years of ministry, I was offered the opportunity to pastor another start-up church, and I agreed. We left our first church on good terms. Yes, we had had our struggles and our misunderstandings. Some had left the church for various reasons and that hurt me, but my overall assessment of our years of service was positive.

After a few years of ministry in the new church, I had the occasion of being in the city in which my first church was located. I decided to drive by and see what changes had taken place while I was gone. When I arrived, I noticed that things looked the same. The building was locked so I had to look through a window to see inside. When I did, I was shocked to see that in the space where we met for worship the chairs were gone and the pews were back. You can imagine my chagrin when I realized that the change that I led the congregation to adopt was not change at all. It was simply tolerance.

I realize now that the real message behind the questions and the resistance was, "Pastor, we can't really have a church unless we have pews." What I failed to recognize was that although the change for me was functional, the change for the people was cultural. These dear people had a deep seated belief of what worship was and what was required to have worship. They tolerated my wild ideas until I left and then moved back into their cultural norm where things looked like church.

If I could teach one lesson to young seminary students regarding how to operate within the church, I would teach them how to recognize, operate within, and change organizational culture. If I had known that all organizations have a culture, I could have saved myself and those to whom I ministered a tremendous amount of grief and heartache. Every church, whether old or newly planted, has an organizational culture that must be recognized if long-lasting change occurs. In my first church I had successfully changed the furniture, but I had failed to change the culture. If we are to embrace the followerfirst perspective of leading within a church, the change must begin at the deepest level of the church's culture.

What is Organizational Culture?

Initially, I hesitated to introduce this subject. Organizational culture and how to change it are such important aspects to every organization I did not think that a cursory introduction of the subject would do it justice. Yet, if we embrace a followerfirst perspective of ministry in our churches, such a way of looking at life and ministry is so different from the norm that there is no way the church culture would not be impacted. Therefore, the following is a brief overview of how to embed a followerfirst perspective in the church with the hope that you will study the matter in more detail later.

Edgar Schein's work, *Organizational Culture and Leadership*,[1] is the source from which I draw many of these steps to create a followerfirst culture. Although Schein posits his insights from a leader's perspective, the followerfirst perspective recognizes that every follower in the organization has the responsibility to understand, operate within and, if necessary, change his/her organizational culture. It may be that the recognized leaders of an organization have an advantage in effecting the organization's culture but, as we will see, followers have an important part to play in this process as well.

Organizational culture is defined as:

A pattern of shared basic assumptions that was learned by a group as it solved its problems of external adaptation and internal integration that has worked well enough to be considered valid and therefore to be taught to new members as the correct way to perceive, think, and feel in relation to those problems.[2]

233

Breaking this definition into a few key phrases, perhaps we can gain a better grasp of the idea of organizational culture. The first phrase is, "A pattern of shared basic assumptions that was learned by a group...." When Schein writes of "basic assumptions," he refers to three specific levels of organizational culture.

1. *Artifacts* – "... the phenomena that one sees, hears, and feels when one encounters a new group with an unfamiliar culture."[3] These phenomena include architecture, language, technology and artistic creations. In the church setting we might include pews, stained glass, crosses, certain furniture, etc. as evidence of certain beliefs and assumptions that a group of people have. One must be careful, however, not to draw too many conclusions based on these evidences without investigating the deeper values and assumptions attached to these artifacts.

2. *Espoused Beliefs and Values* – originate through a process where persons agree with a recognized leader what ought to be done, act on that approach and, finding that the approach is successful, incorporate the approach or belief as a part of the organizations 'way of doing things.' The longer these actions continue to work "they gradually become transformed into nondiscussible [sic] assumptions supported by articulated sets of beliefs, norms, and operational rules of behavior."[4] In others words, the espoused beliefs and values of an organization are the, "That's just the way we do things around here," types of activities and actions that all organizations have. Such espoused beliefs may or may not be congruent with the next level of organizational culture.

3. *Basic Underlying Assumptions* – "...the implicit assumptions that actually guide behavior, that tell group members how to perceive, think about, and feel about things."[5] Another way of addressing this level of culture is to recognize this as the organization's predominate world view. Depending

234

on the church, this worldview may be formed by the Bible, the church's history, or even denominational tradition.

It is important to note that this pattern of basic underlying assumptions, according to the definition above, was learned by a group. Each one of us has a personal set of values by which we live our lives and interpret life events. However, it is when individuals of like values gather together as a group for a stated purpose that the group will decide which of the individual group member's values will be incorporated into the DNA of the newly formed organization. Leaders arise from the group because the group is willing to vest certain persons with the responsibility of guarding these congruent values. It is these values that the group adopts as those that can address the next part of the definition.

The group adopts this pattern of shared values because this pattern seems to have "solved its [the organization's] problems of external adaptation and internal integration."[6] When the group initially agrees on shared values for the organization, the organization immediately faces problems related to its existence. The underlying question is, "How will we survive?" This is a question that is faced by every church, whether new or old, and is answered by the group's shared values and assumptions. The question of survival concerns itself with external adaptation; that is, how will the organization relate to and thrive within the surrounding environment. The question of survival also includes issues of internal integration, or, stated another way, how we get along with one another. The issue of survival gives organizational culture its power. This pattern of shared survival values has worked well enough to be considered valid and therefore is taught to new members as the correct way to perceive, think, and feel in relation to those problems. Those who enhance the survival of the organization are lauded and, conversely, those who dare introduce new and untested ideas that might question or contradict previous held values are vilified or rejected because they are perceived as threats against the survival of the organization. Thus, the young pastor who tries to make some changes and cannot seem to make any headway needs to understand that the resistance to change, in some way, is a response to the congregation's desire to survive.

Understand that when change is presented to the church and there is pushback from the congregation, this resistance is more than likely a reflection of the organizational culture. The church culture is a stabilizing factor in the lives of the members, and any suggested change results in high levels of anxiety. My suggestion is if you truly want to change a church at its core, it will take time, persistence, and a willingness to endure the misunderstandings of others. Make no mistake; because a followerfirst perspective is antithetical to much of how businesses and churches operate in the United States, if not around the world, you can expect some people initially to embrace the followerfirst perspective, but most will have questions.

For our purpose, organizational culture gives the followerfirst individual a necessary perspective regarding how difficult changing a church culture can be. For hundreds of years, churches have been established based upon leader-centered philosophies of operation. It would be unwise to think that such an engrained culture can be changed overnight through preaching a few messages on followerfirst thinking or teaching followerfirst principles of behavior, but this is a start.

One other important aspect of understanding organizational culture allows us to see that resistance to change may be more a product of the prevailing organizational culture rather than, as I unfortunately and naively had assumed, a lack of faith, an unwillingness to respond biblically, or even the devil. I do not mean to imply that the source of resistance may not indeed be from these motivations. What I mean to say is that understanding organizational culture will give those who wish to influence the church an understanding of some people's responses that does not imply some sinister spiritual design. Therefore, we can embrace those who disagree or resist, and be patient with them because we know they may simply be battling and fearing for their own and their group's survival.

How Do I Embed a New Culture?

Two key words for embedding a culture are *wisdom* and *understanding*. You might recall that Solomon was asked what he wanted above all things. His response in 1 Kings 3:9-13 was:

Therefore give to Your servant an understanding heart to judge Your people, that I may discern between good and evil. For who is able to judge this great people of Yours?" The speech pleased the LORD, that Solomon had asked this thing. Then God said to him: "Because you have asked this thing, and have not asked long life for yourself, nor have asked riches for yourself, nor have asked the life of your enemies, but have asked for yourself understanding to discern justice, behold, I have done according to your words; see, I have given you a **wise and understanding** [emphasis mine] heart, so that there has not been anyone like you before you, nor shall any like you arise after you.

Solomon asked for understanding in order to discern between good and evil. God answered his prayer and gave him both wisdom and understanding. Wisdom is "the knowledge and ability to make right choices."[7] Understanding carries the idea of being able "to separate mentally."[8] Applied to our context, if we are to understand our churches, it is imperative that we spend the necessary time digging into the lives of the people who make up the organization in order to discern where *they* are.

After thinking critically and separating out what might be espoused values from actual underlying assumptions, we make the right choices. Solomon's grasp of the necessity of wisdom and understanding in dealing with people can be seen in the multitude of times he references wisdom and understanding in the Proverbs.[6] I encourage you to ask God for wisdom and understanding before attempting to influence others at the level of organizational culture. It is not by accident that James, writing with an understanding of the trials of being a follower of Christ, wrote these words in James 1:2-8:

My brethren, count it all joy when you fall into various trials, knowing that the testing of your faith produces patience. But let patience have its perfect work, that you may be perfect and complete, lacking nothing. If any of you lacks wisdom, let him ask of God, who gives to all liberally and without reproach, and it will be given to him. But let him ask in faith, with no doubting, for he who doubts is like a wave of the sea driven and tossed by the wind. For let not that man suppose that he will receive anything from the Lord; he is a double-minded man, unstable in all his ways.

1. *Understand Yourself*

In order to create real, lasting change, what is needed is to know and better understand the organization beneath the surface. Such understanding comes only as we are willing to invest the time to investigate the core values of the organization and confront the espoused values and underlying assumptions of the church that may be in conflict with Scripture.

How can we discover these core values? Where do we begin? Let me suggest we begin with ourselves. As a Following-Leader, it does me little good to try and discern the values of others when I have not taken the time to address my own values and determine whether or not they are congruent with Scripture. This process of self-introspection can be accomplished if we are willing to be deadly honest with ourselves. Here are a few steps we can take to facilitate this personal values assessment:

1. Set a date on the calendar for a weekend retreat with only you. If we do not set this date and guard it, the other more urgent affairs of our lives will scream too loudly, and we will never find the time to evaluate.

2. Find a quiet place with no phones or televisions. This process will be difficult enough without the constant ringing of phones or temptation to relax in front of the TV.

3. Bring your Bible and a writing pad or laptop to record your personal core values. You will not be able to remember all that comes to mind. Write it down. BE HONEST. Find a biblical validation for each value without taking Scripture out of context. Write down an application of each value to your life. Write down the consequences that will likely result as you live out your values.

4. Once you have completed your assessment, share your findings with a trusted friend and get his or her input with regard to its accuracy and biblical authenticity.

5. Listen to your friend and ask questions with regard to how your values can be applied in your life.
6. Finally, take the steps necessary to apply your core values in each area of your life.

Done correctly, you are likely to find this values discovery exercise one of the most difficult disciplines you have ever attempted. However, once you have experienced the discord, uneasiness, and quite possibly the pain of discovering and applying your biblical core values to your personal life, you will have some idea of the discord, uneasiness, and pain those in the church will undergo when you ask them to go through this process. Values discovery is not for the faint-hearted. It is a process that needs to be empowered by the Holy Spirit and conducted solely for the glory of God.

2. Understand the Church

I do not want you to do what I did: waste precious time changing the furniture but not the church. When inheriting an older, established congregation, I often counsel young ministers to be patient and take the time needed to know the people before introducing change. Love them. Seek understanding of the *whys* behind the actions. I realize that a pulpit committee may have told you that the church was ready to grow and make changes, but please realize that a pulpit committee often does not represent the overall underlying assumptions of the congregation. The wise pastor, whether old or young, will take the time to ask good questions of everyone. I might go so far as to say that it might be wise to ask questions of those who might have left the church during the time it was without a pastor. What dynamics took place that precipitated their leaving? Understanding the current organizational culture represents an initial step that must take place before trying to embed a new culture.

Remember, we said that in order to understand people you have to stand-under them. Hear their stories. Listen to their past, present, and try to hear their fears of the future. On a personal level, the Lord gave me the privilege of caring for my parents in their old age until they passed. I spent hours talking and reminiscing about the past stories and glories and failures of our family. Those were precious moments. While listening to their stories I discovered that in the heart of my eighty plus year old Mom and Dad there was still a twenty year old boy flying planes over Japan, and there was still a sixteen year old girl "noodling" for catfish in the river. I discovered that, just like me, their bodies were older but not their minds. Life still mattered and the relationships they had forged were more important than ever. Most of these precious relationships had begun and developed through their church, and like many in their generation, they weren't about to let some new ideas mess it up.

For those starting a new church, the same counsel applies. Although the new church will not have a history to investigate, the people who are joining the new work certainly will have a history. It is imperative that you recognize that new ministries are often very attractive to those in other churches who are displaced, discouraged, or even disturbed. Understanding the personal and church histories of those who would join you in the new church is vitally important lest the church with the new culture you wish to plant become subsumed by those who bring their bags full of artifacts, espoused values, and basic underlying assumptions to the new work.

Below are a few questions you might want to ask when you are new to an established church or interviewing potential church members when planting a new church:

- **Established:** What is the history of this church?
  New Work: What is your church background?

- **Established:** What activities are of primary importance to you and this church and why?
  New Work: What church activities are of primary importance to you that you might like to see this church participate in and why?

- **Established:** What was the last big change that took place? How was it conducted? How was it received by the church? What were the results?
  New Work: At your last church what was the last big change that took place? How was it conducted? How was it received by the church? What were the results?

- **Established:** What is your view of worship? The Bible? The purpose of the church?
  New Work: What is your view of worship? The Bible? The purpose of the church?

- **Established:** Who are some of the people in the church you respect and why?
  New Work: In your previous church, who are some of the people in the church you respected and why?

- **Established:** How do things get done in this church? Why are they done this way?
  New Work: How should things get done in a church? Why do you believe this is the best way?

- **Established:** What are your personal core values?
  New Work: What are your personal core values?

3. Understand the Process

I suggest that followerfirst cultures be embedded incrementally. Embedding a new way of thinking about how you understand the functioning of any organization, much less the church, is a daunting task. I don't believe we can be naïve and think that those within the church who exercise control and power based upon a leader-centered perspective are likely to yield lightly, regardless of the amount of biblical evidence to support the followerfirst position. Incremental is the way to proceed.

The beauty of this process is that the change to a followerfirst perspective can begin with any follower willing to exhibit the behaviors of a follower of Christ. What this means is that change within the church can occur through the rank and file membership and does not have to wait upon the recognized leaders to begin making changes. The followerfirst perspective may be more easily disseminated, perhaps, if the leaders in the church were to embrace it. However, as a change agent within the body, I submit that the smallest and the least within the Body of Christ can begin to operate with a followerfirst perspective, and these actions will begin to influence others, who, in turn, will embrace the followerfirst way of thinking and acting within the church. In this instance the cliché is true, followerfirst thinking is more caught than taught.

Building upon Schein's list of primary embedding mechanisms[9] I want to broaden this list to include the role followers play in the embedding process. The following steps are the beginning point from which followers can embed a followerfirst culture within the church. The practical application of some of these steps can be seen in the RETHINK section of Chapter 8.

Step One:
Pay attention to, measure, and take account of biblical responses.

Developing a system of incentives for people to work toward is a practice that many businesses incorporate to try and motivate their workforce toward greater productivity. In turn, some churches have embraced similar types of systems such as contests to see which Bible study group can raise the most money, have the most new members, or have the highest percentage of attendance. Such contests within the church are intended to be good clean fun and yield results. However, these results are usually short lived as the contest ends and people return to their normal activities which are indicative of their underlying assumptions.

When it comes to motivating people within the church, I suggest we think through the dynamics of what we are actually accomplishing. First, contests do not teach cooperation within the church. They teach competition. You have one group competing against another, and you set up a win-lose scenario. One group will win and get the steak dinner. The other groups will lose and have to serve the group that won. Don't get me wrong. I am not anti-competition. In fact, I am as competitive as they come. However, I believe we have to be careful where we establish competitive cultures, and the church is not one of those areas.

From a biblical perspective, what is the benefit of creating competition within the church? The Bible speaks of loving one another (John 13:34) and encouraging one another to love and good deeds (Hebrews 10:24), but nowhere have I found that establishing competition within the church is an example of the way Christians ought to work together or become motivated for ministry. One scenario that might work, if you insist on having competitions, is for the group that wins to have the joy of serving the losing groups. This would reflect and embed a more biblical approach where, "If anyone desires to be first, he shall be last of all and servant of all" (Mark 9:35).

A followerfirst perspective seeks to pay attention to and measure faithfulness, not necessarily results. Perhaps we would do well to take account of those who faithfully share their faith, those who encourage others, the person who refuses to spread gossip and slander, or especially those who faithfully teach the truth day in and day out. Such a focus would place the emphasis on the only incentive that truly has lasting results: an unwavering love for the Lord Jesus Christ. Devotion cannot be manufactured. When we see it, we need to recognize these people and pray that they will influence others.

Step Two:
React biblically to critical incidents and organizational crises.

The one reaction that is primary in a followerfirst perspective is love. Paul said in 1 Corinthians 13, "Love never fails." Love recognizes that all persons within the church are humans and prone to failure. At the same time, the love with which we are to love one another must not tolerate sin. Because the essence of church culture seeks to ensure the survival of the organization, nothing poses a greater threat to the church than a moral failure on the part of a leader or member of the church. The Bible gives guidelines on how we are to lovingly respond to those who have experienced failure, but it is the responsibility of the followerfirst believer to make certain that sinful actions are not glossed over or tolerated. As difficult as it may be, church discipline is required if the church is to remain a church and not a social club. Followers are to hold their leaders and each other accountable to the Word of God as the standard for organizational faith and practice. This may require the follower to personally confront the leader and risk rejection. However, from the followerfirst perspective, the reputation of Christ is more important than being accepted, and the time may come when, sadly, the follower has to leave the church if the moral failure is not addressed.

Step Three:
Evidence biblical stewardship over all resources.

Leaders are usually given the responsibility of allocating resources to different ministries within the church. As Following-Leaders, it is important that ministries and programs reflecting the core values and mission of the church are financially supported.

On one occasion as a pastor, I became aware of a financial situation in which we were spending more on maintenance than on outreach. Over time, the finance team and I agreed that, although maintaining a beautiful building and campus was important, it should not exceed the outreach portion of our church budget. Adjustments were made so that outreach and missions ministries would be funded first. As a result, the church made the decision to move from a culture of maintaining and surviving to growing and thriving. A new organizational culture was birthed that moved the focus of the church from self to others and guaranteed that money would always be available to those who wanted to reach others with the gospel.

Followers understand that all resources are from the Lord and are to be used to bring Him glory. What resources they are given are welcomed with gratitude and should be used wisely. This attitude of gratitude rather than grumbling is a powerful influence in the lives of those within their sphere of influence.

Step Four:
Model, teach, and coach from a followerfirst perspective.

The best way to influence the culture of an organization is to be a followerfirst. When given the opportunity to serve others, serve from a followerfirst perspective. When teaching others, emphasize the aspects of what it means to be a follower of Christ first in all things. Let the people see you in the way you respond, speak, listen, and live. When others come to you for assistance and advice, share with them the freedom you have being a followerfirst. Being a *real* person before others gives you a credibility by which others may desire to embed these same characteristics in their lives.

Step Five:
Receive rewards and status as temporal and fleeting.

More than likely, as a followerfirst you will get noticed by others and be given positions of responsibility within the church. After all, who is not going to notice the humble servant, the tireless worker, and the person with a loving demeanor who supports the direction and purpose of the church? As you gain responsibility however, never forget that you are a followerfirst. Our place as followers of Christ will be a constant reminder of the humility we must have if we are to influence others. Additionally, any accolades need to be received with an eternal perspective. Nothing on this earth is eternal except the Word of God and the souls of men. Paul had this eternal perspective when in 2 Timothy 4:8 he wrote:

> For I am already being poured out as a drink offering, and the time of my departure is at hand. I have fought the good fight, I have finished the race, I have kept the faith. Finally, there is laid up for me the crown of righteousness, which the Lord, the righteous Judge, will give to me on that Day, and not to me only but also to all who have loved His appearing.

Step Six:
Support those who evidence a followerfirst perspective.

Unlike the teaching from the leadership literature, we are not looking for particular people with potential. Everyone in the church is a candidate to participate in the followerfirst perspective. By holding each other accountable, each follower can encourage and promote the work of those who embrace the followerfirst perspective.

It is important to reiterate that these six steps outline not only what followerfirst followers can do but who followerfirst followers are. We are to be the people who serve others, take note of the faithful, evidence stewardship, respond biblically, model, teach, coach, and seek the good of others over ourselves. By being this person, we influence the entire organization toward a followerfirst perspective.

Step Seven:
Give the process time.

Being patient and working with others to make the needed changes may be the most difficult step. Internal organizational changes often move at the speed of glaciers. The weight and importance of organizational culture requires that it change slowly. For those seeking to embed a followerfirst perspective, do not become discouraged. It may be that you are in your church for the specific reason of beginning a process that another will complete.

Conclusion

Whether you are ministering in an existing church or beginning a new one, the process of embedding an organizational culture is the most important determiner of whether or not a church will fulfill its purpose. Every follower needs to recognize and understand the aspects of the church's culture in order to make substantive changes that will last beyond a lifetime. A followerfirst organizational culture can only be fully embedded as every person embraces a followerfirst identity and moves away from an identity based upon leader position and power and control.

Remember, this change usually takes time. The weight and importance of organizational culture requires that it change slowly. For those seeking to embed a followerfirst perspective, do not become discouraged. It may be you are in your church for the specific reason of beginning a process that another will complete. Continue to live the followerfirst life, and God will use you as a catalyst for change.

RETHINK

The challenge of culture change is to move the church toward a biblical way of thinking regarding how an organization should operate. As mentioned before, this is a daunting task. Still, whether you are a leader in the church or a follower with no title, you can begin to change the culture around you. Consider the following:

1. Resolve to live each day with the same purpose of the Lord Jesus Christ (i.e. do the will of the Father).
2. Resolve to not DO church but to BE church.
3. Resolve to be an 'infectious' follower to those around you.
4. Resolve to respond biblically to life events.
   a. Love our enemies
   b. Patient when wronged
   c. Forgiving those who do not understand and speak ill of us
   d. Defer all praise the God
5. Resolve to be a peacemaker.
6. Resolve to not be 'front and center' at every event.
7. Resolve to lovingly persevere in the face of opposition.
8. Resolve to connect with and encourage others who embrace the followerfirst perspective. (Don't try to walk this journey alone.)

Chapter 10

The Church: A Holistic Perspective

One way to change church cultures from power and control cultures to role and responsibility cultures is by consistently teaching a biblical organizational perspective. What I mean by this is that a followerfirst perspective presents a biblical picture to the church of its purpose for existence and how, as an organization, every person and process works together with the Holy Spirit to the glory of God.

To that end I submit to you a model of the church from the followerfirst perspective that supports equipping and training both leaders and followers to be their very best. As you look at Figure 12, the left side of the illustration represents the relational aspects within the church and the right side represents the organizational aspects. It is impossible in such a small volume to encompass all the biblical support for each aspect of the model. However, I have tried to share a few Scriptures in order to give the model biblical credibility. I also hope to show how each aspect of the model builds upon the previous aspect, adding order to the church organization, and creating respectful, loving, relationships among the members.

God begins the process and ends the process. He is the "one God and Father of all, who is above all, and through all and in you all" (Ephesians 4:6). The primary focus of the church is God.

Organizationally, He is the Creator and has created all things for His pleasure (Genesis 1:1, Revelation 4:11). As the designer of the universe, God has organized creation at both the macro and micro levels. There is an order to the stars and the planets. There is also an

Figure 12. **Leader and Follower Training in the Church**

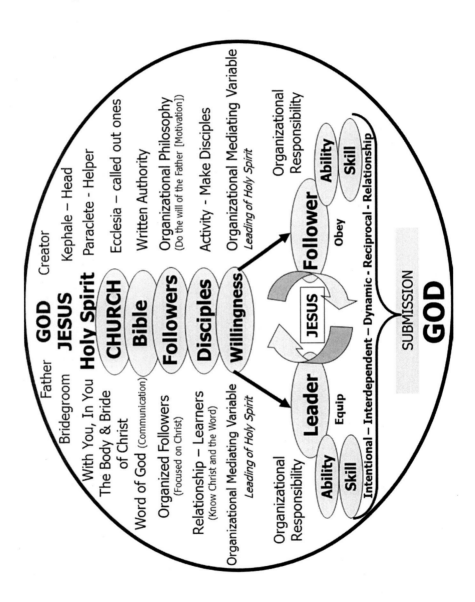

order to the cell and the genetic code. We should not be surprised that God also has an order for His church (1 Corinthians 12:28). It is this sense of order that results in harmony, security and peace.

Relationally, God has revealed Himself as Father to those who believe in Christ. God, as Father, presents a picture that is conceptually different from all other religions in that an intimate, life giving relationship is established between God and mankind. Believers' hearts are enabled by the Holy Spirit to cry out "Abba, Father" (Romans 8:15, Galatians 4:6). This is the same way Jesus called on God in the Garden of Gethsemane (Mark 14:36). Within this familial relationship with believers, God constantly wills and works within the believer for His good pleasure (Philippians 2:13).

Jesus is the Word made flesh and was in the beginning with God and is God. Nothing has come into being apart from Him (John 1). Jesus declares himself to be, "the Alpha and Omega, the beginning and the end, the first and the last" (Revelation 22:13).

Organizationally, Jesus represents the head of the church (Ephesians 1:22, 4:15, Colossians 1:18, 2:10, 19). When referring to Christ, the Greek term, *kephale*, implies that He is "accompanied by the entire command and government of the universe. The metaphor of a head denotes the highest authority."[1] This organizational position is consistent with Jesus' proclamation that "all authority in heaven and earth has been given to Me" (Matthew 28:18).

Relationally, Jesus is the Bridegroom of the Bride, His church (John 3:29, Revelation 21:2). We who have believed are betrothed to Him Who is to come. He has captured our hearts and all our love and desire is for Him. He is the lover of our souls. We are covenanted to Him. Through his sacrifice we are sealed in Him for all eternity.

The Holy Spirit is the spirit of God and Jesus. He participated with the Godhead in creation. He is God, the Holy Spirit.

Organizationally, the Holy Spirit is the "Helper" (John 14:26). The Greek word, paraclete, describes one who is called alongside to help.[2] Jesus promises the Holy Spirit whose function will be to "teach you all things…" (John 14:26). Thus, God's people are dependent upon the Holy Spirit to superintend over the affairs of God's church.

He gives certain individuals to the church so that the church might fulfill her purpose and build herself up on love (Romans 12: 3-8, 1 Corinthians 12). He enables the believer to submit to God's order for His church. He takes the Word declared and communicates it to the heart of the hearer. He draws others to this wonderful relationship of God's love in Christ Jesus.

Relationally, the Holy Spirit is the "Spirit of truth" and not only dwells with believers but in believers (John 14: 16-17). Our bodies are His dwelling place (1 Corinthians 6:19). The presence of the Holy Spirit guarantees that the believer is never alone. He empowers believers to submit to the commands of God so that they might gain a growing intimacy in the knowledge of God and Jesus (John 14:21). He gives gifts to believers so that they might be more fulfilled in serving Christ, understanding they are an important part of His church (1 Corinthians 12). He enables believers to walk worthy of the calling with which they have been called (Ephesians 4:1, Philippians 1:27, Colossians 1:10).

Church is people. Church is bought with the price of the death of Jesus Christ (1 Corinthians 6:20). Without Christ, there is no church. As Peter declares,

> "But you are a chosen generation, a royal priesthood, a holy nation, His own special people, that you may proclaim the praises of Him who called you out of darkness into His marvelous light; who once were not a people but are now the people of God, who had not obtained mercy but now have obtained mercy (1 Peter 2:9-10)

Organizationally, the church is composed of those who have been redeemed by the substitutionary atonement of the Lord Jesus Christ. The Greek word, ecclesia, is translated as "the called out ones."[3] It is not by accident that church is plural. Individuals are a part of the church but singular individuals cannot, by definition, be church. The church does not belong to itself. There is a church universal, those who are Christ's regardless of organizational affiliation. However, the pattern of the New Testament is that those who are "called out" assemble in local assemblies we call churches. These churches operate under the direction of its head, the Lord

Jesus through the leading and empowerment of the Holy Spirit in obedience to the Word of God. The organization of the church, as depicted in the New Testament, allows it to remain grounded in accurate teaching while having the freedom to meet needs and make disciples of all nations.

Relationally, the church is the body and bride of Christ. As a bride, the church is the fulfillment of the desires of the Savior. We are the focus of His love. We await His coming with eager anticipation. As His Body, the church is composed of different and varied parts. Each member of the 'body' has an important and specific responsibility to exercise all that God has given to them individually for the benefit of the whole. This includes our time, talents, treasure and giftedness. As every joint supplies what is needed, the body builds itself up in love.

The Bible is the gift of God's written word to the church. It serves as the authority for faith and practice within the organization and applies to the lives of every believer while interacting with the world.

Organizationally, the Bible serves as the final authority for the church. Each person submits to the teachings of the Bible in order to glorify God, bring unity to the body, and sustain the smooth functioning of the church organization in a spirit of mutual submission.

Relationally, the Bible serves as the Word of God, communicated clearly in written form. It serves as God's 'love letter' to His Bride and offers insights in how to gain greater intimacy with Jesus and the Father. It clearly communicates God's heart and His desire for His church.

Followers are those persons who make up the church. Before we are anything else we are followers.

Organizationally, following the Lord and His Word becomes the organizational philosophy behind every act of service. The church follows the Lord by obeying His Word in the power of His Holy Spirit. Regardless of role or title, the church is composed of followers whose desire is the same as the Savior's, to do the will of the Father

(John 6:38). This desire provides the motivation needed to fulfill God's purpose for His church. This alignment of a God-given organizational purpose with a Holy Spirit led follower philosophy is crucial to the church's mission.

Relationally, the followers in the church are organized in order to focus on Christ. It is this sense of commonality among all within the church that provides a unity of focus, purpose, and direction. Followers respect each other for the unique contribution each follower makes to the body.

Disciples are those followers who, by definition, are learners. Organizationally, these learners are to study the Word and practice its teachings. The primary activity of the church is to "make disciples" (Matthew 28:18-20). This activity is not a program but a lifestyle of the disciples as they model obedience to the teachings of the Word (as you are going).

Relationally, followers present themselves to learn of Christ and His teaching. Encouraging each other, disciples follow Christ and give their lives to honor Him. Each follower seeks to be faithful in order to learn as much as possible of Christ so that they might be able to teach others also (2 Timothy 2:2).

Willingness is described as the organizational mediating variable. This is a social science term that, simply put, speaks to how or why certain events occur. In this case it answers the questions of why some disciples become leaders and other disciples become followers.

In some leadership literature the implication is made that followers do not choose to become leaders because they do not have the 'stuff' of leadership. Leaders, on the other hand, step up to take the mantle of leadership and responsibility. What seems to be implied is that leaders are better than followers. Leaders have what it takes and followers don't. What Figure 12 reveals is that such implications could not be further from the truth.

The biblical order of the church indicates that the point at which a disciple decides to be an organizational leader or an organizational follower is not one of self-perceived capacity, but willingness. This willingness is instigated under the leading of the Holy Spirit in the life of the follower/disciple.

Because this willingness is Spirit led, there is no right or wrong decision. There is only an obedient decision. If the Spirit leads some to assume the responsibilities of an organizational leader, they have made a blessed and obedient choice. If the Spirit leads some to assume the responsibilities of an organizational follower, they have made a blessed and obedient choice. One choice is not 'better' than the other. Each choice is based upon Spirit-directed willingness, and both choices honor God.

I may also add that in the course of working within the Church, the Spirit may lead a person to lead at one point and then to follow at another point. As I pointed out with the Mobius Strip (Chapter 2), the Spirit is free to direct us where we need to be and the roles we need to assume according to His good pleasure and what brings greater glory to God.

Leader – Once the decision is made, disciples seek to hone their abilities and skills in being a leader. As previously stated, one person may be more gifted or more prepared than another to take on certain leader roles and responsibilities within the body. Whatever the level of preparation, the disciple seeks to increase both abilities and skills in order to be most effectively used in the leader role to equip others. This is their organizational responsibility

Follower – In the same way, once the decision is made to be a follower, disciples seek to hone their abilities and skills in being the most faithful follower they can be. Again, one person may be more gifted or more prepared than another to take on certain follower roles and responsibilities within the body. Whatever the level of preparation, the disciple seeks to increase both abilities and skills in order to be most effectively used in the follower role to obey the leaders and bring them joy in their leading (Hebrews 13:17). This is their organizational responsibility.

Jesus serves as the central focus and purpose of all leader and follower relationships. He said He would build His church. (Matthew

16:18). In submission to Him, both leader and follower are willing to move to whatever position is needed in the organization in order to fulfill the purpose of the church. This focus, coupled with leader and follower willingness to obey the leading of the Holy Spirit evidence the intentional, interdependent, dynamic, reciprocal, relationship process of leadership.

Submission – With Christ as their model, responsible, faithful followers of Christ live in a constant state of submission to God (Philippians 2:8). Both leaders and followers find their place under the church to undergird her, build her, and love her to the glory of God. We are to submit ourselves to one another in the fear of God (Ephesians 5:21). Living with a submissive heart invites no chance of "lording over" those within the body. As Jesus said,

> Yet it shall not be so among you; but whoever desires to become great among you, let him be your servant. And whoever desires to be first among you, let him be your slave — just as the Son of Man did not come to be served, but to serve, and to give His life a ransom for many" (Matthew 20:26-28).

God is the end of all things. Two benedictions state this fact beautifully:

> Oh, the depth of the riches both of the wisdom and knowledge of God! How unsearchable are His judgments and His ways past finding out! "For who has known the mind of the Lord? Or who has become His counselor?" 'Or who has first given to Him and it shall be repaid to him?" For of Him and through Him and to Him are all things, to whom be glory forever. Amen (Romans 11:33-36).

> Now to Him who is able to keep you from stumbling, and to present you faultless before the presence of His glory with exceeding joy, to God our Savior, who alone is wise, be glory and majesty, dominion and power, both now and forever. Amen (Jude 1:24-25).

RETHINK

Failure is a part of learning. As disciples of Christ we will fail in our leading as well as in our following. The church needs to find a way to break out of the 'everything must be successful' syndrome.

I remember one instance in college when I went on a summer mission trip to spend the summer working and sharing my faith with the people in the area. I had heard that these experiences were the best experiences one could have in his/her Christian life.

What I experienced, however, was the exact opposite. Instead of being a wonderful time of excitement and spiritual mountain tops, my journey was to slough through the valley of despair and discouragement. My experience was no fault of the organizers of the trip. I blame the entire experience on God. He used that summer to reveal more shortcomings in me than I had previously thought. It was a time of personal brokenness, self-assessment, and redirecting. It was not fun, but it was exactly what I needed.

Needless to say, upon my return to college I was not one of those who bubbled with enthusiasm. But what I remember vividly was that every person who went on a mission trip from that organization was asked to share their experience with the large group. That is, everyone but me. You see, I didn't fit the narrative.

Even though I made some of the greatest strides in my personal walk with the Lord, because they were framed in dark colors of gray and black and did not fit the desired narrative, I was not allowed to share my story. No, everything needs to be victory, success, wonderful.

I am afraid our churches have become susceptible to this same marketing idea. We don't like failure. When we come up short we don't know how to handle it. We don't know how to give glory to God when someone fails while attempting to be obedient to the Lord. We are not taught how to respond when, after a person preaches and lives out the Gospel that bad things happen to them. Does Stephen come to mind (Acts 7)? We usually try to ignore it or marginalize it. But the people who experienced the defeat need some way for it to be redeemed and used as a teaching tool in their lives.

Let me suggest we develop our churches to be safe zones. What I mean by that is that fellow followers make it safe for others to risk, to step out, to trust God in ways that we ordinarily would not. When a person wants to take the lead with an idea they have for a ministry, let's have a safe place for them to fall back to earth when their idea plummets like a meteor and burns up in the atmosphere. Let's create churches where, instead of making excuses for why something or someone did not work out, we embrace these daring followers who put self on the line and learned a lesson on how to die to self. Resurrections only occur after death. The church ought to be a place that knows how to celebrate and look forward to resurrections.

Once, while the interim pastor at a church, a talented young man sought to audition for a national talent show and made it to the second round. After further honing his skills he was prepared to move to the next level. The Sunday before the audition I asked this young man, a strong believer in the Lord, to stand with me at the close of the service and we had a joint prayer before the entire church that God would enable him to sing his best and that God would reveal His will for the young man. On audition day I received a text, "He didn't make it."

The next Sunday as I stood to preach I called out to the young man, "So, how did it go?" His response was, "I didn't make it." To which I replied, "Then let us rejoice with you that God has indeed directed your path. You dared to risk, and put your talent out there for others to judge. They did not see fit to move you on. However, God saw your risk. He saw your obedience. He saw your desire to honor Him and He has directed your life." With that I asked the congregation to join me in thanking the young man for his courage and obedience and thanking God for His faithfulness. The applause went on for quite some time.

How many more risk takers for Jesus would we have if, when they are met with failure, they knew there was a group of fellow followers, fellow risk takers who would not judge them as failures, or rejects. But rather, they would be embraced, encouraged and built up to take on another risk, another challenge to the glory of God? I just wonder.

Chapter 11

Identifying
followerfirst Behaviors

In order to establish a greater understanding of the followerfirst perspective of leading, I sought to codify a group of behaviors, supported by Scripture that identify those who operate with a followerfirst type of thinking. With this desire in mind, I developed the Followerfirst Profile (FFP) that identifies two categories of biblical follower behaviors: (a) relationship oriented behaviors and (b) responsibility oriented behaviors. Additionally, the Followerfirst Profile identifies five specific biblical follower behaviors: (a) commitment to the leader, (b) intimacy with the leader, (c) faithfulness and/or loyalty, (d) obedience and/or supporting, and (e) persistence and/or consistency. By using the FFP, each follower can determine his or her level of biblical following and construct a plan to improve areas of weakness and more readily use areas of strengths.

Relationship Oriented Behaviors

One of the unique qualities of Christianity is that the worship of God involves more than mere servitude. The Bible teaches that God loves the world (John 3:16) and reconciles the world in relationship to Himself through the follower's faith in the life, death, and resurrection of His Son, the Lord Jesus Christ (2 Corinthians 5:18; Romans 5:10). During Jesus' earthly ministry, He emphasized this relational aspect of belief and worship by speaking of those who follow Him as "friends" (John 15:14). This relationship aspect is further emphasized when Jesus, speaking metaphorically of those who believe upon Him, said, "My sheep hear my voice and I know them, and they follow Me" (John 10:27). Jesus even defined eternal life in terms of relationship: "And this is eternal life, that they may know Thee, the only true God and Jesus Christ whom Thou hast sent" (John 17:3).

Relationship oriented behaviors revolve around certain relational factors. The call to, "follow Me," taken in its historical context is a call to walk in close physical proximity with the Savior. Today, even though it is impossible for followers to walk in close physical proximity, it is not impossible to walk in close spiritual proximity. Of this closeness Jesus said, "I will never leave you nor forsake you" (Hebrews 13:5). It is through these and other statements of the Lord Jesus we can deduce the Savior's desire for continuing a deepening relationship with His followers. This deepening relationship manifests itself through specific follower behaviors.

Commitment to the Leader

As we have studied, the primary word in the New Testament for *follow* is *akoloutheo* (ακολυqε)w). This compound Greek word is formed from the prefix *a* which expresses union, or likeness, and the root word, *keleuthos*, which means *a way*.[1] Thus, a possible reading of this term could yield the construct of someone going in the same way. The term is used 77 times in the Gospels and always refers to following Christ. The term follow is sometimes used in the literal sense of actually following Christ (see Matthew 4:25) as well as metaphorically with the concept of discipleship (see Mark 8:34, 9:38, 10:21).

The New Testament concept of following as "commitment to the leader" is demonstrated by the disciples, Peter and Andrew, when, at the command of Jesus to follow Him, they, "...immediately left their nets and followed [Jesus]" (Matthew 4:20). John the Baptist declared his commitment to the Lord when he said, "He must increase and I must decrease" (John 3:30). Peter's walking on the water (Matthew 14:28) is another example of one who is committed to the leader, even to the point of risking one's own life. These sometimes radical and counter-intuitive actions on the part of the follower indicate a level of commitment to the leader regardless of personal cost.

Intimacy with the Leader

In the New Testament, the disciples of Jesus were identified as those who were closely associated with Jesus. On one occasion, Peter and John had been accused by the religious leaders, and together had given a strong defense of their activities. The Scriptures note that, "when [the religious leaders] saw the courage of Peter and John and realized that they were unschooled, ordinary men, they were astonished and they took note that these men *had been with Jesus*" [emphasis mine] (Acts 4:13-14). Jesus emphasized this close proximity of relationship with His followers when before ascending into heaven he told His disciples, "I am with you always, even to the end of the age" (Matthew 28:20). The follower's understanding of intimacy with Christ appears to engender a sense of oneness that Christ seeks to have with His followers. Thus, Christ can say to his followers, "I will not leave you as orphans; I will come to you. After a little while the world will behold Me no more; but you will behold Me; because I live, you shall live also. In that day you shall know that I am in My Father, and you in Me, and I in you" (John 14:18-21). This willingness to be taught by Christ and to apply His words to one's life is indicative of those who continue to grow in an intimate relationship with the Savior.

Responsibility Oriented Behaviors

Relationship oriented behaviors are complimented by responsibility oriented behaviors. From a biblical perspective, the idea of relationship naturally results in the follower having certain responsibilities toward the leader. This concept was emphasized when Jesus stated, "He who has my commandments and keeps them, he it is who loves me, and he who loves Me will be loved by My Father, and I will love him, and will disclose Myself to him" (John

14:21). Additionally, Jesus made the connection between relationship and responsibility when He said, "You are My friends if you do what I command you" (John 15:14). The following responsibility oriented behaviors evidence a life that is truly committed to following the Lord Jesus.

Obedience

The Greek word, *epakoloutheo*, is a compound Greek word. The root word for follow (*akoloutheo*) is preceded with the prefix *epi*, a preposition with the meaning *upon*. This prefix allows the word to be translated with the idea of following after or close upon a person or a concept.[2] The Apostle Peter expresses this concept in 1 Peter 2:21 when he wrote, "For you have been called for this purpose, since Christ also suffered for you, leaving you an example for you to follow in His steps...." This concept of following after Christ is further clarified by Peter's continuing statements in chapter 2 verse 22 describing the person and activities of Christ:

> Who committed no sin, nor was any deceit found in His mouth; and while being reviled, He did not revile in return; while suffering, He uttered no threats, but kept entrusting Himself to Him who judges righteously; and He Himself bore our sins in His body on the cross, that we might die to sin and live to righteousness for by his wounds you were healed.

From the context of these verses it is clear that Peter was aware that followers who are obedient to the commands of Christ would experience suffering and hardship. Obedience to the commands of Christ in the face of hardship, suffering, and even persecution are based upon the follower's understanding of the sovereignty of God and that God the Father would always judge righteously.

A similar Greek word, *parakoloutheo*, is also a compound Greek word that uses the root word for follow (*akoloutheo*) with the prefix *para* which signifies "to follow close up, or side by side, hence, to accompany or to conform."[3] The word is used to describe character qualities that accompany believers who are sharing the gospel and following good doctrine in their lives and ministries. This idea is conveyed in 2 Timothy 3:10 when the apostle Paul proclaims, "You followed my teaching, conduct, purpose, faith, patience, love, perseverance...." It is clear that obedience to the commands of Christ and the teaching of the Scriptures is indicative of a follower of Christ.

Faithfulness

The New Testament often speaks of the abiding faithfulness of God (1 Corinthians 1:9; 2 Corinthians 1:18; 1 Thessalonians 5:24; 2 Thessalonians 3:3) and has many references to faithfulness being a characteristic of those who follow Christ (see Ephesians 1:1; 6:21; Colossians 1:2; 4:9). Paul stated in 1 Corinthians 1:2, "It is required in stewards that a man be found faithful." The Greek word *pistos* is often translated *faithful* but may also carry the meaning of trustworthiness.[4] Followers are entrusted with the gospel of Jesus Christ, gifts of the Spirit, positions of responsibility within the church, and the name of Jesus. A person's faithful stewardship of these constructs is an indicator of their faithfulness to the Lord. Those in the Bible who have been designated faithful are those whose lives have given evidence of keeping a promise and being diligent in their service to others in the name of Christ (Timothy - 1 Corinthians 4:17; Tychicus – Ephesians 6:21; Epaphras – Colossians 1:7; Onesimus – Colossians 4:9; faithful men – 2 Timothy 2:2). Faithfulness is an indispensible characteristic of a follower of Christ.

Persistence

Exakoloutheo, is another compound Greek word that takes the root word for follow *(akoloutheo)* and precedes it with the Greek prefix, *ek*, which is the Greek word for *out*. This creates a word that carries the idea of following certain teachings *out* to their end. Peter presents this concept in the negative by stating that the apostles did not "follow cleverly devised tales when we made known to you the power and coming of our Lord Jesus Christ..." (2 Peter 1:16). From this negative statement, we can imply the positive that Peter and the other apostles *did* follow out to the end the accurate teachings of the Lord Jesus.

The Greek word *dioko* has two meanings. The first denotes *driving away* in the sense of persecution. The second means "to pursue without hostility, to follow after."[5] In this second sense, the word describes the means by which followers of Christ are to pursue the character of Christ. To that end, followers are directed to follow: (a) that which is good (1 Thessalonians 5:15), (b) righteousness (1 Timothy 6:11), (c) peace with all men and holiness (Hebrews 12:14), and (d) righteousness, faith, love, and peace (2 Timothy 2:22). The intensity of the verb is captured when *dioko* is translated, "I *press on* toward the goal for the prize of the upward call of God in Christ Jesus" (Philippians 3:14). Persistence is a behavior of all who follow. However, let me be quick to add that persistence includes recognizing our complacency and mediocrity in the things of God. Once recognized, the persistent follower is quick to confess these to the Lord and continue to pursue the Lord Jesus Christ.

What Would Other People Think?

Because the FFP is a self-report instrument, there is the possibility that "respondents may answer questions in such a way as to represent themselves favorably…[thus] the validity of self-reports becomes suspect as the amount of self-presentation increases relative to self-disclosure."[6] To evaluate the respondent's tendency to give socially desirable responses, the FFP incorporated five questions which have been validated as a social desirability response set. These questions are added to the FFP to assess our capacity to assess ourselves. As followers of Christ, we need to be honest with God, ourselves, and those whom we serve, in that order. These questions help measure how much we may be looking over our shoulder and wondering what other people think.

I measured the face validity[7] of the Followerfirst Profile and have used it with many different churches in many different contexts. I present a portion of the survey in Figure 14 and invite you to complete one free copy of the entire thirty-five item profile with answer sheets by accessing www.followerfirst.com.

The Followerfirst Profile

The primary measurement of the Followerfirst Profile (FFP) is a person's commitment to following Christ. From the followerfirst perspective this commitment to Christ is a prerequisite for following other leaders in the church.

The response options in the FFP are worded so that positive responses produce higher numerical values using a five-item response ordinal Likert scale. The terms used for the responses are: to little or no extent, to a slight extent, to a moderate extent, to a great extent, and to a very great extent. These responses relate to a numerical scale of 1 to 5 respectively. A lower score would indicate a lower presence of biblical follower behavior and a higher score would indicate a higher presence of biblical follower behavior.

The answer sheet (Figure 13) allows the person completing the FFP to identify strengths and weaknesses in their own follower behaviors (Commitment, Intimacy, Obedience, Faithfulness, Persistence) and develop a personal plan for enhancing the indicated strengths and strengthening the indicated weaknesses.

Figure 13: Followerfirst Profile Answer Sheet

A Commitment	B Intimacy	C Obedience	D Faithfulness	E Persistence
30	30	30	30	30
25	25 X	25	25	25
20 X	20	20 X	20	20
15	15	15	15 X	15 X
10	10	10	10	10
5	5	5	5	5
0	0	0	0	0

Figure 14: Followerfirst Profile

Instructions

Each of the following survey statements describes a particular behavior of a follower of Christ. Read each statement carefully and circle the response that best describes to what extent that statement accurately characterizes your actual behavior. Each response relates to a numerical scale of 1 to 5: (1) to little or no extent, (2) to a slight extent, (3) to a moderate extent, (4) to a great extent, and (5) to a very great extent.

	to little or no extent	to a slight extent	to a moderate extent	to a great extent	to a very great extent
1: In my work I serve Christ.	1	2	3	4	5
2: I pray to God through Christ throughout the day.	1	2	3	4	5
3: I confess my sins to Christ.	1	2	3	4	5
4: I obey Christ regardless of the circumstances.	1	2	3	4	5
5: I am consistent in telling others of Christ.	1	2	3	4	5
6: I am consistent with my spiritual disciplines of prayer, Bible reading and Scripture memory.	1	2	3	4	5
7: I obey Christ because of my love for Him over all things.	1	2	3	4	5
8: I always obey Christ.	1	2	3	4	5
9: I have a daily quiet time of fellowship with Christ.	1	2	3	4	5
10: I serve Christ where I live.	1	2	3	4	5

Applying the Followerfirst Profile to the Church

The Followerfirst Profile measures follower behaviors as they relate to following after Jesus Christ. One might ask, "How can these behaviors be applied when, as a part of the Body of Christ, we are called upon to follow leaders within the church?" My initial response is… very carefully. Although there are many wonderful church leaders in the world, there are still charlatans and fakes who capture people with slick presentations, supposed special knowledge, and/or promises of blessing and success. Paul warns of these people even in the first century church:

> But know this, that in the last days perilous times will come: For men will be lovers of themselves, lovers of money, boasters, proud, blasphemers, disobedient to parents, unthankful, unholy, unloving, unforgiving, slanderers, without self-control, brutal, despisers of good, traitors, headstrong, haughty, lovers of pleasure rather than lovers of God, having a form of godliness but denying its power. And from such people turn away! For of this sort are those who creep into households and make captives of gullible women loaded down with sins, led away by various lusts, always learning and never able to come to the knowledge of the truth. Now as Jannes and Jambres resisted Moses, so do these also resist the truth: men of corrupt minds, disapproved concerning the faith; but they will progress no further, for their folly will be manifest to all, as theirs also was (2 Timothy 3:1-9).

As a follower of Christ, I am commanded to follow only those persons whom God has called to lead His church, not those who presume to lead His church. As the above scripture stated, the non-leaders or self-called individuals will be revealed over time because they will refuse to follow the Lord Jesus Christ and obey His commands. Therefore, before I follow anyone, I must know as best I can who the leaders follow. This will not be learned simply from what the leaders say, but what they do over time. I don't have to have a personal conversation with the leader to determine whom he/she is following, although a personal conversation is a good place to start. All I need do is observe their lives. Whom human leaders follow is the best indicator of how they will lead and whether they ought to be leading in the first place. As a follower, it is always my choice whether or not I will follow. I call this the follower's prerogative. If over the course of a few months the leader appears intent on following the Lord, I will put in my lot with the leader and follow.

Commitment

Followerfirst pastors are desperately looking for believers who are committed to the Lord Jesus Christ and His church. The work of ministry is just that: work. The work requires a commitment on the part of the member that goes beyond good intentions. Church members need to be committed to their leaders. However, in this cynical world, this is very difficult. One way for members to be committed to their leaders is by remembering the One to whom we can fully commit ourselves, the Lord Jesus.

When we get involved in our churches, we should join a congregation with the understanding that this is the place where we are entrusting our most important aspect of living, our spiritual livelihood. By understanding what it means to be a biblical follower, perhaps we can begin to change the perspective of many that the church is merely another organization that can help us raise our kids, entertain our students, marry our adult children, and bury us when we die. As a committed follower, I will trust Jesus to have oversight of His church, His bride. I will never be a part of a church that is not led by persons who are not sinners forgiven by the grace of God. This fact will always be in the back of my mind. However, I will also keep in the forefront of my thinking that the church, its people and its leaders, are all followers operating ultimately under the sovereign hand of an almighty God. I can always trust God. I can expect to be disappointed by my human leaders many times. However, my primary commitment is to Christ, and He never disappoints.

Intimacy

Intimacy is another word we do not use very much with regard to our church leaders. Our busy worlds make it difficult to find the time to slow down and spend time with our leaders. The same is true for the leader. How can one person take a meal with hundreds, if not thousands, of people? Such an expectation is not feasible, and if a follower has this expectation, he or she is going to be disappointed and may be guilty of placing an expectation on the leader that the Bible does not. Church leaders are commanded to care for the flock. How they do this is not spelled out in the Scriptures, and if we place an expectation from our own personal lives or from a traditional cultural perspective on what it means for the pastor to care for us, then we will be operating outside the Bible and will find ourselves not following Christ in the process.

There are ways the follower can be intimate with the leader. Emails that simply say you are praying for the leader, short notes through the mail, making certain that the church appreciates her ministers regularly are just a few ways we can bless our leaders and build intimacy with them. It is appalling the number of churches that never recognize the loving care given by their ministers. We muzzle the ox (1 Timothy 5:18) when it comes to gaining intimacy with our leaders. Many pastors and church leaders tell me that the greatest intimacy is built when church members participate in ministry activities. Witnessing, visitation, mission trips are all available for the follower if he or she wants to rub shoulders with their leaders.

The most important activity of intimacy with the leader is praying for the leader. Asking for prayer from the leader, praying for the leader on the spot, and praying for the leader in your personal prayer time, all lead to a greater intimacy. As followers of Christ we want our leaders to hunger after intimacy with Christ. Giving our leaders time to have that intimacy is a blessing to the leader. However, there is little time for extended personal devotion if the pastor is expected at the hospital, nursing home, funeral home, baseball game, visitation, business committee, etc. If prayer is our vital life, as followers of Christ we need to be certain of our prayers, and we need to make certain our leaders have time to pray. We do not want to be guilty of expecting our leaders to minister to us before our leaders have time to minister before God in prayer. We love our leaders when we don't require our leaders to beckon to our every call. Let us seek to take our leaders to the prayer closet with us in praying for them before we require them to meet with us.

Obedience

Obedience - The word sounds rather harsh doesn't it? Yet, in God's economy, obedience is the currency of love. Jesus said that if we love Him we will obey His commandments (John 14:21). If I love Christ I will obey His commands. If I love my leaders I will obey them. When the writer of Hebrews 13:17 said, "Obey those who rule over you, and be submissive, for they watch out for your souls, as those who must give account. Let them do so with joy and not with grief, for that would be unprofitable for you," the Holy Spirit used a Greek word translated obey that carries the meaning of having confidence in those who lead.[8] Followers are to assent to the positional authority of those who have the responsibility before God of watching over their souls. By having confidence in God, the follower of Christ can have confidence in the God called leader as long as the leader has given proof of being a follower of Christ and His Word. Follower obedience to the leader results from: (a) the leader's integrity in following the Lord and (b) follower trust in the sovereignty of God.

I can recall one of several instances during my years as a pastor that the church had come to a place of decision. In one instance, the church had out grown the old church building we had rented, and I desired the church to move from a typical church type building in order to conduct services in the local high school auditorium. After several weeks (it may have been months) of discussion, the church decided to follow my lead, leave the confines of the smaller church building, and move our weekend services to the high school cafeteria. The result was that the people grew closer together because the decision required us to move sound equipment and all our materials from storage to the school each Sunday morning. You do gain intimacy with people while you are serving the Lord. Also, the extra space allowed us to have more visitors. The parking was almost unlimited, and we saw the church continue to grow.

I share this story because after several years, one of the older members of the congregation and I were talking and he related a story of how he came to grips with the whole idea of moving the church to the school. This gentleman confided that he was not too keen on the idea from the start. He participated in the discussions.

He read the material presented, but this was not convincing. What convinced him was the consistency he saw in me and the desire God had placed in my heart to reach the people of our community, even to the point of making ourselves uncomfortable. His words to me were, "I didn't have any confidence in you because you were just a young whipper-snapper. But I did have confidence in God and what He wanted to do in our community and because of that, I agreed to go." That is being a biblical follower. The church made a decision to follow me only because they had the confidence in God that reaching people even at the expense of their own comforts was what God had called them to do. It appeared on the surface that they were obeying me and my wishes when in reality, they were obeying God. I can't tell you how glad I am that I was actually following the Lord's lead with that idea.

Faithfulness

The concept of faithfulness carries with it the idea of keeping a promise. As followers of Christ, we have been entrusted with the treasure of the gospel of Jesus Christ (2 Corinthians 4:7). As good stewards we faithfully share this gospel with others (1 Corinthians 4:1-2). Even though this is our duty as servants of Jesus Christ, we gladly carry out this duty and others from a heart of love for the Savior.

With this backdrop of loving responsibility, followers of Christ have the joy of being faithful to others within the church. From my own experience as a pastor, I can say that nothing is more gratifying than to have a member of the church commit to perform a certain work and then have them complete the task without being reminded, begged, or cajoled into compliance. The faithfulness of the follower to complete a task is one way we can bring joy to the hearts of those who lead.

As followers first, we must understand that our commitment to a task within the church is more than just a task we hope to fulfill for the leader. We are actually making a commitment to the Lord to perform a work for His church. Followers are people who follow through on their commitments. When followers make a promise, followers keep a promise.

271

Persistence

One key to determining perseverance and persistence is to ask the question, "What will it take to make me quit?" Followerfirst believers understand that all churches are composed of humans and that there is no perfect church. Followers understand that leaders in the church will make mistakes and they will sometimes disappoint. However, as long as the mistakes are not of a moral nature nor violate clear biblical teaching, staying in a fellowship of believers for the long haul is a gift that the leaders greatly appreciate. Standing beside the leader through difficult times and not cutting and running at the first sign of trouble usually results in a bond of friendship with the leader that leads to even greater degrees of intimacy and trust.

I recall fondly those friends who were members of my churches who decided to stand with me during difficult times. When seeking to grow a new church, it is all the more important to find those persons who will persist through the difficult, embryonic times that new churches go through as they mature. I still treasure their persistence that evidenced their faithfulness to Christ, His church, and me. It was a persistence that was based on a love for the Savior and a desire to see the church succeed. As we have already stated, followers hold the keys to whether the leader succeeds or not. By both leader and followers being present through the good and bad times, the likelihood of growing a healthy church increases.

Conclusion

How can a person really tell if someone has a followerfirst perspective? I hope the Followerfirst Profile will be a starting point for discovery. However, the truth is that we can never truly know the thinking, the perspective, or the worldview of a person until we have spent time with them through good times and bad. In fact, it is through the bad times that we are more likely to see the true thinking of another. It is one thing to be a followerfirst kind of person when it is popular, everyone likes you, the church is going well, and people are happy. But what happens to our thinking when we see people taking advantage of our generosity or not giving us the benefit of the doubt? What happens when the people with whom we work and minister do not hold to the same biblical ethic we do and begin to act in ways that dishonor God? What happens when being a follower costs us something dear, like a relationship, or our reputation, or even our job? Then we will know if we are truly prepared to live according to a followerfirst perspective.

RETHINK

What are some ways to use the Followerfirst Profile in your church:

1. Have each member of the staff team (elder team, deacon team, etc.) complete the instrument and share the results. Develop plans for each person that enhances their strengths and strengthens their weaknesses. Use this plan as a starting point for accountability before beginning the 'business' of the team meeting.

2. As a leader in the church, conduct a 360° assessment of your personal development by taking the instrument yourself and then giving the instrument to those with whom you work in order to assess you. (These would be persons on the organizational chart who may have responsibility for you and those for whom you are responsible.) Collect these anonymously in order to gain an understanding of what others perceive as your strengths and weakness. Meet with the team to discuss the results and the action plans you will take as a result of this process.

3. Teach a series on the development of followers of Christ using the characteristics outlined in this chapter. Have those who were taught the information complete the instrument. Take the necessary time to have each person create an action plan of development based on the results of the instrument. Divide into small groups to have each person share his/her action plan. (Those who are leaders in the church and have previously taken the instrument and developed an action plan should lead and model transparency and humility within these small groups.) Close the small group time with prayer for one another.

Chapter 12

Following
Can Change the World

It was a very good question. The student asked if there were any biblical examples of a church operating according to followerfirst principles. The question gave me pause to think of another question. Are there any biblical examples of a church operating according to the leadership principles often applied today? In other words, does anything in the New Testament give us reason to think that the pastor/teacher and/or elders who ministered in the New Testament churches were vested with the responsibility of getting a vision from God for the ministry, developing a mission statement, and relating this vision to the rest of the church body for it to accomplish? Were they commissioned to set the pace for the ministry, oversee programs, make certain staff members do their jobs, plan new buildings, form the budget and administrate the office? Historically, the Bible gives evidence that when God wanted to do a work, He chose an individual to begin the process. Moses, Nehemiah, and Paul are all examples of this. Yet, God's working through Old Testament patriarchs and New Testament Apostles does not necessarily support the idea that God's model for the New Testament church is to only give the vision for the ministry to one person or a select group. In the absence of any direct teaching regarding the leader's organizational responsibilities in the church, it appears the members of the church have added this template to a list of responsibilities for ministers to accomplish that simply does not have the weight of Scripture behind it. In fact, I would argue that there is more evidence for a followerfirst perspective of operation within the New Testament church than what is currently practiced today.

Acts chapter 6 indicates one instance in which an organizational problem was remedied by choosing certain men to serve those who were being neglected. From an organizational perspective, it appears the apostles knew their main concern was the ministry of the Word of God. Therefore, they instructed the believers to choose seven men to serve and remedy the problem.

Consider Paul's letters to the churches. A broad view of these letters reveals that most of them were corrective in nature. Having been established by Paul in his missionary journeys, these churches were now being led by elders whom the apostle established to oversee the spiritual well-being of those who were coming to faith in Christ. Most of what Paul shares with Timothy and Titus are directives on how to establish spiritually minded leaders, not organizational duties. I have found nothing that suggests that the elders were charged with the sole responsibility of discerning the will of God for the church, but that their primary responsibility was to make certain that the Gospel and the doctrines were taught and practiced without compromise or adulteration.

Given that these elders/pastors obviously would be looked upon to help in making decisions for the church, how would such decisions be made? Those who operate with an elder rule system may say that the elders are charged with decision making and that they will discern the will of the Lord for the church and inform the church with regard to ministry direction. Those who operate with a congregational rule system may say that each member of the congregation would come to a decision and then the majority would rule. I contend that neither of these systems completely conveys the desire of the Lord for His church.

In a leader-centered organizational culture, an elder rule system has the potential of discounting the input and influence of members of the church who might be able to add insight into the decision making process. Similarly, a congregational rule system has the potential of discounting the input of pastors and deacons and relying solely upon parliamentary procedure and majority rule to discern the will of God. The followerfirst perspective, on the other hand, moderates the possible authoritarianism of an elder rule system and the possible political positioning of a congregational rule system, bringing the church organizational decision making into line with the Lord's establishing the church as a body of followers participating with followers in the process.

We have already seen how a followerfirst perspective begins with the premise that all born again members of the Body of Christ are followers of Christ first. By remembering this simple but fundamental truth, the church can engage more persons in ministry activities and make a greater impact on the culture and community. By leveling the playing field of ministry, the invisible wall of separation between clergy and laity is lowered so that all can understand and fulfill their responsibilities as followers of Christ.

Within a followerfirst church, decisions can be made more quickly and with less friction. This is due largely to the congruence already present within the group with regard to core values, mission, and vision. By emphasizing following and followers, the church body can rally around her common purpose as given by the Lord Jesus Christ to make disciples of all nations. Within the Great Commission, the church has her mission statement, "Make disciples." The authority of the Lord Jesus Christ and the Bible give the core values of how church business and ministry are conducted. The vision is the world-wide influence of "all nations." The only need for the church is clarifying the strategic details of how to fulfill the vision. When the church is unified with regard to mission, core values, and vision, she becomes a powerful force of change within the local community and around the world.[1] Lives are changed and the church grows numerically and spiritually as a natural result of the unity of the Body.

Sometimes there may be occasion when the Body cannot come to a unified decision on how to fulfill a specific ministry endeavor. Well-meaning followers on each side of the decision may simply have a difference of opinion on what needs to be done and how. When time in prayer and corporate conversation yields nothing by way of agreement, what is to be done?

In these times, I would suggest exercising the power of submission. Rather than cause a schism in the church, followers could choose to defer to those who are in positions of oversight (i.e. elders, pastors). The followerfirst perspective does not support a consensus type of leadership. Those in positions of leading others sometimes have to make the difficult decisions. The followerfirst perspective does not abrogate this responsibility but seeks to involve as many people in the decision making process as possible. When the time comes to make a decision, those who lead will be responsible to make it. Entrusting the decision to these fellow followers in leader positions and then praying for them can bring about unity within the Body. In addition, once the decision is made, actively supporting the decision, even though it may not have been one's idea, will bless the Body of Christ and honor the Lord. Unanimity may not be possible, especially for large churches. However, unity can be accomplished when followers choose to follow the Lord and trust their fellow followers with the decision. Unity within the Body comes through a congruence of shared values.

Followers Making History

It amazes me to this day how the church has survived through the centuries. The pages of church history are a testimony to the faithfulness of God to sustain His Son's Bride. We know the names of the more famous who, in some extraordinary way, were used of God to preach revivals, establish churches, or simply stand for truth. However, let us not forget that for every famous follower, there are tens of thousands of unnamed souls who have changed the world simply by being who God had called them out of the world to be: followers of Christ.

Followers change history. They may be called leaders by writers, but in reality, they are followers. With the courage of their convictions they are willing to stand against all odds in order to maintain their personal integrity and the reputation of Christ. The eleventh chapter of Hebrews highlights the saints of old. Their place in the Hall of Faith is not granted because of their station as leaders, but because of their faithful following.

Abraham faithfully followed the command of God to sacrifice Isaac, believing that God would raise him from the dead (Hebrews 11:19). Moses' parents faithfully followed the law of God and not the law of Pharaoh and thus, Moses was spared. Moses followed the directives of the Lord and kept the Passover, sparing the lives of the people of God. This list goes on and on. Yet, all of these faithful followers died without seeing the promise of the Messiah fulfilled. By the grace of God, we have seen the fulfillment.

Today, these great saints become for us a great cloud of witnesses cheering us on as we run the race set before us with endurance.

> Therefore we also, since we are surrounded by so great a cloud of witnesses, let us lay aside every weight, and the sin which so easily ensnares us, and let us run with endurance the race that is set before us, looking unto Jesus, the author and finisher of our faith, who for the joy that was set before Him endured the cross, despising the shame, and has sat down at the right hand of the throne of God (Hebrews 12:1-2).

Our primary objective is to look to Jesus and follow Him. We lead the next generation only as they follow our lead. Whether they follow or not will be their choice, their prerogative. Our choice is now. Will we follow the Lord and revel in our following? Will we assuage any thought of position or power and find ourselves fulfilled in humbly following the commands of Christ? Like the saints of old, this journey will require an undying faith. The future of the church depends on those who follow the perfect follower, the Lord Jesus Christ.

How Do You Measure Up?

From what we have studied, it is evident that the Bible views the church as a follower-centered organization. Biblical followers have responsibilities that must be fulfilled if the church is to accomplish her mission. The followerfirst perspective offers a way for believers to view themselves within the church that gives meaning and purpose to each individual member.

Below are a Follower Covenant and a Following-Leader Covenant. There are 67 organizational responsibilities followers have within the church. The Following-Leader Covenant contains 23 additional organizational responsibilities for those who aspire to the position of leader in the church. The number of responsibilities indicates the important role of followers within the church.

On a recent Followerfirst Roundtable weekend, I invited a group of believers to categorize the 67 organizational responsibilities followers have within the church. There were many great suggestions. Below is just one way these organizational responsibilities may be presented to the church.

The Follower's Covenant

As a follower of Christ I willingly:

Follow Christ in all things

- Place Christ's reputation above my own
- Risk my personal relationship with my leader to protect the character and reputation of Christ
- Answer Christ's imperative and not simply volunteer
- Persist in following Christ
- Place total dependence on Christ and seek to grow in the image of Christ
- Die to self and live to Christ
- Serve Christ by serving others
- Become totally committed to the Lord Jesus Christ
- Follow the leading of the Lord Jesus Christ and the Word of God.
- Submit to the authority of Jesus and the Word of God.

Orient my life toward God

- Have an expectant attitude toward the future
- Focus on the future rather than dwell on the past
- Overcome the status quo
- Become a critical thinker regarding what I read and hear
- Overcome evil with good
- Do not repay evil for evil
- Embrace change and encourage others to do the same
- Trust the promises of God's Word
- Do my work heartily as unto the Lord, rather than men
- Seek my "well done" from God, not men

- Study, learn, and apply the teachings of the Word of God
- Act on biblical grounds instead of cultural or personal preferences
- Change internally, spiritually, and emotionally
- Discipline my life toward intimacy with the Lord Jesus Christ

Loyally follow God and man

- Follow-through on my commitments
- Become a follower with integrity
- Keep my promises
- Become a trustworthy member of the team
- Finish the work I am assigned
- Initiate action
- Assume responsibility

Link with my leaders in a respectful relationship

- Challenge my leaders to greatness
- Serve alongside my leaders
- Become a Following-Leader
- Stand up for my leaders
- As much as possible, seek to make ministry a joy for my leaders
- Unburden my leaders when I can
- Trust God by being committed to my leaders
- Talk to my leaders and not about them
- Leave the church and find another in which to serve if the immoral/unbiblical actions of the leaders go unchecked
- Become actively engaged with my leaders and the church
- Do more than simply comply with my leader's requests
- Have only reasonable expectations of my leaders
- Give my time and resources to assist my leader to accomplish the organizational mission
- Reject participating in a rebellion against my leaders
- Hold no expectation of leading regardless of what position I might hold in the business world
- With a humble heart of love, correct my leaders if they violate or stray from the Word of God

Openly embrace my organizational responsibility
- Seek the unity of the Spirit in the bond of peace
- Reject seeking peace at any price but be a peace maker
- Live peaceably with all men
- Put other followers before me
- Resist seeking to avenge myself
- Forbid anger to dictate my actions
- Establish an organizational culture of grace
- Seek reconciliation with my leaders and fellow followers
- Get the facts from the source before forming opinions or conclusions
- Refuse to play the martyr
- Exercise the power of submission
- Resist the temptation of self-preservation
- Give insight to the change process
- Refuse to operate with a quid-pro-quo

Witness to the "Eternal Life" that is knowing Christ
- Fulfill my ministry of reconciliation by sharing the Gospel
- Do the work of an ambassador
- Use my gifts to fulfill the mission of the church to the glory of God
- Be good a steward of all that God has given
- Employ the power with which I have been entrusted to the glory of God
- Follow in the power of the Holy Spirit

The Following-Leader's Covenant

As a Following-Leader I willingly:

- Assume all the responsibilities and characteristics of a follower of Christ
- Interpret accurately the teaching of the Word of God
- Create environments in which followers are encouraged to share their insights

- Create an environment of trust in which the fear of reprisal does not exist
- Create safe environments for those who risk and fail
- Respect all followers of Christ
- Teach and oversee the biblical responsibilities of followers
- Encourage followers to lead in appropriate contexts
- Reject fearing the involvement of followers in the decision making process
- Resist holding on to my position
- Cherish the interdependent relationship with followers
- Lead through the power of submission
- Assess my own frailties and infirmities
- Lead with humility
- Serve Christ by serving my followers
- Become the first to die to self and live for Christ
- Diligently use my delegated authority to the glory of God
- Establish an organizational culture of grace
- Trust God by trusting and being committed to my followers.
- Become a leader of integrity
- Lead in the power of the Holy Spirit
- Make prayer a primary function of my position
- Keep my promises

I will answer the command of my Leader to,

"FOLLOW ME!"

ENDNOTES

INTRODUCTION

[1] A philosophy is a code of values and beliefs by which [a person] lives" Socio, D. J. (2001). *Archetypes of wisdom: An introduction to perspective.* 4th ed., Wadsworth, United Kingdom.

[2] Schein, Edgar H. (2004). Organizational Culture and Leadership. Jossey-Bass, San Francisco, CA

[3] Stowell, J. M. (1996). *Following Christ: Experiencing life the way it was meant to be.* Grand Rapids, MI: Zondervan Publishing House, p. 40.

[4] Tuckman

CHAPTER ONE

[1] NT:2758 keno/w **kenoo** (ken-o'-o); from <u>NT:2756</u>; to make empty, i.e.

> (figuratively) to abase, neutralize, falsify:
> ***KJV*** - make (of none effect, of no reputation, void), be in vain. Biblesoft's New Exhaustive Strong's Numbers and Concordance with Expanded Greek-Hebrew Dictionary. Copyright © 1994, 2003 Biblesoft, Inc. and International Bible Translators, Inc.

[2] Additional verses supporting Christ as head of the Church

> **Eph 1:22**
> And He put all things in subjection under His feet, and gave Him as head over all things to the church,
> **Eph 4:15**
> but speaking the truth in love, we are to grow up in all aspects into Him, who is the head, even Christ,
> **Eph 5:23**
> For the husband is the head of the wife, as Christ also is the head of the church, He Himself being the Savior of the body.

Col 2:10

and in Him you have been made complete, and He is the head over all rule and authority;

Col 2:19

and not holding fast to the head, from whom the entire body, being supplied and held together by the joints and ligaments, grows with a growth which is from God.

[3] NT:4413 foremost (in time, place, order or importance): Biblesoft's New Exhaustive Strong's Numbers and Concordance with Expanded Greek-Hebrew Dictionary. Copyright © 1994, 2003 Biblesoft, Inc. and International Bible Translators, Inc.

[4] Vander Laan,

http://followtherabbi.com/guide/detail/rabbi-and-talmidim

[5] Ibid.

[6] NT:1205 deute (dyoo'-teh); from NT:1204 and an imperative form of eimi (to go); come hither!: NT:3694 opiso (op-is'-o); from the same as NT:3693 with enclitic of direction; to the back, i.e. aback (as adverb or preposition of time or place; or as noun): KJV - after, back (-ward), (+get) behind, follow. Biblesoft's New Exhaustive Strong's Numbers and Concordance with Expanded Greek-Hebrew Dictionary. Copyright © 1994, 2003 Biblesoft, Inc. and International Bible Translators, Inc.

[7] Instances of the use of the word "come" (duete pisow)

Matt 11:28-30

Come to Me, all *you* who labor and are heavy laden, and I will give you rest. Take My yoke upon you and learn from Me, for I am gentle and lowly in heart, and you will find rest for your souls. For My yoke *is* easy and My burden is light."

Matt 22:4-5

Again, he sent out other servants, saying, 'Tell those who are invited, "See, I have prepared my dinner; my oxen and fatted cattle *are* killed, and all things *are* ready. Come to the wedding."'

Matt 25:33-34

And He will set the sheep on His right hand, but the goats on the left. Then the King will say to those on His right hand,

'Come, you blessed of My Father, inherit the kingdom prepared for you from the foundation of the world:
Matt 28:5-6
But the angel answered and said to the women, "Do not be afraid, for I know that you seek Jesus who was crucified. He is not here; for He is risen, as He said. Come, see the place where the Lord lay.
John 4:29
"Come, see a Man who told me all things that I ever did. Could this be the Christ?"
John 21:12-13
Jesus said to them, "Come *and* eat breakfast." Yet none of the disciples dared ask Him, "Who are You?" — knowing that it was the Lord.
Rev 19:11-18
Now I saw heaven opened, and behold, a white horse. And He who sat on him *was* called Faithful and True, and in righteousness He judges and makes war. His eyes *were* like a flame of fire, and on His head *were* many crowns. He had a name written that no one knew except Himself. He *was* clothed with a robe dipped in blood, and His name is called The Word of God. And the armies in heaven, clothed in fine linen, white and clean, followed Him on white horses. Now out of His mouth goes a sharp sword, that with it He should strike the nations. And He Himself will rule them with a rod of iron. He Himself treads the winepress of the fierceness and wrath of Almighty God. And He has on *His* robe and on His thigh a name written:

KING OF KINGS AND LORD OF LORDS.

Then I saw an angel standing in the sun; and he cried with a loud voice, saying to all the birds that fly in the midst of heaven, "Come and gather together for the supper of the great God...

[8] NT:190 akoloutheo (ak-ol-oo-theh'-o); from NT:1 (as a particle of union) and keleuthos (a road); properly, to be in the same way with, i.e. to accompany (specially, as a disciple): KJV - follow,

reach. Biblesoft's New Exhaustive Strong's Numbers and Concordance with Expanded Greek-Hebrew Dictionary. Copyright © 1994, 2003 Biblesoft, Inc. and International Bible Translators, Inc.

[9] H. L. E. Luering. Suffering belongs to the discipline of all Christ's followers (Rom 8:17; 2 Cor 1:7; Gal 3:4; Phil 3:10; 1 Thess 2:2; 2 Thess 1:5; 2 Tim 2:12; 3:12; James 5:10; 1 Peter 2:20 f; 3:14,17; 4:1,13,16; 5:10). Such suffering is called a suffering for God's or Christ's sake (Jer 15:15; Acts 9:16; Phil 1:29; 2 Tim 1:12). This fellowship in suffering unites us with the saints of God in all times (James 5:10), and is indeed a fellowship with the Lord Himself (Phil 3:10), who uses this discipline to mold us more and more according to His character. From International Standard Bible Encyclopaedia, Electronic Database Copyright (c)1996 by Biblesoft

CHAPTER TWO

[1] Chaleff, Ira. (1995). *The Courageous Follower.* San Francisco, CA: Barret-Koehler Publishers, Inc.

[2] Bible Knowledge Commentary/Old Testament Copyright © 1983, 2000 Cook Communications Ministries; Bible Knowledge Commentary/New Testament Copyright © 1983, 2000 Cook Communications Ministries. All rights reserved.

[3] Kelley, Robert (1988). In Praise of Followers. *Harvard Business Review*, p. 146.

[4] Ibid, p. 143

[5] Kelley, Robert (1992) *The Power of Followership*, New York, Doubleday Currency.

[6] Chaleff, Ira. (1995). *The Courageous Follower.* San Francisco, CA: Barret-Koehler Publishers, Inc.

[7] Rost, Joseph (1991) *Leadership for the Twenty-first Century.* Praeger, New York, New York.

[8] Ibid. p. 108

[9] Ibid. p. 109

[10] Rost, p. 109

[11] Ibid. p. 109

[12] Ibid. p. 10

[13] Hughes, R. L., Ginnett, R. C., & Curphy, G. J. (2006). *Leadership: Enhancing the Lessons of Experience.* Boston: McGraw-Hill/Irwin, p. 12.

[14] http://scidiv.bcc.ctc.edu/MATH/Mobius.html This curious surface is called a **Möbius Strip** or Möbius Band, named after August Ferdinand Möbius, a nineteenth century German mathematician and astronomer, who was a pioneer in the field of topology. Möbius, along with his better known contemporaries, Riemann, Lobachevsky and Bolyai, created a non-Euclidean revolution in geometry. Möbius strips have found a number of surprising applications that exploit a remarkable property they possess: one-sidedness. Joining A to C and B to D (no half twist) would produce a simple belt-shaped loop with two sides and two edges -- impossible to travel from one side to the other without crossing an edge. But, as a result of the half twist, **the Möbius Strip has only one side and one edge!** To demonstrate this, (1) start midway between the "edges" of a Möbius Strip and draw a line down its center; continue the line until you return to your starting point. Did you ever cross an edge? (2) Next, hold the edge of a Möbius Strip against the tip of a felt-tipped highlighter pen. Color the edge of the Möbius Strip by holding the highlighter still and just rotating the Mobius Strip around. Were you able to color the entire edge?

[15] Blanchard, Ken, Leading at a Higher Level. Upper saddle River, NJ: FT Press, 2010

CHAPTER THREE

[1] Barna Research Grouphttp://theologica.blogspot.com/2005/06/how-many-americans-really-attend.html and

http://www.barna.org/FlexPage.aspx?Page=Topic&TopicID=10

[2] King, Marty (2013) http://www.lifeway.com/Article/news-2012-southern-baptist-annual-church-profile-report

[3] We are inadvertently short-circuiting the ministry of the Church by our use of terms that do not accurately portray the activity we are called to act upon. We create ships and isms that are made up of different activities and we call those these discipleship, evangelism, leadership. Because we have created them as intellectual, academic types of constructs, they have lost their biblical thrust. Inspection of the scriptures shows that the bible knows nothing of discipleship or evangelism. These are constructs which have been extrapolated from the Word. The Bible teaches much about following, disciple making, leading, and evangelizing. However, when we seek to capture the essence of these activities by making them a list of prescribed activities, the life inherent in the active participle form and verbal noun (gerund) aspect of the word is killed. The construct becomes sterile. We begin to look upon the activities as the fulfillment of the command rather than the actual product of the activity. Discipleship becomes a prescribed number of meetings and plans and memorized outlines instead of the actual product of an obedient disciple. One might argue that these activities are a means to and end. However, most churches who say they are concerned with discipleship would point to the number of discipleship classes rather than point to the number of disciples. The same might be said for evangelism. This is not to say that classes and activities surrounding the process of disciple making are wrong. It is to say that classes for such purposes simply to give us cause to pat ourselves on the back and say that we are fulfilling the Great Commission is an exercise in self-aggrandizement. I propose we do away with such false constructs and stay with the biblical terms of making disciples, evangelizing and leading. Then, when we are asked to give an account, we will not point to our activities but rather to the activity that the Lord has already prescribed.

Leadership does not exist in the Scriptures. Leading does exist. The idea is that there is a complete, definable list or group of concepts and activities that indicate these areas is a construction that is pressed upon the Scriptures. What we are left with are anecdotal assertions of one person's way of acting within a particular context. There are no didactic teachings on leading and how to lead. Writers and pastors must extrapolate principles that appear to make sense and then apply them to a current context. When this is done often enough, we have a tendency to codify many of these principles and ascribe to them merit. We are prone to want to declare THIS is leadership. Such declaration s may give us comfort and closure on the idea of what leaders are supposed to do. However, to codify one list is to leave out the dimensions of another's list. Then we have dueling lists of concepts and ideas regarding what leadership is. Leadership scholars have written a paper outlining over 200 definitions and ideas on what leadership is. Others state that many of the leadership theories we are discussing today are still the same concepts that have been discussed through the last half century. The reasons for all these discussions may be due to the fact that leading can be identified but leadership varies with regard to context. Do servant leaders have an advantage over transformational leaders? Or is serving others merely an expression of how to be a transformational leader? The concepts of leading and following may be too fluid to be captured within the pages of a book. The best I can ask of you is that you consider looking at life from a different perspective. Embrace who you are as a followerfirst. Don't succumb to the fear of not becoming the leader that everyone seems to teach is the ultimate goal of life. Be the person God has created you to be and then act according to His best interest in the positions of responsibility He gives.

[4] McIntosh, Gary L. (2003). Biblical Church Growth. Grand Rapids: Baker Books, p. 39. Knowledge gained through general revelation is God's truth. It is true because it is sourced in the life-giving God. As such, it is biblical to make full use of empirical research in the fields of anthropology, sociology,

and other sciences. Why? Because God's general revelation reflects his character; it is intelligible, coherent, and discoverable. Truth discovered from the natural realm of creation, human development, and history is God's truth held in common with all people – believing and nonbelieving. We are free to explore, discover, and use common truths.

[5] Maxwell, John C. (1995). Developing the Leaders Around You. Atlanta: Thomas Nelson Publishers, p. 7.

[6] Ibid. p. 10

[7] Maxwell, John C. (1993). *Developing the Leader Within You*. Atlanta: Thomas Nelson Publishers, p. 58

[8] Maxwell, John C. (1998). *The 21 Irrefutable Laws of Leadership*. Nashville: Thomas Nelson Publishers. p. 36.

[9] Ibid. p. 51.

[10] Ibid. p. 136.

CHAPTER FOUR

[1] WORSHIP. The act of paying honor to a deity; religious reverence and homage. The rendering of the following Heb. and Gk. words:
1. Heb. shaha (to "bow down"), to prostrate oneself before another in order to do him honor and reverence (Gen 22:5; etc.). from The New Unger's Bible Dictionary. Originally published by Moody Press of Chicago, Illinois. Copyright (c) 1988.

[2] Used with permission, Faith, Prayer, & Tract League: Tract #76; Grand Rapids, MI 49504

CHAPTER FIVE

[1] Kubicek, Jeremie (2011). *Making Your Leadership Come Alive*. New York: Howard Books.

[3] Kouzes, J. M, & Posner, B. Z. (2012). *The Leadership Challenge: How to make Extraordinary Things Happen in Organizations*, (fifth ed.), San Francisco, CA. Jossey-Bass.

[3] Ibid, p.30

CHAPTER SIX

[1] 1 Corinthians 16:16; Ephesians 5:22; Colossians 3:18; James 4:7; 1 Peter 2:13; 1 Peter 5:5

[2] NT:3401mimeomai (mim-eh'-om-ahee); middle voice from mimos (a "mimic"); to imitate:KJV - follow.(Biblesoft's New Exhaustive Strong's Numbers and Concordance with Expanded Greek-Hebrew Dictionary. Copyright © 1994, 2003 Biblesoft, Inc. and International Bible Translators, Inc.)

IMITATE, IMITATOR
A. Verb. mimeomai NT:3401, "a mimic, an actor" (Eng., "mime," etc.), is always translated "to imitate" in the RV, for KJV, "to follow," (a) of imitating the conduct of missionaries, 2 Thess 3:7,9; the faith of spiritual guides, Heb 13:7; (b) that which is good, 3 John 11. The verb is always used in exhortations, and always in the continuous tense, suggesting a constant habit or practice. Vine's Expository Dictionary of Biblical Words, Copyright (c)1985, Thomas Nelson Publishers)

[3] I am grateful to my colleague, Brad Arnett, Ph. D. for his insights regarding this passage of Scripture.

[4] Kouzes, J. M, & Posner, B.Z. (2012). *The Leadership Challenge*. San Francisco: Jossey-Bass, p. 35.

[5] Ibid. p. 36.

[6] Ibid. p. 40.

[7] 1 Chron 29:14 For man of himself can give nothing: "What am I, and what is my people, that we should be able to show ourselves so liberal?" kowach (OT:3581) `aatsar (OT:6113), to hold strength together; both to have power to do anything (here and 2 Chron 2:5; 22:9), and also to retain strength (2 Chron 13:20; Dan 10:8,16; 11:6), only found in Daniel and in the Chronicle. hitᵃnadeeb (OT:5068), to show oneself willing, especially in giving. kaazo't (OT:2063) refers to the contribution to the building of the temple (vv. 3-8). From Thy hand, i.e., that which is received from Thee, have we given. From Keil & Delitzsch Commentary on the Old

Testament: New Updated Edition, Electronic Database.
Copyright (c) 1996 by Hendrickson Publishers, Inc.
[8] Sanders, J. Oswald *Spiritual Leadership* p. 79.
[9] Ibid. pp 81-82
[10] Kouzes & Posner, p. 78

CHAPTER SEVEN

[1] I am indebted to my colleague, Scott Henderson, Ph.D. for the
information regarding Will to Power.
[2] Northouse, P. G. (2013). *Leadership: Theory and Practice* (Sixth ed.),
Thousand Oaks, CA: Sage, p. 9.
[3] The types of power mentioned in this section are taken from
Ivancevich & Matteson, *Organizational Behavior and Management.*
McGraw-Hill, New York, New York p. 388-393
[4] NT:2634 katakurieuo (kat-ak-oo-ree-yoo'-o); from NT:2596 and
NT:2961; to lord against, i.e. control, subjugate: KJV -
exercise dominion over (lordship), be lord over, overcome.
Biblesoft's New Exhaustive Strong's Numbers and
Concordance with Expanded Greek-Hebrew Dictionary.
Copyright © 1994, 2003 Biblesoft, Inc. and International
Bible Translators, Inc.
[5] Ivenecivich & Matteson, p. 392
[6] For further study:
Romans 2:2 - Romans 2:8 -, 1 Corinthians 13:6 - 2
Corinthians 4:2 - 2 Corinthians 6:7 - 2 Corinthians 11:10 - 2
Corinthians 12:6 - Galatians 2:5 - Galatians 2:14 - Galatians
3:1 - Galatians 4:16 -Galatians 5:7 -Ephesians 1:13 -Ephesians
4:15-Ephesians 4:21-Ephesians 4:25 -Ephesians 5:9 -
Ephesians 6:14 - Philippians 1:18 - Colossians 1:5 -
Colossians 1:6 - 1 Thessalonians 2:13 - 2 Thessalonians 2:10 -
2 Thessalonians 2:12 - 2 Thessalonians 2:13 - 1 Timothy 2:4 -
1 Timothy 2:7 - 1 Timothy 3:15 - 1 Timothy 4:3 - 1 Timothy
6:5 - 2 Timothy 2:15 - 2 Timothy 2:18 - 2 Timothy 2:25 - 2
Timothy 3:7 - 2 Timothy 3:8 - 2 Timothy 4:4 - Titus 1:1
[7] One source to consider is the article on AUTHORITY IN
RELIGION International Standard Bible Encyclopedia

[8] Ivancevich & Matteson, *Organizational Behavior and Management.* McGraw-Hill, New York, New York p. 389

[9] Ibid. p. 389.

[10] The New Unger's Bible Dictionary. Originally published by Moody Press of Chicago, Illinois. Copyright (c) 1988.

[11] NT:1849 exousia (ex-oo-see'-ah); from NT:1832 (in the sense of ability); privilege, i.e. (subjectively) force, capacity, competency, freedom, or (objectively) mastery (concretely, magistrate, superhuman, potentate, token of control), delegated influence. KJV - authority, jurisdiction, liberty, power, right, strength.Biblesoft's New Exhaustive Strong's Numbers and Concordance with Expanded Greek-Hebrew Dictionary. Copyright © 1994, 2003 Biblesoft, Inc. and International Bible Translators, Inc.

[12] Ivancevich and Matteson. p. 388

[13] Means, James E. (1989). Leadership in Christian Ministry. Grand Rapids: Baker, p. 97

[14] Malphurs, A. and Will Mancini (2004). *Building Leaders.* Grand Rapids: Baker Books, p. 86

[15] Clinton, J. Robert (1988). *The Making of a Leader.* Navpress, p. 167

[16] http://www.lectlaw.com/def2/q003.htm

[17] Ivenecivich & Matteson, p. 392

[18] http://www.merriam-webster.com/dictionary/statusquo

[19] The idea of compliance may also be a cause for so many disillusioned people who 'walk the aisle' or 'prayed the sinners prayer', thinking that by complying with the request of the preacher, friend, or mother, that this was what it means to be saved. There is no commitment of heart to Christ only compliance with a prescribed set of actions. Responding to Christ's call to salvation is an act of obedience not merely compliance. Perhaps we would do well to make certain that those who are responding to the gospel know the difference.

CHAPTER EIGHT

[1] Northouse, Peter (2007). *Leadership Theory and Practice.* Thousand Oaks, CA: Sage Publications, Inc., p. 2

[2] Maxwell, John C. (1995). *Developing the Leaders Around You.* Thomas Nelson Publishers, Atlanta, Georgia, pp. 47-60.

[3] See http://www.ichthus.info/Disciples/intro.html

[4] Murray, Andrew (1981) *With Christ in the School of Prayer.* Springdale, PA: Whitaker House, p. 7.

[5] Maluphurs, Aubrey (2004). *Values-Driven Leadership.* Grand Rapids: Baker Books, p. 44.

[6] Compassion - NT:4697 splagchnizomai (splangkh-nid'-zom-ahee); middle voice from NT:4698; to have the bowels yearn, i.e. (figuratively) feel sympathy, to pity:KJV - have (be moved with) compassion.
Biblesoft's New Exhaustive Strong's Numbers and Concordance with Expanded Greek-Hebrew Dictionary. Copyright © 1994, 2003 Biblesoft, Inc. and International Bible Translators, Inc.

[7] Russell, R. F. (2001). The role of values in servant leadership [Electronic version]. *Leadership & Organization Development Journal, 22*(2), 76-84. Retrieved October 28, 2004, from ABI/INFORM Global database.

[8] Graen, G. B., & Cashman, J. (1975). A role-making model of leadership in formal organization: A developmental approach. In J. G. Hunt & L. L. Larson (eds.), *Leadership frontiers* (pp. 143-166). Kent, OK: Kent State University Press.

[9] Northouse, Peter G. (2007). *Leadership Theory and Practice.* Thousand Oaks, CA: SAGE, p. 159.

[10] Weber M. (1947). The theory of social and economic organization (T. Parsons, Trans.) New York: Free Press.

[11] Kouzes & Posner, (1995). *The Leadership Challenge.* San Francisco: Jossey-Bass.

[12] House, R. J. (1976). A 1976 theory of charismatic leadership. In J. G. Hunt & L. L. Larson (Eds.), *Leadership: The cutting edge* (pp. 189-207). Carbondale Southern Illinois University Press.

[13] Taken from Northhouse, P. G. (2007). Leadership Theory and Practice. Thousand Oaks, CA: SAGE, p. 178-179

[14] Burns, J. M. (1978). *Leadership*. New York: Harper & Row.
[15] Northouse, Peter G. (2007). *Leadership Theory and Practice*. Thousand Oaks, CA: SAGE, p. 176.
[16] Bass, B. M. (1985). *Leadership and performance beyond expectations*. New York: Free Press.
[17] Northouse, Peter G. (2007). Leadership Theory and Practice. Thousand Oaks, CA: SAGE, p. 181=182
[18] Ibid p. 183
[19] Ibid p. 183
[20] Ibid p. 183
[21] Greenleaf, R. K. (1977). *Servant leadership: A journey into the nature of legitimate power and greatness*. New York: Paulist.
[22] The Understanding and Practice of Servant-Leadership - Spears http://www.regent.edu/acad/sls/publications/conference_proceedings/servant_leadership_roundtable/2005/pdf/spears_practice.pdf
[23] For a complete explanation of these constructs see: Servant Leadership Research Roundtable – August 2003, 7 http://www.regent.edu/acad/sls/publications/conference_proceedings/servant_leadership_roundtable/2003pdf/patterson_servant_lead ership.pdf

The following excerpts are from this article, used with permission.

Agapao – Love is the cornerstone of the servant leadership/follower relationship, specifically *agapao* love, which according to Winston (2002) is *agapao* love, or the Greek term for moral love, meaning to do the right thing at the right time and for the right reasons. *Agapao* love means to love in a social or moral sense and includes "embracing the judgment and the deliberate assent of the will as a matter of principle, duty, and propriety" (p. 5).

This is in deep contrast to the idea that servant leadership is merely a subset of transformational leadership where the focus of the leader is on the organization, or organizational objectives. Servant leadership stands alone in regard to this follower focus. This type of love applies to today's leaders, in that leaders must consider the needs of their followers. This love is shown by leaders who consider each person as a total person -- one with needs, wants, and desires. *Agapao* love is alive and well in organizations today and it is the foundation for what Winston (2002) calls the "platinum rule" (or do unto others as they would want you to do). *Agapao* love is consistent with servant leadership to the extent that servant leaders must have such great love for the followers that they are willing to learn the giftings and talents of each one of the followers. The leader that leads with *agapao* love has a focus on the employee first, then on the talents of the employee, and lastly on how this benefits the organization

Humility - Humility is the ability to keep one's accomplishments and talents in perspective, which includes self-acceptance, and further includes not being self-focused but rather focused on others (Sandage & Wiens, 2001). Humility, therefore, is a peaceful virtue that rejects self-glorification (Lawrence, 2002). Bower (1997) linked servant leadership with the unassuming behavior of being humble; he believed that humility is a necessity for chief executives, or leaders. The virtue of humility causes one to consider moderation, to listen to the advice of others, and to come with the realization that the right use of power means rejecting the dictatorial (Harrison, 2002).

Altruism, according to Monroe (1994), is not merely having good intentions or being well-meaning; altruism is more about concern for the welfare of another. DeYoung (2000) also concurred with the traditional view of altruism as an unselfish concern for others often involving personal sacrifice; however, he believed that the personal pleasure derived from helping others should also be included in our understanding of altruism. In contrast, Hattwick (1986) placed altruism at one end of the spectrum with personal self-interest at the other end. Altruism seeks the fulfillment of others with behavior directed toward the benefit of others and identifies this behavior as consistent with servant leadership. Bishop Desmond Tutu, Sam Walton, Mother Teresa, and Princess Diana are among Sosik's (2000) examples of altruistic people.

Vision. Vision is most often regarded as the organizational vision, or a vision of the future destination of the organization. However, Patterson (2003) offers the servant leader's focus is on the individual member of the organization and the vision component is about how the organizational members future state. This vision refers to the idea that the leader looks forward and sees the person as a viable and worthy person and seeks to assist each one in reaching that state. Harvey (2001) saw this same ability as inherent in Greenleaf's (1977) formulation of servant leaders as healers, making the person whole by helping that person to because they help others attain the larger vision or purpose than they otherwise might be able to attain for themselves. This visionary process includes seeing each person's unique gifts and influences the decisions of the leader and helps the leader shape a plan for the future, all while asking if the people are being served. Patterson (2003) states that servant leaders learn to know people's abilities and see where they are headed in order to serve them. The visionary servant leader also is able to know the followers and help them develop a clear sense of purpose, direction, dignity and direction (Batten, 1998). Servant leaders enrich lives, build better human beings, and encourage people to become more than they ever believed, and that this is more than a job; this deep-rooted leadership is about mission, the mission to serve (Melrose, 1995).

Trust is a building block for servant leaders (Patterson, 2003), one that is an important element for the servant leader (Wis, 2002); this is due to the belief of the servant leader in trusting in others, which produces a standard of excellence for the entire organization. Respect for and goodwill towards others is the foundation on which trust is built, which is built on goodwill towards others according to Fairholm and Fairholm (2000); further, without trust, discord and disharmony exist. Fletcher (1999) advocated that servant leadership's basis is trust, which is supported by Kezar (2002) who described a servant leadership perspective as helping people to feel comfortable and creating an open environment where everyone has a voice, and everyone works collaboratively and collectively while using skills such as truth telling. Russell (2001) concurs, noting that trust is essential for servant leaders and that the values of integrity and honesty build interpersonal and organizational trust and leads to credibility. Patterson (2003) offers that trust is a building block to work from for servant leaders, a trust in the unseen potential of the followers, believing they can accomplish goals, a self-fulfilling prophecy. Story (2002) agrees, noting that trust is an essential characteristic of the servant leader.

Empowerment. Greenleaf has been called "the father of the empowerment movement" because empowerment is one of the most important characteristics of servant leadership (Buchen 1998; Russell & Stone 2002). Veronesi (2001) explained that there is no servant leadership where there is no sharing of power. Empowering people, with the best interest of those served in mind, is at the heart of servant leadership (Veronesi; Kezar 2002). Empowerment is entrusting power to others, really giving it away (Patterson, 2003); and involves effective listening, making people feel significant, putting an emphasis on teamwork, and valuing of love and equality (Russell & Stone, 2002). In addition, servant leaders also empower by teaching and developing people (Russell & Stone). The servant leaders' satisfaction comes from the growth of others and that they are willing to hold themselves accountable for the results (Blanchard, 2000). Bennett (2001) stated that servant leaders need to know their followers and understand their needs for the knowledge and experience that they acquire through empowerment. Farling, Stone, and Winston (1999) stated that servant leaders empower followers in accordance with acting on their values and that this relationship is transforming. The idea of empowerment and servant leadership go hand in hand, in that servant leadership puts an emphasis on service, a wholistic approach to work, personal development, and shared decision-making (Lee & Zemke, 1993). Empowering followers is a major goal of servant leaders, who desire to create many leaders at all levels (Russell, 2001). Melrose (1995) believed that servant leadership involves giving people chances to move into new and more powerful roles by preserving their roots, respecting their value, and preserving their dignity. In this empowerment-rich model of servant leadership, the leader empowers followers to find their own paths, and they, in turn, are inspired to help others find their best paths. Empowerment involves helping clarify expectations, goals, and responsibilities, and even more importantly it means letting people do their jobs by enabling them to learn, grow, and progress, and it means allowing for self-direction and freedom to fail; all of this multiplies the followers' strengths and trust (Melrose, 1995). By empowering followers, servant leaders are allowing them freedom to proceed toward their goals, helping them make dreams reality. Empowerment is giving up control and letting the followers take charge as needed. Throughout this process, the servant leader is channeling followers, is balancing the growth of followers, and is aware of what is best for the follower. This empowerment allows the follower to bloom and grow.

Service. The servant leader gives of ones self in service (Swindoll, 1981) which involves personal involvement and authenticity. Service is giving of oneself and requires generosity which can mean giving of time, energy, care, compassion, and perhaps, even one's belongings. Servant leaders exhibit service as they support the frontline, discover the uniqueness of each employee, unleash creativity in people, and contribute to the larger good knowing that this is bigger than themselves, and further, actually seek to opportunities to serve others (Aggarwal and Simkins, 2001; Lyerly & Maxey, 2001; Wis, 2002; Smith, 2003; Patterson, 2003). The servant leader is a role model, in behavior and styles, showing others in the organization how to serve, setting the organizational climate (Lytle, Hom, & Mokwa, 1998; Lynn, Lytle, & Bobek, 2000). Melrose (1995) stated that when this type of example is set, service begets service, ultimately permeating the corporate culture.

[24] Ibid.

[25] Greenleaf, R. K. (1977). *Servant leadership: A journey into the nature of legitimate power and greatness.* New York: Paulist. p. 352.

[26] Winston, Bruce, (2003). Servant Leadership Research Roundtable – August 2003
http://www.regent.edu/acad/sls/publications/conference_p

roceedings/servant_leadership_roundtable/2003pdf/winston_extending_pat terson.pdf

[27] Rom 1:1[A servant] This name was what the Lord Jesus himself directed His disciples to use, as their general appellation; Matt 10:25; 20:27; Mark 10:44. And it was the customary name which they assumed; Gal 1:10; Col 4:12; 2 Peter 1:1; Jude 1; Acts 4:29; Titus 1:1; James 1:1. The proper meaning of this word servant, doulos (NT:1401), is slave, one who is not free. It expresses the condition of one who has a master, or who is at the control of another. It is often, however, applied to courtiers, or the officers that serve under a king: because in an eastern monarchy the relation of an absolute king to his courtiers corresponded nearly to that of a master and a slave. Thus, the word is expressive of dignity and honor; and the servants of a king denote officers of a high rank and station. It is applied to the prophets as those who were honored by God, or especially entrusted by him with office; Deut 34:5; Josh 1:2; Jer 25:4. The name is also given to the Messiah, Isa 42:1, "Behold my servant in whom my soul delighteth," etc.; Isa 53:11, "Shall my righteous servant justify many." The apostle uses it here evidently to denote his acknowledging Jesus Christ as his master; as indicating his dignity, as especially appointed by him to his great work; and as showing that in this Epistle he intended to assume no authority of his own, but simply to declare the will of his master, and theirs. (from Barnes' Notes, Electronic Database. Copyright (c) 1997 by Biblesoft)

[28] Bandura, Albert (1994). Self-efficacy. In V. S. Ramachaudran (Ed.). Encyclopedia of Human Behavior, 4. New York: Academic Press. Pp. 71-81.
Self-efficacy is "the belief in one's capabilities to organize and execute the courses of action required to manage prospective situations."

CHAPTER NINE

[1] Schein, Edgar H. (2004). Organizational Culture and Leadership. Jossey-Bass, San Francisco, CA

[2] Ibid. p. 17

[3] Ibid. p. 25

[4] Ibid. p. 29

[5] Ibid. p. 31

[6] Ibid. p. 42

[7] WISE, SKILLED

> Chokmah is the knowledge and the ability to make the right choices at the opportune time. from Vine's Expository Dictionary of Biblical Words, Copyright (c)1985, Thomas Nelson Publishers.

[8] OT:995 biyn (bene); a primitive root; to separate mentally (or distinguish), i.e.(generally) understand: Biblesoft's New Exhaustive Strong's Numbers and Concordance with Expanded Greek-Hebrew Dictionary. Copyright © 1994, 2003 Biblesoft, Inc. and International Bible Translators, Inc.

[9] Consider the following verses in Proverbs regarding understanding:

> Prov 1:2;Prov 1:5;Prov 2:2;Prov 2:3;Prov 2:6;Prov 2:11;Prov 3:5;Prov 3:13;Prov 3:19;Prov 4:1;Prov 4:5; Prov 4:7;Prov 5:1;Prov 6:32;Prov 7:4;Prov 7:7;Prov 8:1;Prov 8:5;Prov 8:14;Prov 9:4;Prov 9:6;Prov 9:10; Prov 9:16;Prov 10:13;Prov 10:13;Prov 10:23;Prov 11:12;Prov 12:11;Prov 13:15;Prov 14:29; Prov14:33; Prov 15:14;Prov 15:21;Prov 15:32;Prov 16:16;Prov 16:22;Prov 17:18;Prov 17:24;Prov 17:27;Prov 18:2;Prov 19:8;Prov 19:25;Prov 20:5;Prov 21:16;Prov 21:30;Prov 23:4;Prov 23:23; Prov 24:3;Prov 24:30; Prov 28:2;Prov 28:11;Prov 28:16;Prov 30:2

[10] Schein, p. 246

- What leaders pay attention to, measure, and control on a regular basis
- How leaders react to critical incidents and organizational crises
- How leaders allocate resources
- Deliberate role modeling, teaching, and coaching

- How leaders allocate rewards and status
- How leaders recruit, select, promote, and excommunicate

CHAPTER TEN

[1] From Calvin's Commentaries, PC Study Bible formatted electronic database Copyright © 2005-2006 by Biblesoft, Inc.
parakletos (par-ak'-lay-tos); an intercessor, consoler: advocate, comforter. Biblesoft's New Exhaustive Strong's Numbers and Concordance with Expanded Greek-Hebrew Dictionary. Copyright © 1994, 2003, 2006 Biblesoft, Inc. and International Bible Translators, Inc.
[2] ekklesia (ek-klay-see'-ah); from a compound of NT:1537 and a derivative of NT:2564; a calling out, i.e. (concretely) a popular meeting, especially a religious congregation (Jewish synagogue, or Christian community of members on earth or saints in heaven or both): assembly, church. Biblesoft's New Exhaustive Strong's Numbers and Concordance with Expanded Greek-Hebrew Dictionary. Copyright © 1994, 2003, 2006 Biblesoft, Inc. and International Bible Translators, Inc.

CHAPTER ELEVEN

[1] International Standard Bible Encyclopedia (1996). Biblesoft Electronic Database.
[2] Ibid
[3] Ibid
[4] Strong's Exhaustive Concordance (1994). Biblesoft Electronic Database.
[5] International Standard Bible Encyclopedia (1996). Biblesoft Electronic Database.
[6] Hays, R. D., Hayashi, T., & Stewart, A. L. (1989). A five-item measure of socially desirable response set. *Educational and Psychological Measurement, 49*, 629-636. Retrieved November 15,

2006, from SAGE Social Science Collections Database, p. 629.

[7] Validity

The Followerfirst Profile was developed to identify and measure behaviors identified in the biblical literature as belonging to persons who seek to follow after Christ. The BFP employs self-ratings using a forced-choice Likert response. Forced-choice items "do not include responses such as *other, no opinion, not sure, or not applicable* as choices but require respondents to select from among a fixed set of response alternatives" [Dixon, E. N. (2003). An exploration of the relationship of organizational level and measures of follower behaviors. Unpublished dissertation, the University of Alabama in Huntsville, p. 50]. This type of response is popular among researchers [Alreck, P. L., & Settle, R. B. (1985). *The survey research handbook.* Chicago, IL: Irwin.], is easy to count, and allows for multiple sampling of any single factor.

The response options were worded so that positive responses meant a higher numerical value using a five-item response ordinal Likert scale. The terms used for the responses were, to little or no extent, to a slight extent, to a moderate extent, to a great extent, and to a very great extent, which relates to a numerical scale of 1 to 5 respectively. The lower the score would indicate a lower presence of biblical follower behavior and the higher scores would indicate a higher presence of biblical follower behavior. Each of the five characteristics has one reverse coded statement to determine respondent credibility and/or respondent fatigue.

To enhance the content validity of the instrument, a pool of experts was assembled to evaluate the potential assessment items as they related to the operationalized constructs. This pool consisted of a New Testament professor, a homiletics professor, an Old Testament professor, and a leadership professor. Each of these individuals holds a Ph. D. in his field. Each expert was given the literature review and biblical word studies as self-study background material before assessing the accuracy and appropriateness of the assessment items.

Their review of the potential assessment items resulted in several changes. One concern centered on the possibility that the word study of the Greek words could result in a "root fallacy". A root fallacy is described as a "notion that the real meaning of a word is found in its original root" [Duvall, J. S., & Hays, J. D. (2005). *Grasping God's Word*. Grand Rapids, MI: Zondervan, p. 133]. The point was made that the prefixes added to the original root meaning of the word *follow*, did not necessarily result in what would be a literal translation of the Greek word for all instances of the word in the New Testament. Issues of context have a major bearing on the actual translation of the word. It was suggested that the word study be changed to reflect that the Greek words *may* be translated in this manner rather than assert a definitive translation.

Another suggestion resulted in changing statements that reflected more of an attitudinal assessment to statements that assessed specific behavior. Because the FFP is a behavioral assessment tool, it is imperative that all of the statements reflect behaviors. Whereas these behaviors may be based upon certain beliefs and attitudes, there may be occasion when the individual's behaviors are not congruent with the individual's stated beliefs. Therefore, the assessment items were changed to reflect only behaviors.

Additional statements were added so that each construct would be measured by at least six items. There is "widespread acceptance for a ratio of survey item to factors using five or more items per factor to achieve reliable estimates" (Dixon, 2003, p. 54). Additional questions regarding the construct of obedience were added to clarify the motive behind the activity of obedience. Other statements were changed to reflect greater clarity, and the profile items were randomly sorted in order to guard against respondent fatigue. The demographic questions were chosen to allow for cross-sectioning of the survey results from different respondent groups. This will allow for more understanding and value from the survey results [Custom Insight (2006). http://www.custominsight.com/tutorial/survey-using-demographics.asp

To assess the face validity of the instrument, the adjusted FFP was pilot-tested with a group of eighteen Christians composed of ministerial students, pastors, pastor's wives, church members and church staff members. The testing showed that the instrument was simple, straightforward to complete, not time-consuming (approximately six minutes) and generally accepted by the participants. Many of the participants commented on the directness of the statements and how the way the phrasing of the statements did not allow for prevarication. Also, several of the participants commented on how the instrument would be a positive self-assessment tool.

The pilot test revealed that several of the questions needed greater specificity with regard to the subcategory being measured. Suggestions for more specific wording were offered and the changes made to the instrument. Also, the pilot-test suggested an additional demographic question regarding denominational and/or church affiliation would be helpful when making assessments of the findings. The group believed that the answers to some of the questions may be different depending on the theological bias within certain denominations and churches and such a demographic would allow the data to be assessed with regard to these various groups.

The pilot-test revealed that questions regarding the subcategory of *obedience* needed to include additional questions regarding the motive behind a person's obedience. These additional questions were added to clarify the difference between a person's obedience because of intimacy with Christ and a person's duty because of perceived church obligation. The essence of the additional statements is to try and differentiate between obedience with regard to the area of relationship and obedience with regard to legalistic duty. These changes were made to the FFP.

In order to assess the construct validity of the instrument, an exploratory factor analysis would need to be performed to determine if the constructs explained any significant variance in the instrument items. This exploratory analysis "defines the possible relationships in only the most general form and then allows the multivariate technique to estimate relationship(s)… and lets the method and the data define the nature of the relationships [Hair, J. F., Anderson, R. E., Tatham, R. L., & Black, W. C. (1998). *Multivariate data analysis.* Upper Saddle River, NJ: Prentice Hall].

Limitations

The primary limitation of the development of the FFP is that the instrument was developed and pilot-tested by only Baptists and not a variety of Christian denominational representation. This single source for the development of the statements could possibly word items that may be misleading to those in other denominations because of the specificity with which certain words, theological assumptions, and concepts are used within the Baptist faith. To broaden the scope of the applicability of the instrument, Christians from other denominational perspectives should be asked to gauge the content and face validity of the instrument.

[8] NT:3982 pei/qw **peitho** (pi'-tho); a primary verb; to convince (by argument, true or false); by analogy, to pacify or conciliate (by other fair means); reflexively or passively, to assent (to evidence or authority), to rely (by inward certainty): *KJV* - agree, assure, believe, have confidence, be (wax) confident, make friend, obey, persuade, trust, yield. (Biblesoft's New Exhaustive Strong's Numbers and Concordance with Expanded Greek-Hebrew Dictionary. Copyright © 1994, 2003, 2006 Biblesoft, Inc. and International Bible Translators, Inc.)

About the Author

Rusty Ricketson speaks and teaches both nationally and internationally in the areas of Leadership Development and Leader-Follower Relationships. Rusty received his baccalaureate degree with honors from the University of Georgia in Social Science Education, his Master of Divinity degree from Southwestern Baptist Theological Seminary, his Doctor of Ministry degree from Reformed Theological Seminary, and his Ph.D. in Organizational Leadership from Regent University. Coupled with over 30 years of ministry experience, including helping start two churches and serving as senior pastor for 18 years, Rusty is able to blend academic insight with the practical application of one who has experienced ministry at the ground level. He is currently Associate Professor of Leadership at Luther Rice University where he is the Director of the Master of Arts in Leadership degree program. Rusty also serves as President of Foundation of the Faith, Inc., a ministry he founded in 2002 that is committed to developing followers of Christ to impact the world. With a dependence upon the Holy Spirit and an energetic and humorous approach, Rusty facilitates learning and encourages those who hear him. He and his wife, Sharon, live north of Atlanta, Georgia. They have two adult children.

Half-day, full-day, and multiple-day workshops and consultations for churches, non-profit organizations, and businesses are available.

For more information contact:

rustyricketson@gmail.com
www.followerfirst.com
www.foundationofthefaith.org

PERSONAL NOTES

PERSONAL NOTES